PSYCHOLINGUISTICS
A COGNITIVE VIEW OF LANGUAGE

Helen S. Cairns • Charles E. Cairns
Queens College of the City University of New York

PSYCHOLINGUISTICS
A COGNITIVE VIEW OF LANGUAGE

HOLT, RINEHART AND WINSTON
New York   Chicago   San Francisco   Atlanta   Dallas
Montreal   Toronto   London   Sydney

This book is dedicated
to our children,
Rick, Helene, Kristina, and Stewart

Copyright © 1976 by Holt, Rinehart and Winston
All rights reserved
Library of Congress Cataloging in Publication Data
Cairns, Helen S.
    Psycholinguistics.
    1. Creativity (Linguistics)
    2. Generative grammar.
    3. Languages—Psychology.
    4. Children—Language.
    I. Cairns, Charles E., joint author.
    II. Title.
    P37.C3   410   75-25303
    ISBN   0-03-007851-2
Printed in the United States of America
5678   059   987654321

PREFACE

When Noam Chomsky published *Syntactic Structures* in 1957, only a handful of psychologists (such as George Miller) recognized what enormous implications that work would have for the field of psychology. At that time a behaviorist view of language was the most prevalent one among psychologists. Because of the influence of Chomsky's transformational-generative theory of grammar, behaviorist accounts of language have been, in the main, replaced by a cognitive view of language—hence the title of this book.

The purpose of *Psycholinguistics: A Cognitive View of Language* is to present both the orienting ideas and the major findings of research in cognitive psycholinguistics; this includes a presentation of the basic concepts from theoretical linguistics that are relevant to psycholinguistics. The book is self-contained in that no prior knowledge of linguistics or of psychological principles is required of the reader. The book is for any newcomer to the fields of linguistics and psycholinguistics and is especially appropriate for undergraduate courses in psycholinguistics. We hope and expect that more advanced students and professionals in related disciplines will also derive benefit from this book.

Rather than attempt a complete review of psycholinguistic literature, we have arranged our examples to illustrate the tight integration and mutual dependency of linguistic competence and linguistic performance. We have adopted as a basic assumption the notion that adequate theories of competence and performance, while distinct entities, are tightly integrated. We also feel that much of the forthcoming progress in both theories will result from a recognition of this mutual dependency.

The book is organized into two parts. Part One, which consists of four chapters, presents the basic theoretical formulations of transformational-generative grammar. In the first chapter we develop the concept of language as a fundamentally human communication system, rooted in the biology of the human organism. The second chapter explores the methodology of linguistic inquiry and explains how linguistic hypotheses are formulated and tested. Chapter 3 is a brief description of the syntactic component of transformational-generative grammar, and Chapter 4 sketches the interpretive components—phonology and semantics. The particular examples of syntactic, phonological, and semantic processes are drawn from English and are just those processes that are relevant to the psycholinguistic investigations discussed in Part Two.

Part Two, which deals with a number of areas of psycholinguistics, also contains four chapters. Chapter 5 describes psycholinguistics within the context of human experimental psychology and traces its transition from behaviorism to its current status as a branch of cognitive psychology; the role of Chomskyan linguistics in this transition is also discussed. Chapter 6 is devoted to the phonological aspects of language performance, with emphasis on current research in speech perception. Chapter 7 presents a view of syntactic and semantic processing, while Chapter 8 deals with the child's acquisition of a first language.

At the end of Part One and of each chapter of Part Two are suggestions for further readings. These consist of books and journals that may be explored for term papers or for more extensive study of selected subject areas.

The intellectual climate in which we developed the conception of linguistics and psycholinguistics presented in this book has been that of the University of Texas at Austin and, more recently, Queens College and the Graduate Center of the City University of New York. Our thinking about linguistics and psycholinguistics has been greatly influenced by colleagues and students at both these institutions. We are particularly grateful to Robert Fiengo, Michael Studdert-Kennedy, and Alan Keiler for specific suggestions on selected portions of the book. Any misconceptions that remain are, of course, our own.

Helen S. Cairns
Charles E. Cairns

New York
January, 1975

CONTENTS

Part II. Linguistic Performance

5. Psycholinguistics as a Psychological Discipline   95

6. Phonological Performance   112

Contents

PART I
LINGUISTIC COMPETENCE

Introduction:
Language as a Cognitive System

Of all aspects of the human condition Language may well be the most significant. With Language man communicates, creates beauty, expresses his most significant as well as his most insignificant emotions, and passes knowledge and culture on from generation to generation.

There are probably more facets to study in Language than in any other single subject. One can investigate the language arts—poetry, literature, drama. One can study the emotive content of Language, perhaps as an area of humanistic psychology or psychiatry. One can study the effects of Language by investigating rhetorical devices, attitude formation, and persuasion. A person who devoted a lifetime to studying all the facets of human Language would discover, first, that a lifetime is not sufficient for such an enterprise, and, second, that one cannot study human Language without also studying human beings.

This book concentrates on one way of looking at Language and develops that viewpoint independent of other, equally valid aspects of Language. How can we characterize the aspect of Language that we have chosen? Very generally, the scope of this book is the mental processes and capacities that underlie the human ability to use Language in everyday affairs; furthermore, we are interested in a child's natural acquisition of these abilities. This is what is meant by a cognitive view of Language. In order to develop this viewpoint, our investigation must be along two major lines: first, we must look at Language as a system; second, we must look at man as the user of that system.

The investigation of Language as a system is within the academic field of linguistics, whereas the investigation of the use of Language, at least as we shall present it, is known as psycholinguistics. The major aim of this book is to show the relationships between a proper characterization of Language as a system and man as a Language user—that is, we want to explain the main ideas of linguistics and psycholinguistics. In fact, one of the main thrusts of this book is that there exists a central core of ideas that are common to the two studies.

Linguistics and psycholinguistics are comparatively young disciplines, although they have roots going back centuries. As in many fresh areas of study there are several opposing schools of thought. This book is within what has become known as **generative linguistics** (also known as **transformational-generative** linguistics); the meanings of these terms will become clear in due course. From the viewpoint of psychology our position is within the framework of **cognitive psychology.** In Chapter 5 we sketch the development of generative linguistics and the cognitive approach in psycholinguistics, contrasting these viewpoints briefly with the major opposing schools. But it is not our purpose to present a broad survey of the various schools of thought; we intend rather to relate the ideas and research that we believe provide the most promising avenues of study in investigating the cognitive bases of Language.

In the remainder of this book we develop the concept of Language as a human cognitive system. In order to do this we must distinguish between the general notion of Language (which we write with a capital letter) and particular languages (with a lowercase letter), such as English, Navajo, Thai, and so on. To develop the concept of Language we first compare human Language to animal communication systems—while there are some interesting similarities on which we might focus were this a book about communications systems, there are, from our point of view, even more interesting differences. We compare the view of Language as a cultural system (on which we might focus were this a book about cultural anthropology) to the view of Language as a biological system, rooted in the human cognitive system. We hope to show that if Language is viewed as a cognitively based ability and if we focus our attention on the communicative abilities unique to human beings, then we find ourselves in an excellent vantage point from which to study the complex system we call Language.

1.1
Language as a Communication System

Practically all animals possess some kind of communication system. A bee, for example, communicates the location and amount of nectar to the rest of the hive by means of a dance. Some varieties of fish exhibit courtship behavior that also involves communicating by means of a kind of dance. Several species of higher animals have more complicated systems involving calls for such things as mating, signaling danger, or the presence of food.

The most complicated communication system in the animal kingdom is, of course, that of human beings, **Language.**

One purpose of linguistics is to describe those properties of Language that are common to all human beings and that differentiate it from the communication systems of other animals. It might seem odd to characterize human Language as an animal communication system. After all, human Language is so much more creative and flexible than the communication system of any other species. The point is that if linguistics is to describe what is unique about human Language, then this creative aspect of Language must be its central focus. That is, if we are to view the possession of Language as a biological trait of human beings—just as we view the communication systems of other animals as biological traits—then we must explain how a biological system such as the human brain can embody creativity. This is a very exciting prospect; if we can explain, even in a very general way, how a material system, which we hope some day to be able to describe in detail, can account for Language and its creative aspect, then we will have opened the door to a scientific study of all those aspects of mental life that distinguish human beings from our friends in the animal kingdom.

1.2
Linguistic Creativity

Just what does it mean to say that Language is creative? This is a question that has interested philosophers for centuries. In particular Descartes, whose thinking continues to influence linguistics and psycholinguistics (see Chomsky, 1966),[1] indicated three aspects of the creative use of Language. For one thing linguistic creativity means that any human being can say things that have never been said before. This seems straightforward enough; after all, it is obvious that a poet is creative when he puts words together in a way that has never been done before. But what might not seem so obvious is that linguistic creativity is an everyday occurrence for practically everybody.

Think back to the last time you had a conversation with somebody, perhaps before you sat down to read this book. We would wager that most of that conversation consisted of sentences that neither you nor your conversant had ever heard or uttered before! With the exceptions of such stock phrases as 'hello,' 'excuse me,' and 'please pass the butter,' practically every sentence we utter or encounter in the speech of others is a new creation. No other naturally occurring communication system has this property, yet it is present in every human language, even those spoken by the most "backward" communities. This might seem a very prosaic sort of creativity, especially when compared with the work of the poet or the theoretical mathematician. But we should not be misled by the fact that linguistic

[1] References are listed in alphabetical order, and by date, at the end of the book.

creativity is an everyday phenomenon into believing that it is uninteresting. In fact linguistic creativity is all the more amazing just because of its everyday character. Consider for a moment the fact that all normal human brains —and only *human* brains—are capable of embodying a communication system that exhibits creativity of this kind. If we are able to provide a scientific explanation of linguistic creativity, we will have taken a giant step toward understanding the workings of human mental processes.

As Noam Chomsky, a contemporary American linguist who is one of the most influential leaders of the school of generative linguistics, has pointed out, other animal communications also have a kind of creativity that, at first glance, appears seductively similar to the aspect of human linguistic creativity discussed above (see Chomsky, 1972). For example, the bee signals the presence of nectar to the rest of the hive by means of a dance that indicates the direction, distance, and amount of the nectar. Since there is an infinite number of possible directions, distances, and amounts that can be signaled by the bee, then there is an infinite number of possible messages that the bee can communicate to the rest of the hive.

Chomsky notes, however, that the infinitude of bee language is much different from that of human speech because the dimensions along which the bee's communication system can range are closely correlated with the physical dimensions of distance and direction. For example, the duration and intensity of the bee's dance indicates the amount of nectar; there is a direct and fixed relationship between the communication dimensions of duration and intensity and the physical dimension of amount of nectar. Similarly, the type and tempo of the dance indicates the distance of the nectar from the hive; here again the relationship between the parameter along which the communication system can vary continuously—type and tempo—is fixed in relation to the physical parameter of distance.[2] Thus the infinitude of bee language—or of any other animal communication system that is infinite in this sense—is due to the fact that it can vary continuously along a fixed dimension that is closely correlated with a physical stimulus.

Noam Chomsky stated the difference between animal creativity and human creativity succinctly in *Language and Mind*:

A communication system of the . . . bee type has an indefinitely large range of potential signals, as does human language. The mechanism and principle, however, are entirely different from those employed by human language to express indefinitely many new thoughts, intentions, feelings, and so on. . . . The issue is not one of 'more' or 'less' [creativity], but rather of an entirely different principle of organization. When I make some arbitrary statement in a human language—say, that 'the rise of supranational corporations poses

[2] The interested reader who wishes to learn more about the fascinating study of bee language is directed to the works of Karl von Frisch (1950, 1953, 1962) and Martin Lindauer (1967). A readable account appears in DeVito (1970, pp. 207–212).

new dangers for human freedom'—I am not selecting a point along some linguistic dimension that signals a corresponding point along an asssociated nonlinguistic dimension . . . (pp. 69–70)

One way of characterizing the infinite capacity of animal communication systems described above is to say that messages in the animal systems are directly connected to some sort of stimuli, either external or internal. That is, both the fact that a bee will produce a dance and the quality of the dance itself are direct products of the direction, distance, and amount of nectar— as well, of course, of the genetic makeup of the bee itself. When a human is presented with either an external or internal situation, however, he is free to choose whether or not to speak and what to say if the decision is made to speak. Thus, if one becomes hungry, he can remain stoically silent or perhaps say something like: 'I'm hungry', 'I'm famished', 'I want a peanut butter and jelly sandwich'. He can even lie and deny that he is hungry.

The point is that the form and content of human linguistic expressions cannot be described as direct reflections of the nonlinguistic situations that prompt them but rather have a much more complex and subtle relationship to the nonlinguistic world. Thus only humans can hold discourse about events that are either geographically or temporally remote, about such abstractions as scientific theories, or about events that may occur after death. (We should point out that it is presently beyond the ability of modern science to explain this immensely complicated relationship between the linguistic and the nonlinguistic worlds.) This, then, is the second aspect of linguistic creativity that attracted the attention of Descartes and his followers. In *Language and Mind (p. 12)* Chomsky, using the term 'stimulus' in a rather specialized sense, has termed this aspect of Language 'freedom from stimulus control' and says: "It is because of this freedom from stimulus control that Language can serve as an instrument of thought and self-expression, as it does not only for the exceptionally gifted and talented, but also, in fact, for every normal human."

The third aspect of the creative use of human Language has to do with the appropriateness of linguistic expressions to situations. Consider that the possession of only the first two aspects of linguistic creativity discussed above would also be characteristic of, say, a computer that was programmed to produce English sentences at random. Such a computer might be programmed to produce novel utterances by following rules of some sort, which were completely independent of events external to the machine. If it were not for the fact that human utterances are usually appropriate either to the external context or at least to the thought going through the mind of the speaker, human Language might possess infinitude and freedom from stimulus control, though it would consist of random productions resembling the speech of some mentally ill people.

A fourth characteristic of human Language that illustrates its creativity and sets it apart from other animal communication systems is the ability of every culture to create new vocabulary for its language. If a society discovers or invents a new concept, it is well within its power to make up a new word to refer to the new concept or idea. Sometimes this is done by joining words or parts of words that had previously existed, sometimes by changing the meaning of previously used words, sometimes by borrowing words from other languages, and sometimes by simply making up words. The point is that all languages have the ability to innovate freely in the area of vocabulary.

We have seen four aspects of linguistic creativity: the infinitude of linguistic expressions, the relative freedom from stimulus control, the appropriateness of speech to situations, and the ability to create new vocabulary. Linguistics and psycholinguistics have not yet advanced to the point where a satisfactory analysis of the last three aspects of creativity can be provided, but we have reasonably good insights into the ability of every normal person to deal with novel utterances as if they were familiar. The way to approach this problem is to consider the kinds of linguistic rules all humans follow unconsciously when speaking and understanding natural Language.

1.3

Linguistic Rules

How can we explain the fact that we do not regard most new sentences as odd or strange? After all, the appearance of phenomena that we have never encountered before usually causes surprise or bewilderment. The answer, of course, lies in the fact that although a sentence in our language may be entirely novel, its principles of construction are familiar. For example, you probably have never before encountered a sentence identical to the one you are now reading, but you have no trouble understanding it because you are familiar with the principles that underlie its construction. By principles we mean the linguistic rules that describe such things as sentence structure, word order, the form of word endings, and so on. Such principles of construction, which are shared by the members of any linguistic community, are necessary in order for people to communicate in their native tongue. It is *not* the case that linguistic communication takes place by the exchange of sentences drawn from a commonly shared list somehow stored in everybody's mind—there are simply too many sentences.

To reinforce the point that there are far too many sentences for any one person to have heard, much less memorized, them all, consider how many English sentences there are that contain twenty words. We pick the number twenty because it is not at all uncommon for sentences to run at least that long. The sentence immediately preceding this one, for example, contains exactly twenty words. George Miller, a well-known psycholinguist, has estimated that there are approximately 10^{20} such sentences—that is, a '1' followed by twenty zeroes (Miller, 1967, pp. 79–80). If you heard one sentence every second, with no time out for sleeping or eating, it would take you 31,688,087,000,000 (3.1688087×10^{13}) years to hear all the sentences twenty words in length. That is more years than many astronomers believe the solar system has existed!

Clearly, even if there were a limit on the length of sentences to twenty words, it would not be possible to characterize any individual's knowledge of English by claiming that he carried around a list of all its sentences in his head! But there is in fact no limit on the length of a sentence. A sentence twenty words in length can be made into a sentence twenty-one words in length by adding, say, an adjective or some other modifier. A sentence twenty-one words in length can be made longer by adding another modifier or a subordinate clause of some kind—and so on. (Analogous arguments are made in mathematics to show that the set of integers is infinitely large; for any given integer there is always a larger integer.) Of course, if we were to continue this too long, we would eventually get to the point of dealing with sentences so ridiculously long that a person could not utter one of them without taking time out to eat and sleep and perhaps even to grow old and die. The point here is that there is no purely linguistic limit on the length of sentences—the only limits are the practical ones imposed by biological properties not part of the linguistic system proper. Of course any individual deals with only a finite number of sentences (or integers) in a lifetime. But the fact still remains that there is an infinite number of English sentences, a finite subset of which might be encountered by an individual during his lifetime. Every human language has this property.

We conclude, then, that each individual possesses a set of linguistic principles or rules that account for the structure of each of the infinite number of sentences in the language. These **rules** are unconscious and were acquired in childhood by processes that are not well understood. (See Chapter 8 for a discussion of the child's acquisition of his native language.) As will be discussed, these linguistic rules are certainly not explicitly taught to children.

The fact that these rules are unconscious is important. The philosopher Michael Polanyi (1958) has made a crucial distinction between those aspects of human knowledge that are conscious (**explicit** in Polanyi's terminology) and those that are unconscious, or **tacit.** An example of explicit knowledge is the math student's knowledge of the rules of calculus, learned after many hours of study. Although after considerable experience these rules can be applied more or less automatically and with little thought, they are learned by conscious study and can always be explicitly stated. Tacit knowledge is exemplified by the handball player's knowledge of the direction in which a ball is likely to bounce off a wall. The ballplayer may have no knowledge of the rules of physics and be unable to explain why the ball will bounce in one direction or another. He nevertheless has some unconscious knowledge, based perhaps on experience with bouncing objects since early childhood, that enables him to form such predictions. Knowledge of one's native language is clearly an example of tacit knowledge.

In addition to being tacit, it is important to realize that the application of linguistic knowledge in everyday speech is automatic. Philip Lieberman (1973), a contemporary linguist, has termed this aspect of human cognitive ability **automatization.** He points out that speech production and perception involve a massive number of incredibly intricate gestures of the speech organs as well as many complicated grammatical operations. He points out:

> None of these processes is, however, what the speaker or listener is directly concerned with. The semantic content of the message is the primary concern of the speaker or hearer. The sending and receiving processes are essentially automatic. No conscious thought is expended in the process of speech production, speech perception, or any of the . . . grammatical stages that may intervene between the semantic content of the message and the acoustic signal. (p. 64)

The study of these unconscious and automatic structures and processes is of course the main task of theoretical linguistics and psycholinguistics.

1.4
Infinite Capacity with Finite Means

No matter how children learn the rules of their languages, and no matter how they are represented in the brain, one thing is certain: There is a finite number of linguistic rules for each language. They were acquired over a finite period of time, during the few years of childhood. Furthermore they are stored within the finite limits of the brain. Therefore a characteristic of Language in general is an infinite capacity with a finite means; an infinite number of sentences are accounted for on the basis of a finite set of rules.

The overall goals of a theory of Language can be deduced from the discussion in the preceding few paragraphs. Recall that we said earlier that linguists hope to describe those properties of Language that are common to all humans and that differentiate it from other animal communication systems. We now see that in order to accomplish this end, it will be necessary to characterize linguistic rules. A theory of Language will have to say what kinds of linguistic rules there are and how they are organized. In particular, such a theory will have to explain how the rules of any language, which must be finite in number, can account for the production or perception of an infinite number of possible sentences.

The goal of explaining the infinitude of Language by means of a finite rule system is comparatively recent in linguistics. In fact it is this idea that distinguishes generative linguistics from other schools of thought in linguistics. The first publication of importance that put forth this viewpoint was Noam Chomsky's *Syntactic Structures* (1957). This book detonated a revolution in linguistics and psychology by creating a new approach to problems within these disciplines that differs radically from what had gone on before.

1.5
Particular Languages and Language in General

We have seen that it is necessary to characterize a language by means of a set of rules that are somehow represented in the brain of each speaker of that language. Any two people can understand each other only if the rules possessed by each are sufficiently similar to each other. But we have been using the word 'language' in a way that is perhaps rather unfamiliar. In everyday usage the word 'language' is used to refer to some language, such as French, Chinese, Navaho, Swahili. How can we reconcile the notion of Language that we have developed in the preceding paragraphs to the existence of a number of different languages? Is it not a contradiction to say that possession of Language is a biological trait but that there exists a large number of different languages? (Actually, there are well over 3,000 different languages spoken on the face of the globe today.) If Language is a biologically based phenomenon, then why doesn't everybody speak the same language?

We commence a systematic answer to these questions by recalling that it is necessary to assume that each person who knows a language possesses a set of linguistic rules that enable him to produce and understand the sentences of that language. The rules of the English speaker differ from the rules of the Navaho speaker. The person who speaks both Navaho and English possesses two sets of rules, Navaho rules and English rules. Although each human language must be characterized by a set of rules, each language requires different rules.

It is a remarkable fact that there are numerous characteristics common to the rules of all the world's languages. These common characteristics are called **linguistic universals.** For one thing every human language has the creative capacities discussed above. There are many more universal properties of human Language, however, ranging from general properties of linguistic rules and rule organization to rather specific features, such as the fact that all languages contain consonants and vowels. We will examine some linguistic universals in the course of this book. The point is that the rules of each language conform to a general pattern, the pattern of Language. Within the general framework of Language, there is a certain amount of room for diversity. We are claiming, then, that the differences among the world's languages are only rather superficial and that what is biologically based is the general framework of Language. Generative linguists maintain that this universal system of Language exists because the human brain is organized in such a way that only languages of a particular kind can be represented in it. Thus, when we speak of Language, we mean a general capacity of human beings to possess a communication system with certain specific properties; however, when we speak of a language like French or Chinese, we refer to a particular instance of this general phenomenon. All languages conform to the general principles that characterize Language in general.

Generative linguists claim that since the general characteristics of Language alluded to in the preceding paragraph are universal, it is reasonable to think that they are common to every child and that some universals may be due to more general cognitive or intellectual properties of all normal human beings. We will amplify this view and present some arguments in its favor in the course of the remainder of this chapter. If we accept the generativists' view, we consider the child's acquisition of his native language as an interaction between his innate capacity for Language and the speech that he hears in his environment. Both innate linguistic capacity and exposure to speech are necessary conditions for the child's acquisition of his native language. We are saying, then, that the child's brain contains certain rather general cognitive or intellectual properties that underlie the development of the universal principles of linguistic structure.

Given the claim that universal linguistic principles are general properties of the human mind rather than derived by each child directly and solely from his exposure to speech, the child's acquisition of his native language can include only those features of the language spoken in his environment that characterize that particular language. The considerations discussed in the above paragraph indicate how the distinction between Language in general and particular languages is reflected in the individual.

One might object at this point that we are making entirely too much of the fact that human beings are the only creatures with Language. The reader might suggest that the uniqueness of Language is completely accounted for by the fact that humans are the only creatures with a sound-producing apparatus (vocal tract) ideally suited for producing speech. Indeed, if those features of the human communication system that are unique in the animal kingdom could be entirely accounted for on the basis of physiology of the vocal tract, then the study of linguistic universals would be quite uninteresting. But there is some rather compelling evidence that the human brain is specifically designed for Language.

Consider the example of the unfortunate child who suffers from congenital anarthria, an organically induced condition that prevents the victim from willfully manipulating the muscles of his speech organs. Eric Lenneberg, a neurophysiologist who has made important contributions to the understanding of the relationship between Language and the brain, has

studied such a case (Lenneberg, 1967). He reports that ¡
precludes not only the development of speech but even ¡
babbling. (By speech we mean the production of linguistic
means of the vocal tract.) One might think that such a chilc
chance of acquiring Language as some lower animal. The f
by Lenneberg, however, speak otherwise. Although such children obviously
do not learn to speak, many do acquire normal receptive language skills
(and without special training, at that). The example of the anarthritic
child demonstrates that the human linguistic capacity is independent of
the ability to produce speech.

As we said above, linguistics is concerned with a characterization of
the human communication system. It is now evident that this means that
a central focus of theoretical linguistics is on the general capacity for
Language—i.e., on universals of Language—as opposed to the description
of individual languages. A major goal of linguistics, then, is to formulate
a general theory of Language that characterizes linguistic universals. Since
any given language conforms to the general principles of Language, the
rules the linguist proposes as a description of any language must be formulated within the framework provided by the general theory of Language.

In attempting to gain insight into linguistic universals, the linguist must
have descriptions of several languages available. Linguists who are concerned with characterizing a general theory of Language and linguistic
universals are interested in descriptions of particular languages primarily
for what they reveal about general properties of human Language and
about the types of linguistic structures that exist in individual languages.

1.6
The Origin of Language

It is interesting to speculate about the possible origins of Language in
man's evolutionary history. We have argued that the capacity to represent
Language in the brain is a uniquely human capacity, just as is the use of
a bipedal gait, the possession of an opposed thumb, and numerous species-
specific characteristics of bone and muscle structure. Contemporary linguists believe that Language was not possible until *Homo sapiens* was established as a species. However, anthropologists have produced evidence
of the prior existence of creatures intermediary in many physical dimensions between early forms of the higher primates and man himself. There
were ancient near-humans whose dentition and/or cranial dimensions were
between those of ape and man. It is not inconceivable that such creatures
had some kind of communication system more structurally complex than
the communication systems that exist naturally in the animal kingdom
today, but still less complex than human Language (see Lieberman, 1975).
This speculation becomes more tempting when we see that a number of

chimpanzees have been taught—in experimental situations—rather complicated systems of communication even though there is no evidence that chimpanzees have a naturally occurring communication system with the creative capacities of human Language. While the laboratory "languages" learned by the experimental chimps do not have the structural complexity and the possibility for creativity embodied in human Language, they do represent a considerable improvement over typical animal communication systems. (See Gardner and Gardner, 1969, and Fleming, 1974, for a description of the laboratory languages of the chimpanzees.) In the light of the chimp experiments it is not difficult to imagine a now-extinct species of creatures brighter than apes but still less than human, speaking some sort of rudimentary language less complex than that of *Homo sapiens.*

One might ask whether or not we can reconstruct the communication system of the ancestors of *Homo sapiens* by attempting to determine earlier forms of human Language, operating under the assumption that the further back in time we could reconstruct languages, the closer we would be to the communication system of our ancestors. A specific type of linguistic inquiry, known as **diachronic**—or **historical**—**linguistics,** attempts to characterize ancient languages and general principles of linguistic change over time. For example, historical linguists have studied the manner in which Indo-European languages have changed over time and have reconstructed portions of the dead language from which English, French, Russian, Hindi, and all the other contemporary Indo-European languages evolved. Aspects of the "mother languages" have been reconstructed for other language families as well. It is useless to hope, however, that historical linguistics will ever be able to construct the communication system of a protohuman species. For one thing the procedures of historical linguistics allow us to reconstruct features of languages spoken only a few thousand years ago. The evolution of man took place at least a million years ago. The inability of historical linguistics to trace the development of languages back more than a few thousand years is not due to a lack of techniques or theory, but rather to the irretrievable loss of direct information about now-dead languages.

1.7
Language and Culture

The claim that the most interesting properties of Language are those that are universal is at odds with the commonly held view that the basic, structural properties of any given language are a reflection of the culture in which that language is spoken (or vice versa). Thus it is frequently argued that since the particular language that children acquire is determined by the society in which they are reared, it follows that Language in general is a purely cultural phenomenon.

As further support for the argument that Language is rooted solely in culture it is frequently pointed out that children removed from human society would not acquire any human language, if they would survive at all. Contrast this situation with a purely biologically acquired trait such as walking. Children would learn to walk in essentially the same way in any society in which they were reared, or even if they survived childhood in an environment entirely removed from human society. Edward Sapir, an important anthropologist and linguist who made many important contributions early in this century, was an exponent of this view (Sapir, 1921).

The viewpoint expressed in the preceding two paragraphs seems compellingly plausible yet quite incompatible with the claim that Language is a biologically based phenomenon. To resolve this contradiction, observe that there is no inconsistency between the claim that Language is biologically based and the statement that some aspects of particular languages are reflections of the cultures that speak them. In fact some examples of how individual features of particular languages are correlated with characteristics of the societies where they are spoken are discussed below. Recall also that we are claiming that humans have a biological basis for Language in general, not that specific languages are innate. In other words all children, and only human children, have brains designed in such a way that they *can* learn a language, provided that they are exposed to the appropriate environment.

It is possible that unique features of particular languages may be connected to unique features of the societies that speak them. For example, Eskimo and Lapp societies have a rich vocabulary for different varieties of snow; the inhabitants of the Faroe Islands in the North Atlantic speak a language that has many words relating to ships and fishing; English, a language spoken by an advanced industrial society, has an extensive scientific and technical vocabulary not shared by the languages spoken in more "backward" times and places. But these differences relate only to vocabulary and are not connected with any of the structural principles of languages. The specific rules of a language which characterize its grammatical structure are generally independent of vocabulary and of cultural influences.

There is a well-known and very interesting idea that the world-view of a society is determined by the structure of its language. This idea is frequently referred to as the Whorf hypothesis after its principle recent proponent, Benjamin Lee Whorf (see Carroll, 1956). Whorf himself referred to this idea as the **linguistic relativity principle.** Less emphasis was put on the importance of linguistic universals at the time of Whorf's writing (in the 1930s) than today. A contemporary version of the Whorf hypothesis might be the claim that at least some differences among the world-views of societies are due to those aspects of linguistic structure that are free to vary within the limits imposed by the general plan of Language.

If there is any truth to this idea, it must be admitted that only rather marginal aspects of a society's world-view could be involved. One area of Language that has been put forth as a possible candidate for such a connection is the system of tenses. In the familiar European languages the tense system usually is based on a partition of the time dimension into past, present, and future. But not all languages relate the universe of discourse to the dimension of time in this manner. Although it would take us too far astray to investigate in detail the different systems of tense that occur among the world's languages, suffice it to say that they are quite diverse and, from the Western viewpoint, sometimes quite exotic. It is not inconceivable that an individual's psychological perception of time is influenced by the tense system of the language he speaks. There is no conclusive proof of a causal relation between linguistic features and such perceptual phenomena, however. Even if such a connection were to be established, we would be faced with an example of the chicken-and-egg problem: Does the language have the system of tenses it has because of the way the society relates to time, or vice versa? It is unlikely that this is a resolvable issue. In any case the fact that any time relationship can be expressed in any language (even though some languages require cumbersome expressions for some relationships that are relatively simple to express in other languages) casts doubt on the idea that a person's perception of time is locked in by his linguistic system.

Before leaving the topic of the relationship between Language and culture, consider the popular notion of "primitive" languages and "inadequate" dialects. Linguists have long recognized that no language is inferior to any other in terms of its expressive capacity. No language has ever been discovered in which it is impossible to express any given idea. All languages, even those spoken by societies usually considered the most "backward," possess perfectly adequate devices for expressing such typically rational concepts as causation, contingencies, directness and indirectness of experience—in short, all the finely wrought distinctions characteristic of human thought. Moreover the linguistic devices utilized by various languages for these concepts do not differ from each other in terms of simplicity or primitiveness. All languages possess highly structured linguistic rules for these expressive purposes, and no language is fundamentally simpler than any other in terms of these rules.

There are, as we have seen, differences among languages in terms of vocabulary. For example, it is not possible to talk about atomic energy in a language that lacks the vocabulary appropriate for that topic, at least without frequent and cumbersome circumlocutions. But every human language has the capacity to develop vocabulary to meet new cultural needs. The content of vocabulary has nothing to do with the structure of a language—the stock of words is rather a reflection of the material and historical context of the society that speaks the language. When a society undergoes a change that requires a richer universe of discourse, the vocabulary of its language is always ready to change in order to meet the new situation. And the only changes ever required are in the area of vocabulary; the essential linguistic structure of any language, including the rules of sentence structure, is suitable to any universe of discourse.

It follows from the foregoing that there are no primitive languages. Of course this is just what we are led to expect from the discussion of linguistic universals and the biological basis of Language discussed throughout this chapter. Since it is a fact that the various races of *Homo sapiens* do not differ biologically in any fundamental way, we are led to expect that there are no differences in Language among human communities.

Since there are no primitive languages, it also follows that there are no "inadequate dialects." Although there are frequently obvious differences among the speech patterns of different segments of any large and complex society, no one of these different dialects is better or worse than any other with respect to adequacy of expression. It is a mere accident of history that the dialect of English now taken as standard enjoys this status. If the history of England and/or America had been different, some other dialect of English that is now considered nonstandard could have been the language of the upper classes.

It may be worthwhile at this point to clear up a possible confusion about the notion of the biological basis of Language. There is a theory held by some contemporary researchers that certain groups, such as American Blacks, tend to be intellectually impoverished because of genetic differences between them and the rest of society. Arthur Jensen (1969) is a well-known proponent of this view. We hasten to add that we emphatically disagree with this viewpoint. But we hope that it is clear from our discussion of the biological basis of Language that we do not mean to explain any linguistic differences between groups of people on the basis of genetic differences. Instead, we are saying that there are genetic features of all human beings that account for their general linguistic capacities. These genetic features are part of the set of characteristics that determine, for example, that the offspring of a human will be a baby human rather than, say, a puppy. Linguistic differences between groups are due to historical and sociological factors beyond the scope of this book.

1.8
The Linguistic Communication System

Since the purpose of this book is to present theory and research that attempt to account for the individual's ability to use language as a communication system, let us consider what is involved in linguistic communication. Consider linguistic communication between two individuals, **A** and **B,** where **A** is speaking to **B** and **B** understands what is being said to him (see Figure 1.1). **A** has in his mind some sort of message (or idea), and he wishes **B** to form in his head the same message. This message is transformed ultimately into a series of neural impulses that are sent to the muscles responsible for the actual production of speech, which follows immediately. This process is frequently referred to as **encoding.** The listener, **B,** must **decode A's** message by converting the sounds into a semantic representation.

A minimal requirement for this sort of activity to take place is that **A** and **B** must know the same language. That is, each must have internalized the same set of rules of a particular language. Such a set of rules is called a **grammar.** It is a theory of how a particular language relates sound and meaning, and it is also a theory about the knowledge that a person has if he knows that language. After many years of considering the question, some generative linguists believe that a grammar consists of three main components, each describing a certain set of linguistic rules. The **semantic component** of the grammar specifies the possible meanings for each sentence in that language. The rules of the **syntactic component** are necessary for a description of the general grammatical structure of sentences. Syntactic rules describe, for example, the order of words in sentences and the relationships between parts of a sentence. The **phonological component** consists of a set of rules specifying the actual pronunciation of each of the words and endings, the intonation of the sentence, and so on. In short, the rules of the phonological component describe how each sentence is to be pronounced. We will have a more detailed look at each of these components in later chapters.

A description of a person's grammatical knowledge does not include how he actually uses that knowledge in the production and comprehension of sentences. The grammar does not specify the information-processing

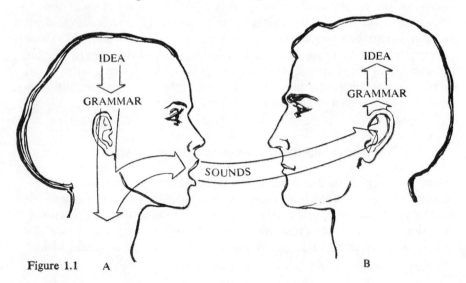

Figure 1.1   A   B

abilities of the human brain that are required for verbal communication.

The concept we are dealing with here has frequently been characterized as the distinction between linguistic **competence** and **performance**. Linguistic competence refers specifically to an individual's knowledge of his language, i.e., to his grammar. Linguistic performance, on the other hand, refers to the cognitive processes the individual employs in actual use of his linguistic knowledge. Bear in mind that competence and performance are technical terms and have meanings in linguistics rather different from what we would expect from the ordinary usage of these terms. Thus in everyday parlance competence is usually taken to mean something like "adequacy, skill, or proficiency"; performance, on the other hand, is usually taken as specific actions or specimens of behavior. As will become clear in the course of this book, linguistic competence refers only to the native speaker's knowledge of his language (i.e., his grammar), whereas performance refers to the set of skills and strategies employed by the language user as he applies his linguistic competence in the actual production and comprehension of sentences.

Before we illustrate and amplify the distinction between competence and performance, a word of caution is in order. The competence/performance concept as presented here derives primarily from an important Swiss linguist of the early years of this century, Ferdinand de Saussure. Saussure, whose conception of the distinction differed in significant ways from later conceptions, described it in terms of his notions of *langue* (literally "language," analogous to competence) and *parole* (literally "speech," analogous to performance). Noam Chomsky interpreted Saussure's ideas in terms of the generative theory of linguistics in the early years of the development of this school, in the late fifties and early sixties. As linguistics and psycholinguistics developed within this framework, the competence/performance idea has undergone a number of revisions. For example, several scholars have pointed out that many aspects of competence and performance seem to be inextricably bound up with each other. In section 2.3 we reexamine the competence/performance distinction and briefly describe some stages in the evolution of this concept.

To illustrate the distinction between competence and performance, it is useful to draw an analogy between Language and chess. Before people can play chess, they must learn all the rules of the game—how to set up the pieces at the beginning of the game and how to move the pieces on the board. The rules of the game describe the legal configurations of pieces on the board—that is, certain configurations are not possible because they could not be attained by any legal sequence of moves. Furthermore the rules of the game dictate which sequences of configurations of pieces are legal and which are not. The analogy between the rules of the game of chess and the rules of grammar should be clear: Just as the rules of grammar describe sentences in the language, the rules of chess define the possible configurations of pieces on the chessboard.

Linguistic Competence

Now suppose that the person who had just thoroughly mastered all the rules of the game attempted to play an experienced player. The novice would obviously be badly beaten, even though he or she might never make an illegal move. What qualities does the experienced player possess that the novice lacks? The experienced chess player possesses a basic knowledge of the rules of the game and a set of skills and strategies for employing this knowledge in order to achieve specific ends. That is, experienced chess players have an image of the configuration of pieces they would like to achieve—i.e., a configuration that means checkmate of the opponent—and attempt to achieve it by a sequence of legal moves. A player who is more skillful than another will succeed in achieving the desired goal. Therefore, in order to actually play a game of chess, players must possess, in addition to chess competence (knowledge of the rules of the game), a set of strategies that enable them to perform as chess players. These strategies are, of course, analogous to linguistic performance.

The analogy between chess and language has its limitations, as do most analogies. Linguistic rules, unlike chess rules, are not usually conscious. In order to learn the rules of chess one must sit down and memorize them; they form part of Polyani's explicit knowledge. It is not possible to learn a language that way; in any case, as discussed above, nobody has ever learned his native language that way. Nevertheless, perhaps this example may help to clarify for the reader the general nature of the distinction between competence and performance. The competence/performance distinction is a recurring theme throughout this book.

1.9
Descriptive Versus Prescriptive Grammar

The foregoing use of the word "grammar" is probably rather different from that familiar to the average reader. This word reminds most people of school experiences with teachers who admonished them to avoid linguistic transgressions such as ending sentences with prepositions. That is, grammar in this sense is a collection of statements that purport to say what is the "correct" or "accepted" way to speak and write. This is called **normative** or **prescriptive** grammar. Although prescriptive grammar may be useful in endeavors like the establishment of literary norms, it is of no value to the scientific study of Language. The linguist is, instead, interested in a grammar that is a description of what he believes to exist in some form in the mind of speakers of the language being described. The linguist is concerned with **descriptive** grammar, as opposed to prescriptive grammar.

To make the distinction between prescriptive and descriptive grammar concrete, consider expressions such as 'It's me'. The prescriptive grammarian might insist that this is incorrect, and would probably try to teach the pupils to say instead 'It's I'. The descriptive linguist, on the other hand, assumes that the speakers who use such expressions (that is, most native speakers of English) possess linguistic rules that underlie the production of such sentences. The linguist would then try to formulate a set of rules that would be a model of what he believes is in the heads of such speakers. From the linguist's point of view, the linguistic rules that a person has internalized are neither correct nor incorrect. The linguist's only concern is to describe them accurately.

The Data and
Methods of Linguistic Inquiry

2.1
The Tasks of the Linguist

In the previous chapter we saw that the goal of the linguist is essentially twofold: First, and most important, he or she wants to develop a general theory of Language that will characterize the commonalities among languages of the world. We will henceforth refer to this as the **linguistic metatheory** or, occasionally, merely as the **metatheory.** Second, the linguist seeks to provide descriptions of particular languages. Another way to describe the first task is to say that a general theory of Language describes the basic pattern to which each individual languages must conform. Thus a general theory of Language—the metatheory—tells us that each individual language must be described in terms of semantic, syntactic, and phonological rules. In addition the metatheory prescribes the general form and organization of the rules and the basic units on which the rules operate.

The metatheory does not specify the particular rules of individual languages; this is the second task of the linguist. In order to describe a particular language, linguists must formulate rules that are unique to the language and that they believe best approximate the internalized rules of its native speakers. Thus the grammar is also a theory with a general form and organization that are determined by linguistic metatheory. The grammar of a particular language, then, is composed of information about Language in general (characterized by the metatheory) and about the particular language being described.

The word "information" in the last sentence of the above paragraph may be misleading. Actually, when linguists come to conclusions about aspects of the metatheory or of a theory of a particular language, they regard those conclusions as hypotheses. By this we mean that the conclusions reached by linguists have the same status as the conclusions reached by any scientist. They represent the linguists' best guesses—based on all the evidence that has been amassed—about the real structure of Language in general or of a language in particular. The sets of hypotheses that constitute linguistic metatheory and those that constitute particular grammars must be justified logically and tested empirically, just as the hypotheses that constitute any scientific theory must be. The next portion of this chapter will be devoted to a discussion of the kinds of evidence that the linguist must examine in order to construct and test hypotheses about the structure of particular languages. In the final section of this chapter we will discuss the competence/performance distinction again in the light of the new material.

2.2

Hypotheses about the Structure of Particular Languages

Linguistics is an empirical science. Linguistic hypotheses are constructed in order to explain and predict events in the real world. Physical theory predicts certain properties of physical objects. Chemical theories predict the reactions of certain substances under a variety of conditions of heat, cold, interaction with other substances, etc. So we must ask: What are the events that linguistic theory must predict, or, equivalently, what is the range of phenomena for which linguistic theory must account? The answer is that in a very broad sense linguistic theory must account for certain judgments that a native speaker makes about sentences in his language. These judgments, which will be described below, are chosen because experience has shown that analyses of them have yielded some insight into the internalized knowledge that a person has about his language. These judgments represent tasks that can be performed by a native speaker of a particular language, but not by someone of comparable age and intelligence who does not have an internalized knowledge of that language. We shall see, for example, that we consider the speaker's judgment that a particular sentence is ambiguous to be a fact for linguistic theory to explain. On the other hand, we do not consider the speaker's judgment that a sentence is spoken in anger to be such a fact. The judgment that a sentence is ambiguous rests on an analysis of its syntactic and semantic content, both of which are aspects of linguistic knowledge. Thus only a person who knows English could reliably report on the ambiguity of an English sentence. The judgment that a sentence is spoken in anger is not a judgment about the sentence, but a judgment about the speaker. Such a judgment is not based on a knowledge of the language, but on knowledge about other aspects of human beings, such as their emotions and how they are manifested. It is thus frequently the case that we can judge the emotional tone of an utterance spoken in a tongue unknown to us.

Notice that in the above paragraph we have used the verbs 'predict', 'explain', and 'account for' interchangeably. We can do this if we assume that events (in this case linguistic judgments of a speaker of some language) are predicted from general theoretical principles rather than from a summary of observed events.

What is the distinction between a scientific explanation and a statement that summarizes observed events? Consider, for example, modern astronomy. Astronomical theory predicts on the basis of general principles that an event we refer to as the sunrise will occur at a time that can be specified for each morning. Astronomers have developed a mathematical theory explaining the orbits of heavenly bodies on the basis of physical principles. Application of this general theory to the earth's orbit around the sun allows them to predict exactly when the sun will seem to rise for any place on the surface of the earth on any given date. Thus the prediction of the time of sunrise and the explanation for that event are inextricably related. One can, however, imagine a society where the people have no astronomical theory but predict that the sun will rise only because they have an expectancy, based on prior experience, that it will do so. In such a case prediction would not be based on explanation and would not be analogous to the kind of prediction we want to achieve in linguistic theory.

To complete the analogy, a grammar of a language (i.e, a theory of that language) should consist of elements that we can apply in such a way that we can predict events. Elements of the grammar—or theory—of a language take the form of rules that can be applied to describe sentences with certain properties. These sentences are then submitted to a speaker of that language for evaluation. The theory, or grammar, predicts that the speaker will judge the sentences to have the supposed properties. Since the sentences are generated from general rules, we claim that certain properties of those sentences—such as grammaticality or ambiguity—are simultaneously explained by those rules. Since it is the native speaker who decides whether those sentences are in fact grammatical, ambiguous, or whatever, we also claim that the rules reflect general principles that the speaker has internalized about his language.

Let us now turn to the data for which the grammar of a language must account—that is, to the linguistically based judgments made by a native speaker about sentences (and parts thereof) in his language.

2.21 The ability to distinguish grammatical from ungrammatical sentences

If one knows a language, one knows that there are strings of words that are not admissible as sentences of that language, though the individual words themselves may be legitimate. A speaker of any dialect of English knows, for example, that (1), (2), and (3) below are grammatical sentences of English, but (4) is not (at least not without extra emphasis on 'him'). In accordance with standard practice in linguistics, an asterisk is placed by sentence (4) to indicate that it is not a grammatical sentence of English.

(1)   The orangutan picked her baby up.
(2)   The orangutan picked up her baby.
(3)   The orangutan picked him up.
(4)   *The orangutan picked up him.

Of course (4) contains perfectly correct English words and is easily comprehensible; however, there is something about the order of the words that violates certain general principles of sentence formation that must be included in the grammar of English. Verbs like 'pick up', 'pour out', 'look over', include a particle ('up', 'out', and 'over'). If the direct object is a noun, such as 'baby', then the particle can appear either before the direct object and next to the verb—as in (2)—or after the direct object, separated from the verb—as in (1). If the direct object is a pronoun such as 'him', however, the particle cannot appear before the direct object; it must follow the object. Compare (2) and (4). The former is grammatical, the latter is not, yet the only difference between them is that in (4) the direct object is a pronoun, while in (2) it is a noun. Now compare (1) and (3). Both are grammatical, showing that the construction in which the object appears before the verb particle produces an admissible English sentence whether the object is a noun or a pronoun.

There are, of course, strings of words that some speakers might differ about or that have an uncertain status. For example, the sentences in (5)–(16) exemplify strings about which English speakers might be uncertain.

(5)   Harry shouted to run.   (Postal, 1970)
(6)   Three of the mere children are in college already.   (Smith, 1969)
(7)   John saw the man running who wore a black homburg.   (Smith, 1969)
(8)   I sent the jug which was from India out.   (Ross, 1969)
(9)   Let's look for Rick a coat at Macy's.
(10) We might could drive to Dallas in three hours.
(11) What we endeavored was not to antagonize him.   (Rosenbaum, 1969)
(12) His keeping chanting ads bugs me.   (Ross, 1972)

(13) The last time I saw the youngster he was growing like a weed, and now I hear he's still at it.

(14) Can I bring you anything from upstairs down?

(15) The men want to be all invited.

(16) Who (or whom) did you send the package?

Are they or are they not sentences? Many of these examples have been discussed by linguists, as indicated. A plausible way to proceed, then, is to restrict our attention to the clear cases, examples of sentences and nonsentences where there would certainly be agreement. If we are able to work out a satisfactory grammar on the basis of clear cases, then perhaps the grammar may provide some insight into the uncertain cases. We will deal only with clear cases in this book, as we feel one should in linguistics in general.

In order to describe the tacit knowledge that the native speaker must have to identify sentences and nonsentences in his language, the grammar must provide a set of rules that will describe, or generate, not only *all* the grammatical sentences of the speaker's language, but *only* the grammatical sentences of the language. In other words it would be inadequate to have a grammar of English that would generate (1), (2), (3), and (4). Such a grammar would not account for the speaker's judgment about the ungrammaticality of (4).

2.22 The ability to recognize ambiguous sentences

Many sentences have more than one meaning. Some sentences, such as (17), are ambiguous because one or more of the words contained in the sentence is ambiguous.

(17) There is a nut behind the wheel.

Thus all the meanings of (17) can be accounted for completely by the various meanings that can be associated with the words 'nut' and 'wheel'. From the viewpoint of syntax, however, sentences that are ambiguous because they have more than one grammatical structure are more interesting. Consider, for instance, a sentence such as (18), which is ambiguous because the words can be grouped together in two different ways.

(18) The man looked up the street.

Any ambiguous sentence has, by definition, two or more interpretations. Each of the two interpretations of (18) is associated with a unique grammatical structure. Thus the interpretation of (18) that means the man consulted a directory of some sort, perhaps to see where the street is, is associated with a grammatical description of the sentence where 'up' is a particle of some sort closely associated with 'looked'. The interpretation that means the man was, for example, standing in the street and looking up it, is associated with a grammatical description where 'up' is a preposition closely associated with 'the street'. The grammar, then, should differentiate between the two kinds of 'up' and, most importantly, show that in one meaning it is bound with the verb 'looked', whereas it is bound with 'the street' in the other meaning.

As will be shown in more detail in the next chapters, the transformational-generative theory of grammar provides devices known as **phrase markers** (PMs) to illustrate the kinds of grammatical information described above. Simplified versions of the PMs associated with the two meanings of (18) are shown in Figure 2.1. In Figure 2.1a 'looked up' is analyzed as a verb–particle combination, whereas 'up' is analyzed as a preposition associated with the 'street' in Figure 2.1b. The verb–particle construction is similar to other constructions such as 'put up' (in the sense of 'to put up preserves'), 'look over' (as in 'look over the examination'), 'put down', 'pick up', and many others. The preposition construction, as in Figure 2.1b, is similar to constructions like 'down the street', and 'in the bookcase'.

The PMs show how the various parts, or constituents, of the sentence are organized with respect to each other. That is, they illustrate the constituent structure of sentences. Starting at the top of Figure 2.1a, this PM shows that the largest constituent of all—the whole sentence itself, abbreviated by the symbol S—consists of a noun phrase, NP, followed by a verb phrase, VP. The constituent labeled VP in turn consists of a verb, V, followed by another NP constituent. The V consists of a verb stem, V_{stm} followed by a particle, prt. Each NP constituent of this sentence consists of an article, art, followed by a noun, N. The two Ns in this sentence are 'man' 'street'; the V_{stm} is 'looked'; the prt is 'up'. The PM illustrated in Figure 2.1b differs

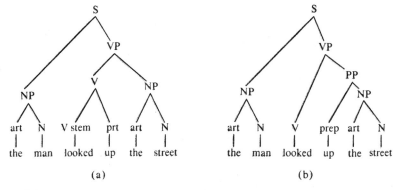

(a)   (b)

Figure 2.1

from that in 2.1a in the structure of the VP. The VP of (b) consists of a V, 'looked', followed by a prepositional phrase, PP. The PP in turn consists of a preposition, prep, followed by the NP 'the street'. The prep, of course, is 'up'.

The point here is that since the grammar must account for the fact that (18) has two possible meanings, it must provide two grammatical descriptions for (18), one for each meaning. Since the difference in meanings between the two sentences can be accounted for in terms of constituent structure, the PMs illustrated in Figure 2.1 characterize the relevant grammatical facts.

There is another type of ambiguity that does not depend on alternative groupings of words and that reveals a further, very interesting aspect of the organization of the grammars of natural language.

(19) Fighting tigers can be dangerous.

Consider sentence (19), whose ambiguity depends on whether one interprets the sentence to mean that the tigers are doing the fighting or that someone (or something) else is fighting the tigers. There are two possible ways in which the words 'fighting' and 'tigers' can be related to each other in this sentence: in the former sense 'tigers' is the subject of 'fighting'; in the latter interpretation 'tigers' is the object of 'fighting'.

There is an important difference between the kinds of ambiguity exemplified by (18) and (19). It is possible to account for the ambiguity of (18) by referring to two possible ways of grouping the words that occur in the sentence. In (19), on the other hand, it is necessary to refer to the more abstract notion of grammatical relations. As the following discussion will make clear, these examples not only show that the grammar must provide a definition of relational concepts, such as subject and object, but also lead the linguist to assume that there is an abstract level of representation for each sentence, usually referred to as **deep structure.**

2.23 The ability to identify underlying grammatical relations in sentences in the language

Whenever a speaker of English hears an English sentence, he is automatically and immediately aware of what is the subject, what is the verb, and what is the object (if present) of the sentence. That is, he is able to figure out who did what to whom. These relationships are characterized as grammatical relations, the relation of subject (or actor) to verb (action), of verb (action) to object (recipient of action), and so on. As a straightforward example, consider the grammatical relations in sentence (20).

(20) The boy hit the ball.

The Data and Methods of Linguistic Inquiry

To characterize these relational notions explicitly, consider the PM associated with (20), given in Figure 2.2. Let us adopt the following definitions of subject and object:

> The subject of a sentence is the NP that is directly connected to the node labeled S, where by 'directly connected' we mean that there is no node between the NP and the S.
> The object of a verb phrase is the NP that is directly connected to the node labeled VP.

With these definitions, the fact that 'the boy' is the subject of (20) and 'the ball' is the object is made explicit. Although these definitions are given as formal aspects of the theory of syntax we are introducing here, it should be borne in mind that they are intended to correspond to our intuitive notions of subject as something like 'performer' and object as 'recipient'. That is, every NP that meets the definition of subject or object, given above, should also bear the intuitive relationship of subject and object, respectively.

Let us now consider some more complicated examples, as illustrated by the relationships between the noun phrase 'the professor' and the verb 'understand' in sentences (21) and (22).

(21) The professor is easy to understand.
(22) The professor is anxious to understand.

Any speaker of English will recognize that it is the professor who is being understood in (21) and is, in a sense, the object of 'understand'. In (22), on the other hand, it is the professor who is to understand something or someone and is, therefore, the subject of the verb 'understand'.

The PMs of these two sentences are illustrated, in greatly simplified form,

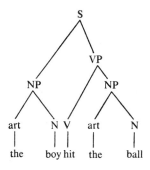

Figure 2.2

in Figure 2.3. Figure 2.3a shows the constituent labeled VP as consisting of a copula, cop, which is always some form of 'be', followed by an adjective, adj, followed in turn by another VP constituent. The latter VP simply consists of the so-called infinitive form 'to understand'. The constituent structure of (22), illustrated by the PM in Figure 2.3b, differs from that of (21) only in that 'anxious' appears in the position occupied by 'easy' in (21).

The point here is that the constituent structures of (21) and (22) do not reveal the crucial differences between the grammatical relations in the two sentences. This is not due to any fault in our definition of the notions of subject and object or to a mistaken analysis of the PMs of these two sentences. No reasonable definitions of subject and object, no reasonable analysis of the PMs of these two sentences, can yield the desired results as long as the definitions and PMs are associated with the actual, occurring forms of these two sentences. That is, the underlying, or logical, grammatical relations in these sentences are not reflected directly in their superficial forms. Despite the apparent similarity between (21) and (22) English speakers perceive the meanings of the two sentences in such a way that 'the professor' plays dissimilar roles in them. The deeper grammatical relations —namely that 'the professor' functions as the object of 'understand' in (21) whereas it functions as the subject of 'understand' in (22)—seem to underlie the superficial form of the sentences. It would be possible to find many more examples like this.

The examples discussed above reveal an extremely important fact about human Language—one that gives us a great deal of insight into linguistic structure. If underlying grammatical relations are not directly reflected at the superficial level, then our hypotheses about the structure of a language must include a level of representation more abstract than the superficial level. Our reasoning is simply this: The grammar must characterize a speaker's linguistic competence, his tacit knowledge of his language. In understanding sentences one must interpret the basic grammatical relations, which are therefore represented in linguistic competence. The examples in

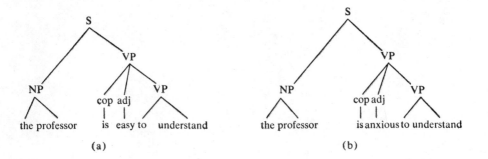

(a)   (b)

Figure 2.3

(21) and (22) illustrate that these relations cannot be identified at a superficial level of analysis for all sentences. Therefore, to characterize the knowledge of the native speaker correctly, we must hypothesize a more abstract (or underlying) level of representation at which basic grammatical relations are invariably identifiable.

The underlying representation of a sentence is described in generative linguistic theory as the **deep structure** of the sentence. It is in deep structure that the basic grammatical relations of the sentence are expressed, as well as much other information necessary to express the meaning of the sentence. The superficial form of a sentence is termed its **surface structure.** These terms will be discussed in more detail in the following chapter.

All of the PMs illustrated so far are the representations of the example sentences at the level of surface structure. Deep structures are also described in terms of PMs. The deep-structure PMs of the sentences in (21) and (22) are given in Figure 2.4. Figure 2.4a indicates that the subject of the entire sentence—that is, that which 'is easy'—is itself the sentence 'for somebody to understand the professor'. Sentences like this, which occur inside other sentences, are known as **embedded clauses.** Notice that the

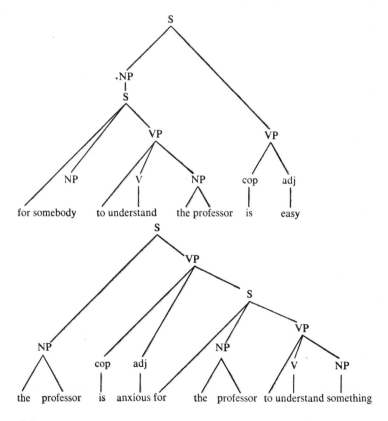

Figure 2.4

definition of object of a verb phrase given above, when applied to the embedded clause in Figure 2.3a, yields the desired results. Thus at the level of deep structure 'the professor' is the object of 'understand' in sentence (21).

Turning now to the deep-structure PM of (22), illustrated in Figure 2.4b, observe that the VP is analyzed as consisting of a cop, followed by an adj, followed in turn by an embedded clause. This embedded clause asserts what it is that 'the professor' is anxious for, namely, 'for the professor to understand something'. Observe that the definition of subject, given above, when applied to the embedded clause in Figure 2.4b, shows 'the professor' to be the subject of 'understand'. Thus here again, when the definitions of subject and object are applied to the level of deep structure, they yield results that correspond to the intuitive interpretations of 'the professor' as object of 'understand' in (21) and subject of 'understand' in (22).

The reader may well wonder where these deep-structure PMs come from and how they are related to the surface-structure PMs illustrated in Figure 2.3. The answer to these questions is that we are working with a theory put forth to explain a range of phenomena about human Language; this theory contains two sets of syntactic rules, one of which, called **phrase-structure rules** (PS rules), generates deep structure PMs. These deep-structure PMs contain grammatical information necessary for the semantic interpretation of a sentence. The second set of syntactic rules, called **transformational rules** (T rules), converts these deep-structure PMs into their surface-structure forms. See Figure 2.5.

In the following chapter we will discuss the form of these rules and give several examples. The point here is that these notions of deep structure

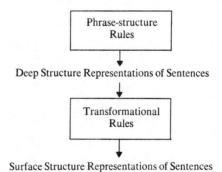

Figure 2.5 The organization of syntactic rules. There exists a set of rules that create deep structure representations of sentences, called phrase-structure rules. It is at the level of deep structure where the basic grammatical relationships necessary for semantic interpretation are defined. Deep structure representations of sentences are then operated on by transformational rules to yield the surface structure representations of sentences, which are more similar to their occurring forms.

and surface structure, as well as the subsidiary definitions of subject, object, and others we will encounter later, are all meaningful only in terms of the general theory of Language in which they are embedded. As such, their status rises and falls with the success of the general theory. If the general theory is successful in explaining the phenomena we wish to account for, if it is free from internal contradictions, and if it is not replaced by a superior theory, then these theoretical constructs are to be taken as claims about the structure of Language in the human mind.

We have attempted to show that in order to account for the ability of English speakers to interpret correctly the relationship between 'the professor' and 'understand' in sentences (21) and (22), it is necessary that the theory of Language contain the levels of deep structure and surface structure. In these examples we saw that the surface-structure PMs differ only slightly from each other (in fact only in the occurrence of 'easy' in one and 'anxious' in the other), yet their deep structures differ greatly from one another. An even more extreme example was illustrated in (19), which we considered before, in which two radically different deep structures, illustrated in Figure 2.6, are paired with two identical surface-structure PMs. In all these cases there exist very general T rules, which are necessary to account for a broad range of phenomena, which apply to the different deep-structure PMs and convert them into the similar surface-structure PMs. The reader must not make the mistake of thinking that it is the purpose of these T rules to create this kind of ambiguity; these rules have the effect of creating ambiguity by chance, as it were. But the existence of these ambiguous sentence types gives the linguist clues as to the underlying structures and the rules that account for the occurring forms. We now turn to another set of phenomena that show the necessity for assuming the existence of deep structure.

2.24 The ability to recognize sentences that are paraphrases of each other

Sentences that mean the same thing are said to be paraphrases of each other, such as sentences (23) and (24).

(23) The boy hit the ball.
(24) The ball was hit by the boy.

Notice that paraphrases are in a sense mirror images of ambiguous sentences. While an ambiguous sentence has multiple meanings associated with one superficial form, paraphrases are multiple superficial forms, all of which have the same meaning associated with them. If sentences that are paraphrases of each other have roughly the same words in them, then it is frequently the case that they are all analyzed as having only one deep structure to which different T rules have applied, relating that deep structure to two or more different surface structures. In terms of the example at hand the

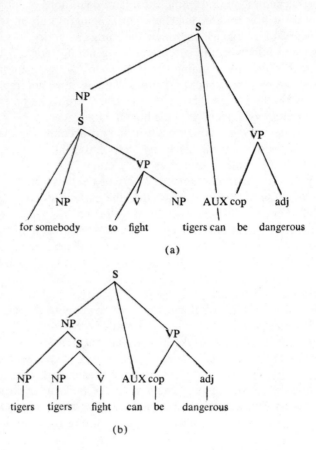

Figure 2.6 Deep-structure PMs of sentence (19). The PM in (a) represents the deep structure of the interpretation of (19), which means that it is dangerous for somebody to fight tigers; the node labeled AUX (abbreviation for auxiliary) contains so-called helping verbs, which will be discussed at length in the following chapter. The PM in (b) represents the deep structure of the interpretation of (5), which means that tigers that fight can be dangerous. The subject NP contains an embedded clause referred to traditionally as a "relative clauses." In this example the relative pronoun 'which' serves as the subject of the embedded clause. These examples, though rather drastically simplified, nevertheless exemplify the main point that the single sentence (19), which has only one surface-structure PM, has two deep-structure PMs.

deep-structure PM that underlies (23) is identical to that which underlies (24). In the derivation of (24) a T rule known as the passive rule applies, whereas no such rule applies to the deep structure of (23). We will reserve for the next chapter the illustration of these PMs, as they involve some considerations not relevant to the present discussion.

2.25 The description of linguistic competence

We are now in a position to characterize more precisely what is involved in describing the linguistic competence of a speaker of English (or of any other language). The linguist must describe the speaker's knowledge of his language by determining the deep- and surface-structure representations of all the various types of sentences in that language and postulating a set of T rules that relate those deep structures to surface forms. The sets of deep structures and T rules must be constrained so that they will produce only sentences that will be judged as grammatical by native speakers. In addition the analyses that the linguist postulates must be in accord with the judgments a native speaker makes about the meanings of sentences when the speaker is exposed only to the superficial forms of those sentences.

We are now in a position to give a more precise definition of the term "grammar of a language":

> The grammar of a language is a finite set of rules that generates all and only the sentences of that language, which are infinite in number; in addition the rules provide one (or, in the case of ambiguous sentences, two or more) structural description(s) for each sentence generated.

We say that the rules generate all the sentences of a language because if we find a string of words that speakers judge to be a possible sentence, and if our proposed grammar is unable to generate it, then that is empirical evidence that our proposed grammar is inadequate. Furthermore we say that the grammar must generate only the sentences of the language because if our hypothetical grammar were to generate strings of words that strike speakers as outlandish, then that is evidence that our grammar is not empirically adequate.

Recall that we said in Chapter 1 that if the theory of linguistic competence is to be empirically adequate, it must be able to relate sound and meaning. We said also that the theory described in this book consists of three components—phonology, syntax, and semantics. Now that we have seen that the syntactic component of a grammar consists of two subcomponents, the PS rules and the T rules, we can give a more detailed account of the organization of a generative grammar. We have argued above that the deep-structure PMs contain information necessary for interpreting the meaning of many sentences which is lost in their surface-structure PMs as a result of T rules that obscure the true grammatical relations. We know from the above that deep-structure PMs are necessary for semantic interpretation, but we have not yet discussed whether or not they are sufficient for semantic interpretation. In other words, do surface structure PMs provide any information necessary for determining the meaning of a sentence that is not contained at the level of deep structure? Linguists had believed for a fairly long time that the answer to this question is no; recently, however, convincing arguments have been put forth to show that surface-structure PMs do contain some semantically relevant information not available at the level of deep structure. For example, although the grammatical relations in (23) and (24) are identical, there are subtle differences between them, an explanation of which requires reference to their surface structures. It is nevertheless clear that deep structure is necessary for a specification of grammatical relations; therefore we are justified in maintaining the assumption that reference to deep structure is necessary for semantic interpretation.

The considerations discussed above suggest an organization of a grammar similar to that in Figure 2.7. Notice from this diagram that the phonological rules receive as input the surface-structure PMs. This is equivalent to the claim that the surface-structure PMs contain all the information necessary for specifying how a sentence is to be pronounced. The evidence for this is so very strong that we will assume it to be true in this book.

To summarize the main point of this section, the linguist who is attempting to describe the linguistic competence of the speaker of a language works within a given theoretical framework, or, to put it differently, assumes a given linguistic metatheory. If the linguist agrees that the transformational-generative theory is the best available, then he will assume that the grammar he intends to propose as a description of that competence will consist of a set of PS rules that generate deep-structure phrase markers and a set of T rules that converts these deep-structure PMs into surface-structure PMs.

The hypothesis the linguist proposes will be subject to the a priori constraint that they adhere to the general form of the linguistic metatheory. It

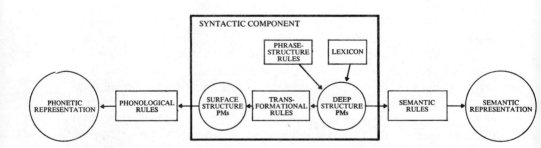

Figure 2.7 The organization of a transformational generative grammar. In this diagram phonological rules determine the phonetic representation of an utterance, while semantic rules underlie the semantic representation. Mediating between these two types of interpretative rules is the syntactic component of the grammar. Hence sound and meaning are related via the syntactic rules that relate deep structures (which serve as input to semantic rules) and surface structures (which constitute the input to the phonological rules). In order to reflect the fact that surface structures also contribute to meaning, an arrow might be drawn from SURFACE STRUCTURE PMs to SEMANTIC RULES.

is, of course, necessary to subject the hypotheses to empirical verification, as illustrated above. Although the linguist assumes the metatheory as an a priori constraint in describing the grammar of a particular language, it should not be assumed that the metatheory is not itself subject to empirical verification. In fact, in descriptions of particular languages details of the metatheory are always put to the empirical test in the sense that it is always a question whether or not the metatheory will provide the mechanism needed to describe a given range of phenomena. A detailed exposition of the methodology involved in testing the linguistic metatheory would take us too far afield here.

2.3
Competence and Performance Revisited

The linguistic judgments of the native speaker discussed so far in this chapter are of a particular sort. They are judgments that give us some insight into the underlying structure of the speaker's native language and thus into the speaker's linguistic competence, or the linguistic knowledge that he has internalized. Possessing internalized linguistic knowledge is necessary, but obviously it is not sufficient for an individual to be a functioning member of a language-using community. The language user must be equipped with an impressive array of cognitive, perceptual, and motor skills that interact with his linguistic competence to enable him to produce and comprehend sentences.

As was discussed in the previous chapter, this array of psychological skills is said to constitute the basis of linguistic performance, while the internalized system of rules of one's language constitutes linguistic competence. The investigation of the structures and processes responsible for linguistic performance is generally regarded as the province of psycholinguistics.

When the concepts of linguistic competence and performance were first formulated in generative linguistics, linguistic competence was regarded as a kind of Platonic ideal that would describe all and only the perfectly grammatical sentences of a language. Linguistic performance, on the other hand, was conceived of as a kind of overlay of human error, producing less-than-ideal sentences due to imperfections of the human organism. Thus actual speech—consisting of false starts, incorrectly completed sentences, and sentence fragments—was conceived of as being produced by a pristine pure competence, sullied by such imperfections of the human performance system as limitations in memory span, shifts in attention, and inertia of the vocal organs. This view is no longer seriously held by linguists or psycholinguists. It is now recognized that in actual language behavior it is absurd to think of either competence or performance structures as being more "basic" than the other—and it is equally absurd to conceive of either operating autonomously in any real sense.

This change in view, plus the recognition of the rather obvious fact that both competence and performance capabilities must be located (at least functionally) in the central nervous system, have led a few psycholinguists to suggest that the distinction between competence and performance is no longer a useful one and should perhaps be discarded. We do not agree with this point of view because we believe that it is theoretically necessary to keep separate, conceptually, the structure of knowledge and the use of knowledge. It is clear, however, that psycholinguistic, or performance, processes are far more complex and far more basic to linguistic behavior than they were once believed to be. It is these processes that enable a hearer to figure out (with astonishing speed) the intended meaning of an utterance from the sensation produced by acoustic wave forms impinging on his ear. The performance system, then, must embody information-processing strategies and skills making possible the nearly instantaneous perception of speech and the comprehension of language. Later chapters in this book will describe current theories that attempt to characterize the operations of the performance system.

An important aspect of the competence/performance dichotomy is that it sets limits on the kinds of language behavior that a theory of language is expected to explain. Consider once again structurally ambiguous sentences —such as (25).

(25) The baby felt good after his bath.

One of the authors (HC) presented this sentence (along with a number of other ambiguous and unambiguous sentences) to a group of about fifty people and asked them to paraphrase it. They all perceived it as meaning that the baby was happy and contented. That is, 'baby' was perceived as the subject of the verb 'feel'. No one perceived it as meaning that the baby felt good to the touch, i.e., no one perceived 'baby' as the object of 'feel'. Since no participant in that experiment perceived (25) as ambiguous, must we conclude that the sentence is not ambiguous? Of course not. Suppose we gave the sentence to a hundred people and none of them perceived the second meaning? A thousand people? No matter how many people failed to perceive the dual meaning, the sentence would still be an ambiguous English sentence. There exist rules of English, devised independently of sentence (25), that predict that (25) is structurally ambiguous, since it can be derived from two deep structures reflecting different meanings. Why, then, isn't the linguistic hypothesis falsified by the failure of English speakers to perceive the ambiguity immediately? The answer is that English speakers do *not* fail to perceive the ambiguity; they only fail to perceive initially the less likely of the two meanings. Any native speaker of English will acknowledge the ambiguity in (25) once it is pointed out to him.

A theory of the linguistic competence of a speaker of English (i.e., a grammar of English) does not—and should not—indicate which of two possible meanings for any particular ambiguous sentence is more likely to be initially understood by hearers. Nor do we expect the grammar to specify how any particular sentence is actually understood. If we demanded such a conclusion of our theory, we would be changing our entire conception of what a grammar should be, i.e., a statement of the general principles underlying the construction of sentences in a particular language. Predictions about the comprehensibility of individual sentences are not derivable from general principles of sentence construction; individual sentences are unique and their comprehension will vary according to numerous factors (linguistic and nonlinguistic) unique to that sentence and the context in which it is spoken. Thus we demand that a theory of linguistic competence characterize the general structural properties of sentences, but we leave to a theory of linguistic performance a characterization of the mechanisms by which those sentences are actually produced, perceived, and understood.

Syntax

3

In the previous chapter we defined the grammar of a language as a set of rules that describes all and only the sentences of that language and the structural description(s) of each sentence generated. We also illustrated various aspects of linguistic description, such as PMs and grammatical relations. A schematic representation of the organization of a grammar within the transformational-generative framework was presented in Figure 2.7.

It is the purpose of this chapter to describe in more detail the character of the syntactic component. We will illustrate the form and application of phrase structure and transformational rules with selected syntactic constructions of English. In particular we will illustrate certain aspects of the auxiliary phrase in English (cf. Figure 2.6) and, most importantly, the related phenomena associated with the passive construction, negative sentences, and the formation of yes/no questions. These constructions played an important role in the development of modern psycholinguistics and figure prominently in the material discussed in Chapters 7 and 8. A brief discussion of relative clauses and complement sentences is also included in this chapter; these constructions, which are discussed in subsequent chapters, are also important to psycholinguistics.

The analysis of the auxiliary and the related phenomena given here follows that proposed by Chomsky in his famous 1957 book, *Syntactic Structures*; the publication of this book, more than any event, revolutionized linguistics and psycholinguistics. The analysis in this chapter is a slightly modified version of that offered in *Syntactic Structures* as one of the early published examples of the transformational-generative theory of grammar.

It is not surprising that in the late 1950s and early 1960s psycholinguistics based its new approach at first on a series of experiments oriented around it; these experiments are described in later chapters.

Subsequent developments in syntactic theory have led to some modifications in the rules presented in this chapter, but nothing essential to the main points to be made is at stake here. In fact the rules described here are of sufficient generality that they could—and did—form a basis for a more extensive analysis of English syntax. It goes without saying, of course, that only a tiny fragment of the syntax of English is described in this book.

3.1
The Structure of the AUX

To illustrate the form and operation of PS rules, we will begin by analyzing sentences that involve either a simple verb or a verb with an auxiliary phrase. These are illustrated in examples (1)–(7). In analyzing these examples, we will make a number of simplifying assumptions, at least partially. For one thing we will at first ignore the endings and pay attention only to the order of words. Furthermore we will temporarily ignore the distinction between deep and surface structure. When we analyze the endings of the words in these sentences, we will see that in order to analyze the facts adequately, it is necessary to invoke the distinction between deep and surface structure and to use transformational rules.

- (1)   The doctor examined the child.
- (2)   The doctor is examining the child.
- (3)   *The doctor examining is the child.
- (4)   The doctor has examined the child.
- (5)   *The doctor examined has the child.
- (6)   The doctor has been examining the child.
- (7)   *The doctor is having examined the child.

A first approximation to the PM of (1) is given in Figure 3.1. This PM can be conceived of as being generated in part by a set of PS rules, the

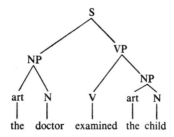

Figure 3.1

first of which is PS–1, below (which will be modified later). The rule should be read as "Sentence (S) is rewritten as (or consists of) an NP followed by a VP." PS rules 1–3 describe the constituent structure illustrated by the PM in Figure 3.1, as well as a number of other PMs in English.

(PS)–1   S → NP + VP
(PS)–2   VP → V + NP
(PS)–3   NP → art + NP

If we supply a lexicon, as illustrated below, we can complete the generation of the PM. The lexicon consists of a collection of words, each with a description of its meanings, an abstract representation of its phonological content, and a specification of the syntactic constructions—as defined by deep-structure PMs—in which it may occur. A word can be added to a deep-structure PM only if the specification of the possible syntactic structures in which it may occur is compatible with the deep-structure PM in question. In the lexicon given here we illustrate the requirement that a lexical entry can be added to a PM only if the symbol specifying its part of speech agrees with the symbol in the PM. In section 3.63 we return to this issue and describe further aspects of the lexicon.

Lexicon   the: [art]   child: [N]
            doctor: [N]   examine: [V]

Sentence (2) is in the progressive aspect; this means that the action described by the verb is continuing at the time specified by the tense in the sentence. The word 'is' serves as a sign of the progressive aspect and is part of what we call the auxiliary phrase **(AUX).** Since we now have a new constituent of a sentence to be generated by the PS rules, we must decide where it should appear. The unacceptability of (3) as a sentence of English shows that the AUX must not appear after the verb. It is an easy matter to demonstrate that the AUX must immediately precede the VP. Accordingly we modify PS–1 as illustrated.

PS–1′   S → NP + AUX + VP

In this example the AUX consists merely of the sign of the progressive, which we will call **PROG.** Therefore PS–4 is a first approximation to a description of the AUX phrase in English. Of course it is necessary to specify that PROG contains some form of the word 'be'; we will return to this problem later.

PS–4   AUX → PROG

Sentence (4) is in the perfective aspect, one of whose meanings is that the action described by the verb is completed. Sentence (4), like (3), contains an auxiliary phrase, which must precede the VP, as illustrated by the unacceptability of (5). Of course in this example the AUX is represented by the word 'has', a sign of the perfective aspect, abbreviated **PERF.** Accordingly PS–4 must be modified to allow for the occurrence of PERF; the question, of course, is how to do this.

Sentence (6) illustrates the occurrence of both PERF and PROG in the same sentence. Notice that when they appear together, they must appear in the order PERF–PROG; the fact that (7) is not a sentence of English shows that this order is mandatory. Therefore the new (but not yet final) version of PS–4 is:

PS–4′   AUX → (PERF) (PROG)

The parentheses around these terms means that either is optional. That is, the AUX may consist of a PERF with no PROG, a PROG with no PERF, both, or neither. When both PERF and PROG appear, they must appear in this order. The PM associated with (6) is illustrated in Figure 3.2.

Rules PS–1 through PS–4 account for the order of words in examples (1)–(7). We now turn to a consideration of the endings attached to the verb and to the words in the AUX.

3.12 Morphemes

Many of the words illustrated in sentences (1)–(7) consist of two parts, a stem and an ending. Stems and endings are both examples of morphemes, which are defined roughly as the minimal syntactic elements that make up a word. Some words in the example sentences, such as 'the' and 'child', consist of one morpheme each, whereas others consist of two morphemes. For example, 'examining' consists of the stem 'examine' and the ending '-ing'.

The rules of syntax must account for the order of morphemes as well

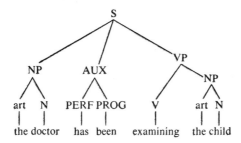

Figure 3.2

as the order of words. When we examine the order of morphemes in these example sentence, we will see that it is a challenging task to discover precise rules to account for these phenomena. This problem is key to the hypothesis proposed by Chomsky in *Syntactic Structures*.

The acceptable sentences from (1)–(7) are represented in terms of their morphemes below:

(1′) the doctor examine + PAST the child
(2′) the doctor be + PRES examine + prog the child
(4′) the doctor have + PRES examine + perf the child
(6′) the doctor have + PRES be + perf example + prog the child

The order of morphemes in these strings is, of course, the order in which they appear at the bottom of the surface-structure PMs.

The symbol PAST in (1′) is simply an abstract representation of the past-tense morpheme, spelled '-ed'. We use abstract representations for the endings since we are dealing with the syntactic representations of the sentences; phonological rules will apply to these representations and specify how they are to be pronounced. Alternatively, spelling rules could apply to these representations in order to produce the written versions of these sentences. But for syntactic purposes it is most convenient to label the suffixes with the abstract symbols that represent their grammatical functions.

Notice that in (2′) the word 'is' is analyzed as consisting of the stem 'be' with the suffix PRES, our symbol for the present-tense morpheme; this simply represents the fact that 'is' is the present-tense form of 'be'. In these examples the present- and past-tense morphemes are represented. We will use the cover term TNS to represent the tense morpheme; the rule that relates PAST and PRES to TNS will be presented shortly.

Before we give a detailed account of the distributions of these morphemes, it is necessary to define the terms **stem** and **affix.** The term **stem** refers to the morphemes 'have', 'be', and any verb stem, such as 'examine'; we are of course ignoring nouns, articles, and other parts of speech for the purposes of the present exposition. The term **affix** will refer to any of the morphemes represented by PAST, PRES (i.e., either TNS morpheme), 'perf', and 'prog'. These last two morphemes, written in lowercase letters, refer to the affixes associated with the ocurrence of PROG and PERF in the same sentence; we will discuss their distribution in due course, after we show the rules accounting for the distribution of the TNS morpheme.

The tense morpheme appears in different words in the example sentences. It is suffixed to the verb stem in (1′), to the stem 'be', which represents the PROG in (2′), and to the stem 'have', representing the PERF in (4′) and (6′). The most general description of the position of TNS is simply that it is always attached to the leftmost stem. Thus, if there is neither a PERF nor a PROG, then the verb stem is the leftmost stem. If there are one or more stems in the AUX, then it is always attached to the first of them.

There is no feasible way of accounting for the location of this morpheme with PS rules. These rules can account for the position of the *words* in these particular examples because each occupies fixed positions with respect to each other; for example, if a sentence contains both a PROG and a PERF, the PROG is always to the right of the PERF and to the left of the verb stem. However, the TNS appears sometimes to the right of the verb stem (see sentence (2')) and sometimes to the left of the verb stem (as in all the other examples). Accordingly we need to invoke T rules, which have the power to move morphemes around. (Later we will see examples of T rules that move around larger portions of sentences as well.)

The hypothesis described in *Syntactic Structures* is, the PS rule that expands the AUX (our PS–4) has TNS as its leftmost element. Accordingly our final version of this rule is PS–4′″.

PS–4′″   AUX → TNS (PERF) (PROG)

Chomsky suggested that there is a T rule that moves the TNS affix around the stem immediately to its right. To visualize this, refer to Figure 3.3. These PMs are basically simplified representations of the deep structures that underlie sentences (1′)–(6′). We are temporarily ignoring the affixes associated with the PERF and PROG and considering these as units. We are also assuming rule PS–5, which rewrites TNS as either PAST or PRES. The curly braces mean that either morpheme inside them may be chosen.

PS–5   TNS →   {PAST, PRES}

The PS rules described so far will generate the PMs illustrated in Figure 3.3. These PMs, then, are simplified versions of the deep structure PMs of the example sentences. The T rule that Chomsky suggested, usually referred to as **Affix-Hopping,** or T-AFF, moves the affix around the stem as indicated by the double arrow. This would then yield the order of morphemes that actually occurs in the surface structures in (1′)–(6′).

We turn now to a discussion of the other affixes, the 'prog' and the 'perf'. Observe that the 'prog', which appears always as the suffix '-ing', appears only in sentences that have the 'be' of the PROG as well. Therefore it is only natural to assume that the 'be' and the 'prog' are both representatives of the PROG constituent and are introduced into the AUX by PS–6.

PS–6   PROG → be + prog

Part of Chomsky's hypothesis is that Affix-Hopping applies to the 'prog' as well as to the TNS morpheme, as illustrated in Figure 3.4b.

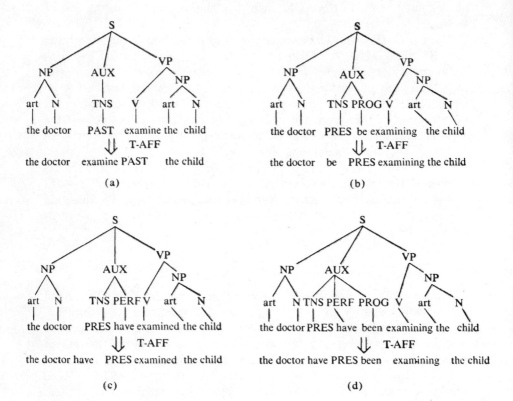

Figure 3.3

The morpheme 'perf' has a number of forms, two of which are illustrated here. It appears as the suffix '-ed' when attached to 'examine', as in (4), and as the suffix '-en' when attached to the stem 'be', as in (6). This morpheme is, along with 'have', the sign of the PERF. Therefore we assume a PS rule 7.

PS–7   PERF → have + perf

If we assume that Affix-Hopping also applies to 'perf' as in Figure 3.4c and d, it follows that Chomsky's hypothesis handles the distribution of the morphemes in (1')–(6'). Moreover this hypothesis also explains the facts that 'have' and 'perf' and 'be' and 'prog' always occur in the same sentence; since 'have' and 'perf', for example, are part of the same deep-structure constituent, the occurrence of each depends on the other. The PS rules given to this point generate the deep-structure PMs illustrated in Figure 3.4. The rule of Affix-Hopping, which is given a more precise description below, applies to each affix, moving it around the stem immediately to its right.

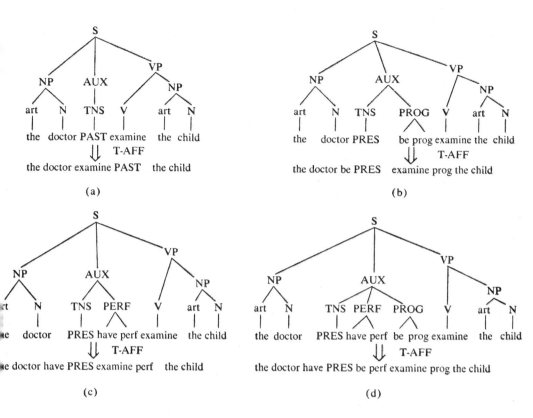

Figure 3.4

Affix-Hopping (T-AFF)
Where AFFIX = TNS, perf, prog; and STEM = have, be, or a verb stem;
attach an affix to the end of the stem immediately to its right. (This rule
will be given a more formal notation on p. 54.)

This is the essence of an important part of the syntactic analysis in Chomsky's early publications which stimulated so much initial excitement among
both linguists and psychologists. An interesting observation that follows
from this analysis is that for every English sentence the deep structure is
always different from the surface structure. Since every sentence has a tense
morpheme in it, and since these rules are involved in the generation of
every English sentence, then every sentence has a deep-structure PM where
the TNS is placed in a different position from its appearance in the surface-
structure PM.

The most important aspect of this hypothesis is its interaction with a
number of other syntactic processes in English. The analysis Chomsky
offered of the passive construction, to which we turn next, is mutually dependent on the Affix-Hopping hypothesis.

3.2
The Passive Construction

Consider the sentences (8)–(11), which are the passive analogs of sentences (1), (2), (4), and (6).

(8) The child was examined by the doctor.
   the child be+PAST examine+pass by the doctor
(9) The child is being examined by the doctor.
   the child be+PRES be+prog examine+pass by the doctor
(10) The child has been examined by the doctor.
   the child have+PRES be+perf examine+pass by the doctor
(11) The child has been being examined by the doctor.
   the child have+PRES be+perf be+prog examine+pass by the doctor

The morpheme 'pass' in these examples represents the affix that is always attached to the verb stem, indicating the passive voice.

In the previous chapter we said that the deep structure of a passive sentence is identical to the deep structure of its active cognate (see section 2.24). Therefore it must be the case that an optional T rule has applied to the passive sentences that did not apply in the generation of the active sentences; we call this rule T-PASS. Our present task is to describe the operation of this rule. In doing so, it is helpful to observe that each of the passive sentences (8)–(11) seems to have been operated on by T-AFF. The strings (8')–(11') illustrate the order of morphemes that would appear in these sentences just prior to the application of T-AFF; that is, the application of T-AFF to (8')–(11') yields the surface structures in (8)–(11).

(8') the child PAST be pass examine by the doctor
(9') the child PRES be prog be pass examine by the doctor
(10') the child PRES have perf be pass examine by the doctor
(11') the child PRES have perf be prog be pass examine by the doctor

Since we assume that only one rule applies in the derivations of the passives that does not apply in the derivations of the actives, it is reasonable to assume that this rule applies to the deep-structure PMs identical to those illustrated in Figure 3.4 and produces the strings (8')–(11'); T-AFF then applies to these strings and yields the desired surface structures. Our present task is to determine the form of T-PASS by asking what must be done to the PMs in Figure 3.3 to yield (8')–(11').

It seems that there are four major differences between the deep-structure PMs and the strings in (8')–(11'). First, the deep-structure object NP appears at the beginning of the sentences in (8')–(11'). Second, the subject NP has been moved to follow the main verb. Third, the morpheme 'by' was inserted to the right of the verb. Finally, the morphemes 'be' and 'pass' were inserted to the right of the AUX. To put it more precisely, T-PASS must have the following characteristics:

1. It may apply optionally to any PM with an NP to the left of the AUX and an NP to the right of the main verb.

2. T-PASS moves the NP to the left of AUX into the rightmost position in the sentence, and the morpheme 'by' is inserted immediately to its left. The morphemes 'be' and 'pass' are inserted to the right of the AUX. Furthermore the NP immediately to the right of the V is moved to the position immediately to the left of AUX. These operations are to be conceived of as operating simultaneously. As a result the two NPs change places, and 'be', 'pass', and 'by' are inserted.

It is customary in theoretical linguistics to state transformational rules in a formal notation. T-PASS described above in words, has the following technical representation:

		X	NP	AUX	V	NP	Y
T-PASS							
(optional)	SD:	1	2	3	4	5	6
	SC:	1	5	3 be pass 4		6 by 2	

X and Y are cover symbols standing for any arbitrary string of constituents that do not have to be present.

The upper part of this rule is known as the structural description, or SD. The SD specifies the structures, or PMs, to which the transformation may apply. This SD says that any PM that consists of any arbitrary string of symbols, X, followed by an NP, followed in turn by an AUX, followed by a V, then an NP, and finally any other arbitrary string, Y, may be operated on by this rule. The numbers under the string of symbols are there simply to specify strings of symbols that are relevant to the operation of the rule. The lower portion of the rule is called the structural change and represents the change carried out by the rule. In this case the SC says that the NP that followed the V in the SD (that is, element 5 in the SD) is moved into the position formerly occupied by the subject NP (that is, element 2). Furthermore 'be pass' is inserted after the AUX (element 3 in the SD), the subject NP is moved into last position in the sentence, and 'by' is placed before it. This rule is, then, a formal notation for stating precisely what was stated in words previously. We will use this formal notation for all the T rules discussed in this book.

The operation of this T rule is illustrated in Figure 3.5. The manner in which the PM is analyzed by T-PASS is shown by the numbers under the constituents. Thus the '1', which stands for an arbitrary string, represents no morphemes in this example (we will see an example later where

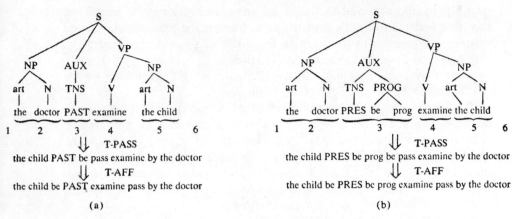

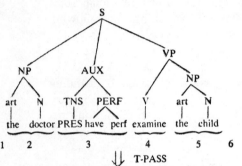

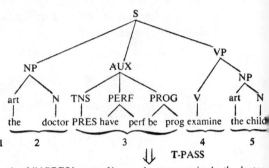

Figure 3.5

the X does stand for some morphemes); the 2 that appears under the NP 'the doctor' corresponds to the 2 under the first NP in the SD of T-PASS. The reader can match the analysis of the rest of the PM against the SD of T-PASS. The application of T-PASS is also illustrated in this diagram, showing the strings that result from applying T-PASS to the PM.

3.3
Negative Sentences

Let us now consider the negative cognates of the sentences in (1), (2), (4), and (6), illustrated by (12)–(15).

> (12) The doctor did not examine the child.
> the doctor do+PAST not examine the child

(13) The doctor is not examining the child.
the doctor be+PRES not examine+prog the child

(14) The doctor has not examined the child.
the doctor have+PRES not examine+perf the child

(15) The doctor has not been examining the child.
the doctor have+PRES not be+perf examine+prog the child

Some of these sentences may strike the reader as somewhat stiff or awkward. A more natural set of sentences would have included contractions such as 'The doctor didn't examine the child'. It would be simple enough to add a rule that contracts a 'not' with a preceding word under certain circumstances, but this process is not pertinent to the present discussion.

These sentences differ from their affirmative counterparts in a number of ways. For one thing they all have the morpheme 'not', which we take to be simply a marker of negative sentences (there are other morphemes and constructions for expressing negation in English, but we will not discuss them here). Second, notice that (12) contains a form of the stem 'do', to which the tense morpheme is suffixed; the 'do' is furthermore the first morpheme of the AUX in the surface structure representations of this sentence.

The third interesting observation about these sentences concerns the location of 'not' in the AUX phrase. In (12), (13), and (14), 'not' appears at the end of AUX, whereas in (15) it appears as the third morpheme in the AUX phrase. A moment's inspection will reveal that in fact 'not' appears in third position of the AUX in each of the example negative sentences; this is the correct generalization.

Our present task is to determine a plausible deep-structure PM for each of the negative sentences and simultaneously to propose a set of T rules that maps the deep-structure PMs into the surface structures illustrated by (12)–(15). We assume that the morpheme 'not' appears in the deep structure of each negative sentence.

It is impossible to account for the location of the 'not' by PS rules alone. We would run into problems essentially like those involved with trying to place the affixes by PS rules. It seems more plausible to locate the 'not' in some arbitrary position in the deep structure of each sentence —say, at the very beginning—and then to posit a T rule—to be called T-NEG—that puts 'not' into the third position in the AUX. (A more precise description of T-NEG is given shortly.) We must, of course, revise PS–1 so that 'not' is optionally inserted in front of a sentence:

PS–1″ S → (not) NP + AUX + VP

According to our analysis the deep structure of (15) is as in Figure 3.6 and is operated on by T-NEG, which moves the 'not' to the third position in the AUX. After that T-AFF applies, yielding the surface structure.

This analysis accounts for all the observations made about the sentences

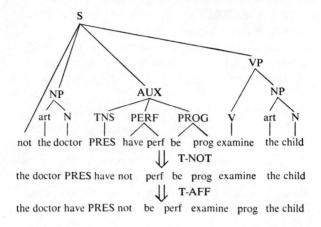

the doctor PRES have not   perf be   prog examine   the child

⇓ T-AFF

the doctor have PRES not   be   perf   examine   prog   the child

Figure 3.6

in (13)–(15). We have yet to account for the occurrence of 'do' and re-lated phenomena in sentence (12). Consider the deep structure of (12) in Figure 3.7. Recall that T-NEG moves the 'not' to third place in the AUX. However, since there is no third place in the AUX in (12) at the level of deep structure, we must change the rule to handle cases such as these. In order to cover all these examples, we must specify that T-NEG move the 'not' to the position immediately following a 'have', if it is present in the AUX. If there is no 'have' in the AUX—if, instead, a 'be' occurs in the AUX in the deep structure immediately after the TNS—then 'not' is to be placed right after the 'be'. If neither 'have' nor 'be' is present, then the 'not' is to be placed immediately after the TNS. The formal notation for this rule is:

T-NEG   X   not   NP TNS$\left(\left\{ \begin{matrix} \text{have} \\ \text{be} \end{matrix} \right\} \right)$ Y   where X and Y
                                                                            represent any
(obligatory)   SD: arbitrary strings
               1   2   3   4   of morphemes
       SC: 1   3   2   4

This is an obligatory rule because it applies to all sentences that have 'not' in the required position in the deep structure. The string labeled 3 stands for the entire string around which the 'not' is to be moved. The braces around the 'have' and 'be' mean that this string may end in either of these two morphemes. The parentheses around the braces mean that if neither of them is present, the 'not' is to be placed directly after the TNS.

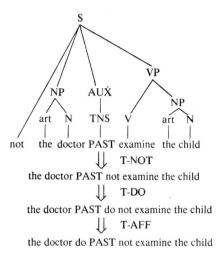

Figure 3.7

The application of T-NEG to the deep-structure PM of (12) in Figure 3.7 will yield the string (12′), representing one stage in the derivation of sentence (12).

(12′) the doctor PAST not examine the child

Observe that T-AFF cannot apply to this form; it only moves an affix around a stem, and 'not' fails to fit our definition of a 'stem'. Thus the 'not' prevents the tense morpheme from becoming suffixed to a stem. Interestingly, it is just in situations like this, where the tense morpheme is prevented from becoming suffixed to a stem, that the 'do' appears; we will see some examples of interrogatives below where this phenomenon reappears. We are led, then, to postulate a rule called **Do Support** (T-DO), which inserts a 'do' immediately to the right of a TNS when it is stranded, separated from a stem so that it cannot get moved by T-AFF. Formally, we accomplish this by positing a rule that inserts a 'do' immediately to the right of an affix that does not immediately precede a stem, as defined. The application of this rule will yield the correct order of morphemes.

T-DO		X	TNS	Y	Z;	where Y is a single
(obligatory)	SD:	1	2	3	4	morpheme, not a stem
	SC:	1	2	do 3	4	

T-AFF		X	AFFIX	STEM	Y;	where AFFIX and
(obligatory)	SD:	1	2	3	4	STEM are as defined on

p. 47, except that the
definition of STEM is
broadened to include
the stem 'do'

SC: 1 3 2 4

T-DO puts 'do' between a TNS and any other morpheme that is not a STEM. T-AFF is merely a formal representation of the rule that has been described discursively on p. 45.

The order of these rules is crucial. Thus T-NEG must precede T-DO so that T-NEG can provide the necessary environments for the application of T-DO. Furthermore T-DO precedes T-AFF in application, since T-DO supplies the stem for the application of T-AFF in sentences like (12).

The preceding discussion illustrates an important principle, known as the **principle of strict linear ordering,** which says that the T rules apply one after the other in sequence, each rule applying to the output of the preceding rule. Furthermore the rules are rigidly ordered in the grammar so that they apply in the same order in each derivation.

T-PASS and T-NEG are also crucially ordered with respect to each other. That is, if one wishes to generate a negative, passive sentence, these two rules must be applied in the correct order to arrive at an acceptable sentence. We leave as an exercise for the reader to determine this order.

3.4
Interrogative Sentences

Turning now to a discussion of simple questions, we first distinguish between two kinds of questions, yes/no-questions and wh-questions. The former, illustrated in (16)–(19), are analyzed here. The latter are formed with wh-words like 'who', 'when', and so on. The child's acquisition of both types of questions are discussed in Chapter 8.

(16) Did the doctor examine the child?
      do+PAST the doctor examine the child
(17) Is the doctor examining the child?
      be+PRES the doctor examine+prog the child
(18) Has the doctor examined the child?
      have+PRES the doctor examine+perf the child
(19) Has the doctor been examining the child?
      have+PRES the doctor be+perf examine+PROG the child

Notice that there is a striking parallelism between the questions and the corresponding negatives. For example, (16) is the only question that has a form of 'do', just as (12) is the only negative with 'do'. In both the negatives and the questions the sentences that contain neither PERF nor PROG contain 'do'. Notice that except for the rising intonation at the end of yes/no-questions, their most striking characteristic is that some of the morphemes from the AUX appear at the beginning of the sentence. In fact it is evident that it is always the first two morphemes of the AUX that appear in sentence-initial position, just as it was always the first morphemes of the AUX that appeared to the left of the 'not' in the negatives. In other words, whereas the negatives are formed by moving 'not' to the third position in the AUX and then applying T-DO and T-AFF, the questions are formed by moving the first two morphemes of the AUX to the front of the sentence and then applying T-DO and T-AFF. We will illustrate this after we consider the deep structure of questions.

It is not reasonable to propose that the deep structures of interrogatives contain some morphemes of the AUX in front of the sentence, as do the surface structures of these sentences. The reasons for this not being a viable proposal are similar to those against the proposal that the deep structures of negative sentences contain a 'not' in the third position of the AUX. As we have seen, transformational rules are better suited to handling this kind of phenomenon.

The analysis of questions we will adopt involves deep structures, essentially as shown in Figure 3.8, and a T rule that deletes the 'Q' and moves

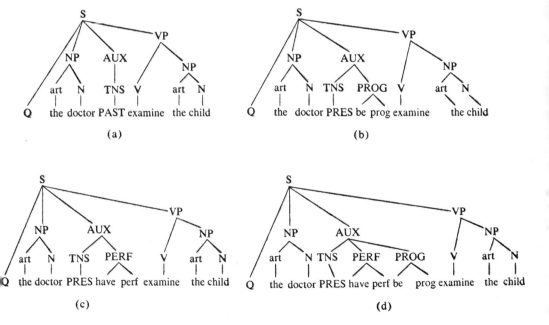

Figure 3.8

the first two morphemes of the AUX to the beginning of the sentence (just the tense morpheme is transposed if the AUX does not contain any other morphemes); this rule is called **T-Q**. The Q at the beginning of the sentence is simply to be taken as an abstract marker of interrogation; the rest of the sentence does not differ from ordinary declaratives, as a comparison of the deep structures of (16)–(19) with those of the sentences in (1)–(6) will show. The phrase-structure rule that introduces 'Q' would have to be modified as in **PS-1'''**. (The relative ordering of 'not' and 'Q' in PS-1''' is entirely arbitrary.)

$$\text{PS-1'''} \quad \text{S} \rightarrow \text{(Q) (not) NP + AUX + VP}$$

T-Q		X	Q	Y	TNS $\left(\left\{ \begin{array}{c} have \\ be \end{array} \right\} \right)$		Z
(obligatory)	SD:						
		1	2	3	4		5
	SC:	1	4	3	5		

Notice that T-Q transposes only the tense morpheme in the event that it constitutes the only morpheme in the AUX. This means that when T-AFF applies in such cases, the tense affix is left stranded in the front of the sentence and cannot be affixed to anything. Therefore here again we find that T-DO comes to the rescue, providing a dummy stem to support the tense affix. The deep structures of (16)–(19) are portrayed in Figure 3.8.

Note that the deep-structure PM of (16) in Figure 3.8a differs from the deep structure for (1), the declarative cognate of (16), only by the presence of 'Q'. This is intuitively plausible since the only semantic difference between (1) and (16) is that one is declarative and the other interrogative; thus at the level of deep structure they differ only by the Q, the interrogative marker.

3.5
The Rules Applied in a Single Derivation

In the preceding discussions of active versus passive, affirmative versus negative, and declarative versus interrogative sentences we motivated the relevant T rules independently of each other. That is, the passive rule was considered in isolation from the negative rule, and so on. If the analyses we presented above are correct, we would expect that sentences that represented combinations of these processes could be generated by the same rules, with little or no modifications of them. We will see that this is so. Consider, for example, sentence (20).

(20) Has the child not been examined by the doctor?

Recall that we are dealing exclusively with sentences where the 'not' has not been contracted; this accounts for the somewhat stilted style of this sentence. It is, of course, fully grammatical.

The derivation of (20) is given in Figure 3.9. Observe that the T rules developed so far apply to this sentence with no modification. Thus we first apply T-PASS to the deep-structure PM; then the T-NEG applies, moving the 'not' into position between the 'have' and the 'perf' in the AUX; next T-Q applies, moving PRES and 'have' into initial position and deleting the Q; finally T-AFF applies, reordering the morphemes into the occurring order.

To summarize the development to this point, all the simple sentences we have shown so far have very similar deep structure PMs, and the differences among their surface structures are largely accounted for by the application of regular T-rules. An important aspect of this discussion has to do with the generality of the rules. That is, we motivated the passive transformation on the basis of a comparison of rather simple active/passive pairs. If we were to proceed with the investigation of more passive sentences we would find that little modification of the rules would be necessary to handle a huge sample of passive construction. It follows that we have

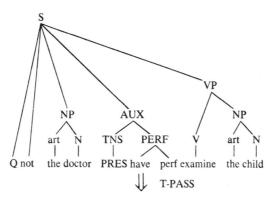

Q not the child PRES have perf be pass examine by the doctor

⇓ T-NOT

Q the child PRES have not perf be pass examine by the doctor

⇓ T-Q

PRES have the child not perf be pass examine by the doctor

⇓ T-AFF

have PRES the child not be perf examine pass by the doctor

Figure 3.9

managed to capture a generalization which is of significance for English syntax with a rather simple rule. This illustrates the concept of a **linguistically significant generalization**—a generalization about the syntactic (or semantic or phonological) structure of a language which obviously must be captured by an adequate grammar.

The negative and interrogative transformations also capture linguistically significant generalizations. We are encouraged in our belief that all these rules correspond to significant generalizations when we note that it is not necessary to modify the rules at all in order to generate sentences which combine passive, negative and interrogative constructions. The conclusion seems inescapable that these rules capture linguistically significant generalizations which in turn reflect psychologically real aspects of English speakers' knowledge of their language.

Recursive Rules and Complex Sentences

In Chapter 1 we pointed out that an essential characteristic of human language is the fact that each language has an infinite number of sentences; this follows from the observation that there is no longest sentence of any language. The rules presented so far do not provide any mechanism for elongating sentences. In order to explain the fact that there is no longest sentence, the transformational generative theory of grammar contains some recursive rules. Recursive rules are phrase structure rules that have the property that a given rule contains a symbol to the right of the arrow that had appeared to the left of the arrow in an earlier rule. For example, we will see rules below that contain the symbol S to the right of the arrow. The PS rules then reapply to the new S, thus providing the possibility of limitless looping.

A complex sentence is a sentence that contains other sentences at the level of deep structure. Complex sentences, then, are sentences that contain embedded sentences, usually referred to as clauses in traditional terms. As we will see in Chapter 7, current experiments in adult comprehension of sentences make crucial reference to clauses and their boundaries; we present in this section the background necessary for an understanding of these experiments.

3.61 Relative clauses

One example showing how simple sentences may combine to form complex ones is given in (21).

(21) The wolf who ate the grandmother scared Little Red Riding Hood.

The phrase 'who ate the grandmother' is known as a relative clause. The deep structure of (21) is given in Figure 3.10. The topmost S in this PM

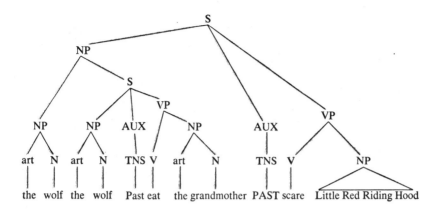

Figure 3.10

is known as the matrix sentence as opposed to embedded sentences.

Observe that in Figure 3.10 the relative clause is attached to the subject NP. The NP immediately to the left of a relative clause is known as the head NP.

The PM in Figure 3.10 indicates that the PS rule that expands the NP node must be modified as shown below. If the first option is chosen (i.e., if NP is rewritten as NP + S), then the rule may reapply and the new NP may either be again rewritten as NP + S or be rewritten as art + N.

PS–S″   NP → $\begin{Bmatrix} NP + S \\ art + N \end{Bmatrix}$

Sentence (22) illustrates a case of multiple embedding, which would result from multiple applications of the first part of PS–3″.

(22) The wolf who ate the grandmother who lived in the cottage scared Little Red Riding Hood.

We leave as an exercise for the reader to work out the deep-structure PM of (22).

Our next task is to determine the T rule that applies to the PM in Figure 3.10 to yield the surface-structure representation. Very simply, a rule known as **T-REL** converts 'the wolf' in the embedded sentence into 'who'. In general this rule applies to any NP in a relative clause that is identical to the head NP.

T-REL is actually considerably more complicated. For example, in (23) we see a sentence where it appears at first glance that the relative clause does not have a direct object.

(23) The wolf who the woodman killed scared Little Red Riding Hood.

Upon closer examination, however, the direct object of the relative clause turns out to be the relative pronoun, which has been moved to the front of the embedded sentence by T-REL; that is, T-REL can move NPs as well as convert them into relative pronouns. The deep-structure PM and the derivation of (23) are given in Figure 3.11.

Observe that the phrase 'the wolf' in the embedded sentence in the deep structure in Figure 3.11 is the NP that is identical to the head NP. It is apparent that T-REL applies to the deep structure PM, converting 'the wolf' into a relative pronoun as well as moving it to the front of the relative clause. In general, then, T-REL finds an NP in a relative clause that is identical to the head NP, converts it into a relative pronoun and moves it to the front of the relative clause.

Sentences which contain relative clauses where the relative pronoun is the subject of the embedded clause are known as **subject relatives;** if the relative pronoun is the object of the embedded clause, they are called **object relatives.** Thus, (22) is a subject relative, whereas (23) is an object relative. This terminology is useful in the psycholinguistic experiments described in Chapter 7.

There is an interesting, optional process, closely associated with relative clauses, that is known as **relative clause reduction.** Under certain circumstances a T rule may apply that optionally deletes a relative pronoun. For example, the 'who' in (23) may be deleted and still yield a grammatical English sentence. However, this is not true of (21) or (22). Some more

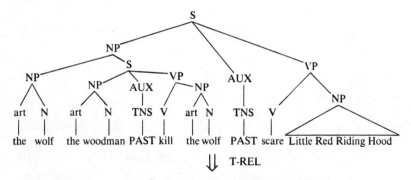

the wolf who the woodman PAST kill PAST scare Little Red Riding Hood

⇓ T-REL

the wolf who the woodman PAST kill PAST scare Little Red Riding Hood

⇓ T-AFF

the wolf who the woodman kill PAST scare PAST Little Red Riding Hood

Figure 3.11

examples of permissible and impermissible applications of relative clause reduction are given in (24)–(27).

(24)   The man who the woman loved robbed the bank.
(25)   The man the woman loved robbed the bank.
(26)   The man who loved the woman robbed the bank.
(27)   *The man loved the woman robbed the bank.

Observe that the relative pronoun may be deleted whenever it immediately follows the head NP and precedes the subject NP of the relative clause. That is, it may delete whenever it was moved by the T-REL into position in front of the subject of the relative clause.

There is one more example of relative clause reduction that differs somewhat from the above pattern, as illustrated in (28)–(31).

(28)   The man who is standing on the corner is my uncle.
(29)   The man standing on the corner is my uncle.
(30)   The car which is in the driveway is a Ford.
(31)   The car in the driveway is a Ford.

Here we see that under certain circumstances a relative pronoun and a following 'is' (or any 'be + TNS' word) may be deleted. Thus 'who is' and 'which is' are optionally deletable in (28) and (30), respectively. Relative clause reduction plays an important role in Chapter 7.

3.62 Complement sentences

Consider sentence (32).

(32)   Mary read that John took the ball.

It is evident that the clause 'John took the ball' is an embedded sentence, but it is not a relative clause. Such embedded sentences are known as **complement sentences.** There is a rich variety of complement sentences in English (and other languages), but we will be concerned only with one type in this section, known as **verb phrase complements.**

Observe that some verbs like 'believe' can take complement sentences, whereas others cannot. Thus (33) is ungrammatical because 'slugged,' like many English transitive verbs, cannot take a complement sentence.

(33)   *Mary slugged that John was guilty.

The deep structure of (32), which does not differ greatly from its surface-structure PM, is illustrated in Figure 3.12.

The PS rules developed in this book so far do not generate the PM in Figure 3.12. Therefore it is necessary to modify PS-2' to allow for complement sentences.

$$\text{PS--2'} \quad \text{VP} \rightarrow \text{V} \begin{Bmatrix} \text{NP} \\ \text{S} \end{Bmatrix}$$

Verbs are then divided into two classes: those that take complement sentences and those that do not. Verbs that take complements can be further subdivided into classes, depending on which **complementizers** each takes. A complementizer is a morpheme like 'that' in (33) which marks the complement sentence. Other complementizers are illustrated in (34)–(38). The asterisked sentences illustrate that the choice of complementizer is dependent on the verb.

(34) Sam claimed that John was the culprit.
(35) Sam preferred that John take the blame.
(36) Sam preferred for John to take the blame.
(37) Sam preferred John's taking the blame.
(38) John resented Sam's telling the truth.
(39) *Sam claimed for John to be the culprit.
(40) *Sam claimed John's being the culprit.
(41) *John resented that Sam told the truth.
(42) *John resented for Sam to tell the truth.

There are basically three complementizers in English, 'that,' 'for–to,' and what is known as 'POSS–ing.' We have already illustrated 'that' in (32) and again in (34) and (35). The 'for–to' complementizer is illustrated in (36); the 'for' precedes the complement sentence and the 'to' precedes the AUX constituent of the complement sentence.

The 'POSS–ing' complementizer is illustrated in (37). 'POSS' means the possessive suffix, as in 'John's book'. This suffix is affixed to the subject NP, and the '-ing' suffix is attached to a verb stem (or 'have' or 'be').

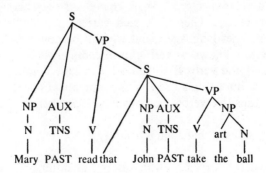

Figure 3.12

As we stated above, some verbs take one complementizer, others take other complementizers. Thus 'claim' may take 'that', as illustrated in (34), but may not take 'for–to' or 'POSS–ing', as illustrated in (39) and (40). The verb 'prefer' may take any of the three complementizers, as (35), (36), and (37) show. The verb 'resent' may only take 'POSS–ing', as (38), (41), and (42) show. (Observe that (41) would be grammatical for some speakers if 'it' were inserted after the verb 'resented'; this illustrates a different type of complement construction, which will not be discussed here.)

3.63 The lexical representation of verbs

In section 3.1 we described part of the lexicon and stated that each morpheme in the lexicon must have associated with it a specification of the grammatical structures into which it may be inserted to form a complete deep-structure PM. The discussion in that section referred only to the parts of speech of lexical entries. However, the facts presented earlier in this chapter suggest that it is also necessary to specify aspects of the environments in which morphemes may occur.

The relevance of syntactic environment can be illustrated clearly by the distinction between transitive and intransitive verbs. A transitive verb is simply a verb that may take a direct object, whereas an intransitive verb may appear without a direct object. (Of course to generate sentences with no direct object NP, we would have to modify PS–2′ by putting parentheses around the NP.) Some verbs may appear as either transitive or intransitive. Sentences (43) and (44) illustrate verbs that are obligatorily transitive and intransitive, respectively.

(43) Mary brought a friend.
(44) Mary slept.

The deep-structure PMs of these sentences, without words, are illustrated in Figure 3.13. The lexical representation of the verb 'bring' must specify that it appear in a VP that has a direct object NP, whereas the lexical

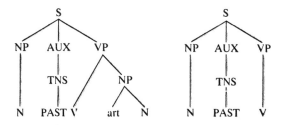

Figure 3.13

representation of 'sleep' must specify that no NP follow the V in the VP in which it is to appear.

The implication of these considerations for complement sentences is that the lexical representation of each verb must specify whether or not it may appear with a complement sentence, and if so, what complementizer(s) may be associated with it. Many verbs may appear with or without complementizers, just as some verbs are either transitive or intransitive. The verb 'read', for example, can be either intransitive or transitive; it may also take a complement sentence. Such verbs have more complicated lexical representations than do those for which it is necessary to specify, for example, that it must always (or never) take a direct object and never take complement sentences. We will see in Chapter 7 that this aspect of verb complexity plays an important role in language comprehension.

3.7
Summary

In the preceding sections of this chapter we have illustrated a number of rules that generate an infinite number of sentences and structural description(s) for each sentence generated. We illustrated the rule of Affix-Hopping, which not only explains a rather complicated set of facts about the structure of the auxiliary phrase in English but also interacts with rules necessary for describing passives, negatives, and questions. An interesting result of that discussion is that in every English sentence the deep structure and the surface structure differ from one another. Another important aspect of the preceding discussion has to do with the fact each rule captures a linguistically significant generalization of English syntax and can apply one after the other to generate sentences which combine the various constructions. We also illustrated the recursive property of Language with relative clauses and complement sentences in English. These constructions are important to the content of Chapters 7 and 8, which deal with adults' comprehension of language and with children's acquisition of their language, respectively.

The Interpretive Components

This chapter consists of two sections—the first is devoted to the phonological component of the grammar; the second, to semantics. Each section is limited to the concepts relevant to the psycholinguistic questions discussed in later chapters.

According to Figure 2.7 the semantic and phonological components convert syntactic representations of sentences into phonetic and semantic terms; that is, these components give phonetic and semantic interpretations to syntactic representations of sentences. This accounts for their being called the interpretive components.

The theoretical view underlying this book maintains that the syntactic component, sketched in the previous chapter, is the source of linguistic creativity; in particular we maintain that the aspect of creativity referred to in Chapter 1 as the recursive nature of Language is explained by the theory of syntax. According to this view the interpretive components are simply passive devices that receive syntactic information and convert it into phonetic and semantic information. No one has seriously raised the possibility that the phonological component might contain some creativity; there is nearly universal agreement that the essential role of phonology is to specify how sentences are to be pronounced (or heard). However, many scholars have raised the possibility that the semantic component is creative; more accurately, there exists a school of thought that maintains that syntax and semantics belong together in a single component. This component is held by this school to be the sole source of linguistic creativity. In the conclusion of the semantics section of this chapter we will return to this question and briefly state what we believe to be the advantage of our point of view.

4.1
The Phonological Component

The main purpose of this section is to describe the phonological rules that convert syntactic surface structures into phonetic representations. Before we discuss these rules, it is necessary to describe phonetic representations. Then, after we consider some phonological rules, in the final paragraphs of this section we briefly describe some segmental and sequential constraints —rules that determine possible speech sounds and sequences of them in words.

4.11 Phonetics

A phonetic description of a sequence is basically a description of those aspects of the pronunciation of a sentence that are determined by the phonological rules. A phonetic representation consists of a string of symbols, called **phones.** Each phone represents an idealization of the pronunciation of each sound in the utterance. Some of the symbols linguists use in phonetic representations resemble the letters of written English; others appear strange. But the reader should not make the mistake of confusing the phonetic symbols with letters of orthography. Ordinary spelling frequently fails to resemble phonetic representations, as a few examples such as 'enough', 'tough', 'thought', and 'through' suffice to indicate. Phonetic representations are given in square brackets [. . .]. Thus, for example, the word 'cat' has the phonetic representation [kʰæt]. Each of the symbols (which are described later) within the brackets stands for a particular set of gestures to be performed by the organs of the vocal tract.

4.111 The vocal tract. Figure 4.1 illustrates the most important organs that can be voluntarily controlled to produce speech sounds. All English sounds are produced by a stream of air passing from the lungs out of the body through the mouth, nose, or both.

The pressure of the outflowing air is determined by the force exerted by the muscles (and other forces) of the chest on the lungs (1); the air escapes from the lungs out of the trachea (windpipe) (2). The air is forced to pass through the larynx, or voice box (3). There are structures within the larynx known as the vocal cords (the term "vocal folds" is preferable), which determine whether or not voicing takes place. You can become aware of voicing by placing your fingers in your ears and producing a prolonged [z] sound. The buzzing sound you hear, which emanates from your larynx, is **voicing,** or **phonation.** Next say a prolonged [s] sound with your fingers in your ears; the buzzing sound is absent. Voicing is produced by bringing the vocal folds close enough together so that the outflowing air causes them to open and close in rapid succession. Voiceless

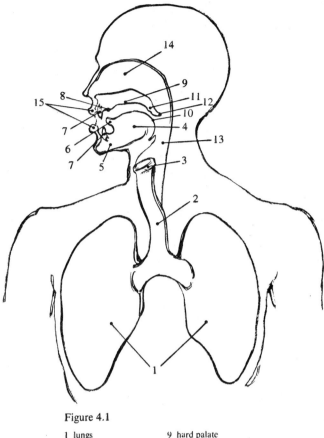

Figure 4.1

1 lungs	9 hard palate
2 trachea (windpipe)	10 dorsum of tongue
3 larynx (voice box)	11 soft palate (velar area)
4 main body of tongue	12 uvula
5 mandible (jaw)	13 pharynx
6 corona of tongue	14 nasal passageways
7 teeth	15 lips
8 alveolar ridge	

sounds are produced by separating the vocal folds so that the air does not set them vibrating.

The main body of the tongue (4) can move forward or backward and up or down. The up-and-down motion of the tongue is usually assisted by the opening or closing of the mandible (jaw) (5).

The corona, or front part of the tongue (6), is capable of movement independent of the tongue body. The corona can protrude from the main body of the tongue and be brought into contact with the upper front teeth (7) or the alveolar ridge (8), which is the hard ridge directly behind the upper front teeth. Actually the alveolar ridge is the front portion of the hard palate (9). Figure 4.1 reveals that the hard palate is rigid because of hard cartilage, shown by the shaded area.

The rear, or dorsum, of the tongue (10) is not capable of movement independent of the tongue body. The soft palate, or velum (11), is a flexible organ that can move back, to close the flow of air through the nose, or forward, to allow air to pass through the nose and the mouth. During rest breathing the velum is usually open. During speech, however, its usual position is closed; it is open only during the production of nasal sounds, described below. The uvula (12) is the flap of tissue hanging down in the center of the back of the mouth. The pharynx (13) is the opening down to the trachea and the esophagus (not shown here).

Finally, the lips (15) can be brought together, as in [p], [b], and [m]; some vowels also involve lip rounding ([u] and [o]; 'boot and boat' are examples of such sounds).

4.112 Phonetic features. We have stated that each phone represents a set of gestures performed by each of the speech organs. The symbol [t], for example, means that the corona of the tongue is in contact with the alveolar ridge such that the air flow is completely blocked, the vocal folds are not producing voicing, and the velum is closed. This description suggests that phones can be classified according to their articulatory characteristics. In fact it has been traditional to view phones as consisting of a number of features rather than as indivisible entities, and this approach is adopted in contemporary phonological theory. We present the most important features necessary for a description of English phones in this section, starting with the vowels.

4.113 Vowel features. We will consider the seven English vowels illustrated in Figure 4.2.

[i]	'beat'	[u]	'boot'
[e]	'bait'	[o]	'boat'
[æ]	'bat'	[ɔ]	'bought'
		[a]	'cot'

Figure 4.2

The vowels [i] and [u] involve raising the body of the tongue more than for any other vowels. Thus these vowels are **high** and the other vowels are **nonhigh.**

The vowels [æ], [a], and [ɔ] are the lowest vowels. The jaw is the most open for these vowels, and the body of the tongue is brought to its lowest position. Therefore these vowels are called **low** and all other vowels are **nonlow.**

Observe that there are now two vowels that are both nonhigh and nonlow; these are traditionally called the **mid** vowels. It is not difficult to observe the three degrees of vowel height—high, mid and low. Hold your head absolutely still and say the three vowels [i], [e], and [æ] in succession while holding your hand lightly under your jaw. You will notice that the jaw position gets progressively lower as you go from the first to the last vowel. You should get the same result if you try this experiment with [u], [o], and [ɔ].

The lips are somewhat rounded and protruded for the production of [u], [o], and [ɔ]. Any phone for which the lips are rounded and protruded has the feature **round;** all other sounds are **nonround.**

Compare the production of [i] and [u]. If you produce one after the other, you will of course notice that [i] is unrounded (in fact the lips may actually be spread) and [u] is rounded. Yet you should also notice that the tongue is farther back in the oral cavity for [u] than it is for [i]. Any phone that has a retracted tongue position is **back.** All the others (sometimes referred to as front vowels) are **nonback.** The back vowels in Figure 4.2 are: [u], [o], [ɔ], and [a].

There are a number of vowels of English that we have not yet discussed. Although we will not discuss all of them, there are four that are relevant to material discussed later: [ɪ], the vowel in 'bit'; [ɛ], the vowel in 'bet'; [ʊ], the vowel in 'put'; and [ə] the last vowel in 'sofa'.

[ɪ] is a high, front, unrounded vowel, like [i], but differs from the latter in that it is lax whereas [i] is tense. In fact all of the nonlow vowels in Figure 4.2 are tense. A tense vowel is produced with muscles of the vocal tract generally tighter. You can sense this difference if you hold your hand against the soft area right under your jaw and pronounce the words 'beet' and 'bit'. You should notice that the muscles tense up more for the former than they do for the latter. The vowel [ɛ] is the lax counterpart of [e]; that is, [ɛ] is a lax, nonhigh, nonlow (i.e., mid) vowel, differing from [e] only in laxness versus tenseness. Similarly, [ʊ] is the lax counterpart of [u]; it is a lax, high, back, rounded vowel.

The vowel [ə] is often referred to as the reduced vowel of English, or 'schwa.' Phonetically it is central (i.e., between back and front), unrounded, and about mid in height, although its precise characteristics vary considerably.

4.114 Obstruent features. Basically an **obstruent** is any consonant that is produced by creating an impedance on the flow of air out of the lungs great enough either to stop the air or to cause a friction noise at the point of constriction. Any other sound is a **sonorant.** The list in Figure 4.3 contains all the English obstruents.

The phones [f,] [θ], [s], [š], [v], [ð], [z], and [ž] are all produced by placing either the tongue or the lower lip against either the teeth or some point on the roof of the mouth in such a way that the air stream is forced to pass through a narrow constriction. Any phone for which there is air flowing out through the oral cavity is **continuant.** Thus in addition to the sounds listed immediately above the vowels are also continuant. The con-

[p]	'pat'	[s]	'sin'
[t]	'tat'	[š]	'shin'
[k]	'cat'	[v]	'vow'
[b]	'bat'	[ð]	'wither'
[d]	'dame'	[z]	'zip'
[g]	'game'	[ž]	'rouge'
[f]	'fame'	[č]	'chin'
[θ]	'thin'	[ǰ]	'gin'

Figure 4.3

tinuants listed here, however, involve forcing the air stream through a narrow constriction, which causes a hissing noise. Such phones are often referred to as **fricatives**. All fricatives are continuants, but not all continuants are fricatives.

If a phone involves the blockage of all air flow through the oral cavity, it is **noncontinuant**. Such phones are often referred to as **stops**. Any obstruent that is not a fricative is a stop.

The phones [č] and [ǰ] can be viewed as a combination of a stop and continuant. They are produced by first producing a complete closure between the corona of the tongue and a point on the roof of the mouth behind the alveolar ridge, in the forward part of the hard palate. This closure, or blockage, is then released in such a way that for a brief period of time during the release there is a constricted opening between the tongue and the roof of the mouth through which air may rush, producing a friction sound. These phones are noncontinuants, but the release of the closure is delayed so that they have a fricative off-glide. These phones have the feature **delayed release**. A traditional term for delayed release phones is **affricates**. [č] and [ǰ] are the only affricates in English.

The phones [s], [z], [š], [ž] have a primary noise source at the point where the air stream rushes through the constriction formed by the tongue against the roof of the mouth. A secondary noise source is created by the air stream striking against the teeth. In the case of [f] and [v] the primary noise source is the constriction between the lower lip and the upper teeth. The secondary source is the air stream striking the upper lip; this can easily be felt by energetically producing a prolonged [f] or [v] sound. Any phone that has both a primary and a secondary noise source is **strident**. [č] and [ǰ] are strident, since the fricative portion of these sounds has the two noise sources.

[θ] and [ð] are the only nonstrident fricatives of English. They are produced by inserting the corona of the tongue between the teeth, at which point the only noise source is created.

Those strident fricatives for which the secondary noise source is the air stream striking the back of the teeth are sometimes referred to as **sibilants**. Thus [s], [z], [š], and [ž] are sibilants.

We have already described the process of voice production. The following obstruents are **voiced:** [b], [d], [g], [v], [ð], [z], [ž] and [j]. All the other obstruents are **unvoiced.** The voiceless obstruents are the only unvoiced phones in English.

A **coronal** phone is any phone produced when the front of the tongue is brought into contact with or close to either the teeth or some point in the roof of the mouth. The coronal obstruents of English are [t], [d], [θ], [ž], [č], [s], [š], [ð], [z], and [j]. This can be verified by producing all of the obstruents one after another and observing that the corona of the tongue is involved in all of these—and only these—obstruents.

The feature **anterior** refers to the general location of the consonantal constriction within the oral cavity. Anterior phones are produced in the front part of the oral cavity—in particular, at or in front of the alveolar ridge. All other phones are nonanterior. The English phones [t], [d], [θ], [ð], [s], [z], [p], [b], [f], and [v] are all anterior; the English phones [š], [ž], [č], [j], [k], and [g] are all nonanterior. In the case of [š], [j], [č], and [j] the tongue is brought into contact (or near-contact) with the hard palate directly behind the alveolar ridge; this region of contact is referred to as the **alveo-palatal** area, and these phones are called the **alveo-palatals.**

Since [k] and [g] are produced by raising the dorsal area of the tongue against the soft palate, or velar area, these phones are nonanterior and noncoronal. Such phones are referred to as **velar.**

4.115 Some further features. There are eight sonorant sounds of English that we have not yet accounted for. These are divided into three groups—the nasals, the liquids, and the glides, illustrated in Figure 4.4.

[m] '*m*oose'	[y] '*y*ack'
[n] '*n*oose'	[h] '*h*ack'
[ŋ] 'ri*ng*'	[r] '*r*ack'
[w] '*w*ail'	[l] '*l*ack'

Figure 4.4

The nasals [m], [n], [ŋ] are distinguished from all other English phones by the feature **nasal.** The velum is open for these phones, allowing the air to pass through the nasal passageways. Since a closure is maintained in the oral cavity, these phones are classified as noncontinuant. And since [m] is produced with a labial closure, it is anterior and noncoronal; [n] is produced with the corona of the tongue against the alveolar ridge and is therefore anterior and coronal; [ŋ] is velar and is therefore nonanterior and noncoronal.

It is possible to divide a spoken utterance into syllables. All utterances consist of sequences of consonants and vowels, where each vowel constitutes the peak of a syllable. Thus all vowels are **syllabic.** Phones that do not serve as syllabic peaks are classified as **nonsyllabic.**

Consonantal phones are produced with a constriction at some point on the center line of the oral cavity; some phones may of course, involve further constrictions. All obstruents are consonantal, as are the nasal stops. The phones [r] and [l] are produced with a sufficient narrow constriction in the center of the oral cavity to be classified as consonantal, although they have rather large openings around the sides. [w] and [y] are non-consonantal.

If a sonorant is nonnasal and consonantal, it is a **liquid;** [r] and [l] are the only liquids in English. A **glide** is any nonnasal sonorant that is non-syllabic and nonconsonantal. The only English guides are [w], [y], and [h]: [w] is back and rounded, like [u]; [y] is nonback and nonrounded, like [i]. Both [w] and [y] differ from the high vowels primarily in that they are higher and nonsyllabic. [h] is a voiceless phone, frequently produced with the articulating organs in position for the production of an adjacent vowel.

A **lateral** phone is any sound for which the entire air stream is shunted around the sides of a center obstruction. The only lateral in English, [l], is produced by a contact between the corona of the tongue and the alveolar ridge, with the sides of the tongue sufficiently lowered that the air stream can pass relatively unobstructed.

We have now shown all the features necessary for providing a gross description of the most important English phones. Figure 4.5 is a chart showing how the phonetic symbols are defined with respect to the features described above.

4.116 Systematic phonetics versus physical phonetics. It is important to distinguish between the levels of systematic phonetics and physical phonetics. **Systematic phonetics** refers to the lowest level of the grammar, the output of the phonological rules. Representations of utterances at this level contain all the phonetic features determined by the rules of the grammar, although they will ignore many physical features of actual speech sounds. For example, a systematic phonetic representation will not distinguish between the speech of a man and a woman or a child and an adult. **Physical phonetics,** then refers to any description of actual physical or physiological events that take place during speech production. A description of the neural impulses traveling to the muscles of the vocal tract during the production of an utterance would be an example of a physical phonetic description. Other examples include a description of the gestures carried out by the speech organs and a description of the acoustic properties of an utterance.

During speech production systematic phonetic representations of utterances are transmitted to some sort of immensely complicated device that can integrate the phonetic specification of the desired utterance with other

	ɔ	æ	u	i	o	e	ɪ	ɛ	ʊ	p	t	k	b	d	g	f	θ	s	š	v	ð	z	ž	č	ǰ	m	n	ŋ	w	y	h	r	l
sonorant	+	+	+	+	+	+	+	+	+	−	−	−	−	−	−	−	−	−	−	−	−	−	−	−	−	+	+	+	+	+	−	+	+
consonantal	−	−	−	−	−	−	−	−	−	+	+	+	+	+	+	+	+	+	+	+	+	+	+	+	+	+	+	+	−	−	−	+	+
syllabic	+	+	+	+	+	+	+	+	+	−	−	−	−	−	−	−	−	−	−	−	−	−	−	−	−	−	−	−	−	−	−	−	−
lateral	−	−	−	−	−	−	−	−	−	−	−	−	−	−	−	−	−	−	−	−	−	−	−	−	−	−	−	−	−	−	−	−	+
nasal	−	−	−	−	−	−	−	−	−	−	−	−	−	−	−	−	−	−	−	−	−	−	−	−	−	+	+	+	−	−	−	−	−
continuant	+	+	+	+	+	+	+	+	+	−	−	−	−	−	−	+	+	+	+	+	+	+	+	−	−	−	−	−	+	+	+	+	+
del. rel.	−	−	−	−	−	−	−	−	−	−	−	−	−	−	−	−	−	−	−	−	−	−	−	+	+	−	−	−	−	−	−	−	−
strident	−	−	−	−	−	−	−	−	−	−	−	−	−	−	−	+	−	+	+	+	−	+	+	+	+	−	−	−	−	−	−	−	−
voice	+	+	+	+	+	+	+	+	+	−	−	−	+	+	+	−	−	−	−	+	+	+	+	−	+	+	+	+	+	+	−	+	+
coronal	−	−	−	−	−	−	−	−	−	−	+	−	−	+	−	−	+	+	+	−	+	+	+	+	+	−	+	−	−	−	−	+	+
anterior	−	−	−	−	−	−	−	−	−	+	+	−	+	+	−	+	+	+	−	+	+	+	−	−	−	+	+	−	−	−	−	+	+
high	−	−	+	+	−	−	+	−	+	−	−	+	−	−	+	−	−	−	+	−	−	−	+	+	+	−	−	+	+	+	−	−	−
low	+	+	−	−	−	−	−	−	−	−	−	−	−	−	−	−	−	−	−	−	−	−	−	−	−	−	−	−	−	−	+	−	−
back	+	−	+	−	+	−	−	−	+	−	−	+	−	−	+	−	−	−	−	−	−	−	−	−	−	−	−	+	+	−	−	−	−
round	+	−	+	−	+	−	−	−	+	−	−	−	−	−	−	−	−	−	−	−	−	−	−	−	−	−	−	−	+	−	−	−	−
tense	−	−	+	+	+	+	−	−	−	−	−	−	−	−	−	−	−	−	−	−	−	−	−	−	−	−	−	−	−	−	−	−	−

Figure 4.5

73

requirements of the speaker (such as the need for oxygen) in order finally to produce the actual speech gestures. The nature of this little-understood integrating device will be discussed further in Chapter 6. The reader should bear in mind, then, that systematic phonetic representations are cognitive structures in the sense that they correspond to a level of grammar and not to articulatory or acoustic levels.

4.12 Phonological rules

The features described in the preceding section are all those that are not predictable by rule. However, some phonetic features are redundant in the sense that their occurrence is determined by other features within the same segment and/or the environment in the utterance. An important example of this phenomenon is **aspiration,** which plays a significant role in speech perception, as described in Chapter 6.

Aspiration can be illustrated by comparing the pronunciation of the words 'pool' and 'spool'. The 'p' of the first word is followed by a small puff of air, which can be felt by dampening the back of your hand and holding it in front of your mouth; this puff of air is known as **aspiration,** and any phone that has it is called aspirated. This feature is absent from the 'p' in 'spool'. In phonetic transcriptions the phonetic feature of aspiration will be represented by a small, raised [ʰ], as illustrated in the phonetic representation of 'pool', [pʰul]; the phonetic representation of 'spool' is simply [spul].

How are we to account for the aspiration in 'pool' and its nonoccurrence in 'spool'? Basically, it is a fact of English that with some exceptions any voiceless stop that begins a word is aspirated. The [p] in 'pool' meets this qualification, whereas the [p] in 'spool' does not. This suggests, then, that we posit a phonological rule that adds the feature of aspiration in the appropriate environment:

$$\text{ASPIRATION} \begin{array}{l} - \text{ continuant} \\ - \text{ voice} \end{array} \rightarrow [+ \text{ aspiration}]; \text{ in the env: } \# \underline{\hspace{2cm}}$$

This rule says that a voiceless stop becomes aspirated when it appears in the position indicated by the bar (_____). The symbol # stands for word boundary; therefore the indicated environment is that of word-initial position. This is the typical form of phonological rules.

PHONEMIC REPRESENTATION	/spɪl/	/pɪl/	/prun/
ASPIRATION RULE	—	pʰɪl	pʰrun
PHONETIC REPRESENTATION	[spɪl]	[pʰɪl]	[pʰrun]

Figure 4.6

The application of ASPIRATION is illustrated in Figure 4.6. The rule is shown applying to words as they would appear in the syntactic surface structure representations of sentences. The symbols at this level, called **phonemes,** are enclosed within slant lines (//). A phoneme, then, is a phonological symbol at the level of syntactic surface structure. Phonological rules apply to syntactic surface structures of sentences that are "spelled out" in phonemes. (Notice the quotation marks around "spelled out." Do not confuse phonemes with letters.) A phonemic representation of a sentence is essentially the same as the syntactic surface structure representation. We use the terms "phonemic representation" and "phonemic level" in this sentence to call attention to the phonological, rather than the syntactic, character of sentences. The phonological rules apply to sentences represented by strings of phonemes (along with some syntactic information as to phrase boundaries, etc.) and converts them into strings of phones. This is exactly the same as saying that phonological rules convert syntactic surface structures into phonetic representations.

All occurrences of aspiration in English are the results of the application of a phonological rule. Aspiration is therefore different from the other features of English described previously. Unlike aspiration, these other features occur in environments where they are not inserted by a rule. Therefore the presence or absence of one of these features conveys some information to the listener. Since the presence or absence of aspiration is predictable, it is said to be redundant.

Another example of phonological rules that is relevant to experiments reported in Chapter 6 involves the relationships among the morphemes in the words presented below.

president [prɛzədənt]	presidency [prɛzədəns+i]
permit [pərmɪt]	permissive [pərmɪs+ɪv]
aristocrat [ærɪstəkræt]	aristocracy [ærəstakrəs+i]

These words are given in their orthographic and phonetic representations but with a plus sign (+) between the stem and the suffix in the phonetic representations. The purpose of this symbol is to indicate where the boundaries between the morphemes are; '+' is not a phonetic symbol in the sense that it represents a phone.

The point is that the stem-final phone is [t] when there is no suffix, whereas the suffixes illustrated here cause the stem-final phone to be an [s] instead. The analysis adopted by most linguists assumes that the phonemic representations of each of these stem morphemes involves a /t/ in stem-final position and that there is a phonological rule that converts a /t/ to an [s] whenever a suffix morpheme follows in the same word, provided the suffix begins with a /y/, an /ɪ/ or an /i/. We will call this rule SPIRANTIZATION and present it in a semiformal notation below. We first consider some further ramifications of this analysis.

Consider the relationship between the words 'abuse' (when used as a verb) and 'abusive'. The phonetic representation of 'abuse' is, roughly, [əbyuz], whereas 'abusive' is [əbyus+ɪv]. Observe that the verb form ends in a [z], whereas the stem morpheme in the adjective form ends in an [s]. The only difference between the two phonetic representations of this stem is that the final phone of one is voiced and the final phone of the other is voiceless. If we assume that the phonemic representation of the stem is /əbyuz/, we can account for the two phonetic representations by postulating a rule that devoices any obstruent that appears before the suffix /ɪv/. We will call this rule DEVOICING.

In order to determine the form and relative ordering of DEVOICING and SPIRANTIZATION, we next consider a pair of forms illustrating the application of both rules, 'intrude' and 'intrusive'. Given the assumption that the phonemic representation of the stem involves a /d/ in final position, it is evident that first SPIRANTIZATION applies, converting the /d/ to a [z]; DEVOICING applies next, converting the [z] to an [s]. (Notice that SPIRANTIZATION must be formulated so that it applies to /d/ as well as to /t/.) The two rules are given below, and the derivations of 'permissive' and 'intrusive' are illustrated in Figure 4.7. These examples were used in an interesting psycholinguistic experiment reported in Chapter 6.

PHONEMIC REPRESENTATION	/ɪntrud+ɪv/	/pɛrmɪt+ɪv/
SPIRANTIZATION RULE	ɪntruz+ɪv	pɛrmɪs+ɪv
DEVOICING RULE	ɪntrus+ɪv	——
PHONETIC REPRESENTATION	[ɪntrusɪv]	[pɛrmɪsɪv]

Figure 4.7

SPIRANTIZATION
$$\begin{bmatrix} + \text{obstruent} \\ + \text{coronal} \\ + \text{anterior} \end{bmatrix} \rightarrow [+ \text{continuant}]; \text{in env:} \_\_\_ + \begin{bmatrix} + \text{syllabic} \\ + \text{high} \\ - \text{back} \end{bmatrix}$$

DEVOICING
[+ obstruent] → [− voice]; in env: ___ + ɪv

4.121 Plural formation in English. Some of the early important psycholinguistic experiments concerned children's mastery of the phonological rules involving the pronunciation of the plural morpheme in English. Therefore, in anticipation of the discussion of how children learn these rules (in Chapter 8), we present the linguistic analysis of plural formation here.

A plural form of a noun is analyzed at the phonemic level as consisting of a stem followed by the abstract symbol PLU; this is of course similar to the syntactic representations of verbs with the TNS, which was presented in Chapter 3. Consider the forms in Figure 4.8. In each of the three sets of data we see three lists of plural nouns. One list indicates the printed form of the word, the second shows the phonemic representation, and the third gives the phonetic representations that result from the application of the rules discussed below to the phonemic representations.

It is evident that there are three rules: one converts PLU to [əz]; one converts PLU to [s]; and one converts PLU to [z]. Observe that all the noun stems in the first column end in coronal, strident phonemes, whereas none of the stems in either of the other two columns end in such sounds. Therefore PLU can be converted to [əz] by the first PLURAL RULE, given below.

PLURAL RULE 1: PLU → [əz]; in env: $\begin{bmatrix} + \text{ strident} \\ + \text{ coronal} \end{bmatrix} +$ _____

The second column contains stems that end in voiceless phonemes (not including, of course, stems that end in strident, coronal, voiceless sounds). Therefore the second rule is as follows:

PLURAL RULE 2: PLU → [s]; in env: [−voice] + _____

Finally, the third column contains stems ending in all the remaining sounds. Notice that all the voiced phonemes except the strident coronals are represented here (this includes all the voiced obstruents and all sonorants; of the vowels, we have included only /o/). Since the preceding two rules have already taken care of all the occurrences of PLU that do not end up as [z], all we need is a rule such as PLURAL 3.

PLURAL RULE 3: PLU → [z]; in all remaining environments

It is important to bear in mind that these rules must be ordered as given here in order to achieve the correct results.

4.13 Segmental and sequential constraints

Not all the possible combinations of vowel features occur as phonemes of English. Thus, although we have a high, nonback, unrounded phoneme, /i/, we do not have a high, nonback, rounded phoneme. Many languages do, however, including French, German, and Finnish. The phonetic symbol for it is [ü] (some transcription systems represent it as [y]). This illustrates, then, that English has rules that set limits (or constraints) on the

PLU represented as [ɪz]

nooses	/nus + PLU/	[nusɪz]
rash	/ræš + PLU/	[ræšɪz]
fuse	/fyuz + PLU/	[fyuzɪz]
rouge	/ruž + PLU/	[ružɪz]
watch	/wač + PLU/	[wačɪz]
badge	/bæj + PLU/	[bæjɪz]

PLU represented as [s]

caps	/kæp + PLU/	[kʰæps]
rats	/ræt + PLU/	[ræts]
racks	/ræk + PLU/	[ræks]
reefs	/rif + PLU/	[rifs]
breaths (noun)	/breθ + PLU/	[breθs]

PLU represented as [z]

cabs	/kæb + PLU/	[kæbz]
beads	/bid + PLU/	[bidz]
figs	/fɪg + PLU/	[fɪgz]
sieves	/sɪv PLU/	[sɪvz]
grooms	/grum + PLU/	[grumz]
loons	/lun + PLU/	[lunz]
beers	/bir + PLU/	[birz]
rolls	/rol + PLU/	[rolz]
sows (female pig)	/sæw + PLU/	[sæwz]
soys	/soy + PLU/	[soyz]
windows	/wɪndo + PLU/	[wɪndoz]

Figure 4.8

possible combinations of features that can occur within a single phoneme. These are known as **segment structure rules,** and their chief role is to prohibit the impossible phonemes in a language. They play a role in some psycholinguistic discoveries reported in Chapter 6.

In addition to rules that prohibit the impossible phonemes, the phonological component of the grammar of every language must also have rules that prohibit impossible sequences of phonemes. As an example of the need for such rules, consider the examples /slip/ and */tlip/. The first is possible—in fact, it is an actual English word—and the second is not a possible word of English. (There are also examples of possible words that just happen, by accident, not to occur. The possible English word /blɪk/ is an example of this.) The rules that accomplish this task are known as **sequential structure rules;** they are also relevant to some of the psycholinguistic material discussed in Chapter 6. It is beyond the scope of this book to describe the form of these rules.

4.14 Summary of Phonology

All the knowledge of phonology relevant to the psycholinguistic material presented in later chapters has been presented in this section. The main points to bear in mind are the following:

1. That it is necessary to distinguish between physical and systematic phonetic representations
2. That phones are to be viewed as bundles of phonetic features
3. That phonemic and phonetic representations are related by phonological rules
4. That phonological rules apply in order, one after the other
5. That phonological rules apply to classes of phonemes, defined in terms of features
6. That some features are distinctive, while others are redundant
7. That the phonological component must contain rules for describing segmental and sequential constraints
8. Most importantly, that the role of the phonological rules is to assign a phonetic interpretation to syntactic representations of sentences.

We now turn to a brief discussion of the other interpretive component, the semantic component.

4.2
The Semantic Component

The role of the semantic component of a grammar is to specify the meaning of each sentence of the language. Although this is accomplished by a set of formal rules, it would take us too far afield to present them here.

Instead we will discuss some basic aspects of semantics that would have to be accounted for by formal rules in a more complete exposition. Many of the key notions described below have been applied in psycholinguistic experiments described in later chapters. We commence with a discussion of semantic representations.

4.21 Information to be contained in semantic representations

In rather general terms the meaning of a sentence is dependent on the meaning associated with its individual words and morphemes and the meaning implied by their combination. The meaning of a group of morphemes is not always simply an amalgamation of the meanings of each individual morpheme. For example, a 'venetian blind' is not the same thing as a 'blind Venetian'. Many words (like 'blind') have more than one meaning, of course, so the grammar must specify which of its assorted meanings may be appropriate in a particular sentential context. Individual meaning selections are determined by the part of speech of the lexical item (i.e., whether a noun, verb, adjective, or adverb node dominates the item in a PM) and also by the environment in which it appears in the sentence. In the above example 'blind' is a noun in the phrase 'venetian blind' and an adjective in the phrase 'blind Venetian'. Therefore, two meanings can be at least partially characterized by noting the difference in form class of the word 'blind'.

To see how the environment of a morpheme can contribute to determining its meaning, consider the word 'bat.'

(1) Florence killed the bat.

In isolation the word 'bat' can mean, among other things, a flying rodent or a stick of some kind for hitting balls. In (1), however, it can only have the flying rodent interpretation because any noun that is the object of the verb 'kill' must refer to an animate object.[1] The same principle that accounts for why only one interpretation of 'bat' is possible in (1) accounts for the anomaly of sentence (2). Furthermore, since there are no such restrictions on the objects of the verb 'love', sentence (3) is ambiguous.

(2) *Florence killed the can opener.
(3) Florence loves bats.

The discussion of (1)–(3) reveals that one task of the semantic component of a generative grammar is to account for how the environment of a word in a sentence can contribute to its meaning. Thus the semantic

---

[1] Of course, there are other uses, such as 'to kill an idea', which we are ignoring for our purposes. A more thorough description would have to specify the classes of all possible nouns that can serve as objects of the verb 'kill'.

component must account for the ambiguity of (3), for the fact that (1) has only one meaning, and for the anomaly of (2). One further task is to explain the fact that (4) and (1) have the same meaning (i.e., that they are synonyms).

(4) Florence killed the flying rodent.

4.22 Semantic features

It is generally assumed that the meaning of an individual word is not an indivisible whole but can be broken down into features of meaning, analogous in some respects to phonological features. We will illustrate these semantic features and the role they play in the grammar of English with the examples 'equation', 'man', 'woman', 'dog', and 'rock'.

The noun 'equation' is an abstract noun, and all the others are nonabstract. Thus the object of the verb 'solve' must be an abstract noun; it may not be a nonabstract noun. Thus the sentence in (5) is a perfectly good English sentence, whereas (6) would be judged odd by any English speaker.

(5) Matilda solved the equation.
(6) *Matilda solved the dog.

The substitution of any nonabstract noun for 'dog' would yield an anomalous sentence.

Among the nonabstract nouns the words 'man', 'woman', and 'dog', are all animate nouns, whereas 'rock' is nonanimate. The object of the verb 'frighten' must be animate, as must the subject of the verb 'admire'. Thus the naturalness of (7) and (8) is accounted for, as is the unacceptability of (9).

(7) The monster frightened the man.
(8) The dog admired his master.
(9) *The rock admired the dog.

Restricting our attention now to the animate, nonabstract nouns, it is possible to distinguish between those that refer to human and those that refer to nonhuman objects. Thus 'man' and 'woman' are both human, and 'dog' is nonhuman. Only a human noun can serve as the subject of the verb 'lecture', whereas only a nonhuman noun can be the subject of 'whelp'. These facts are illustrated in (10)–(13).

(10) The woman lectured brilliantly.
(11) My dog whelped last night.
(12) *The woman whelped last night.
(13) *The dog lectured brilliantly.

The distinction between 'man' and 'woman' is of course one of sex only. The sentences in (14)–(17) demonstrate that there are a few verbs and adjectives that are restricted to male or female nouns.

(14)   This man has sired a fine group of youngsters.
(15)   This woman is pregnant.
(16)   *This woman has sired a fine group of youngsters.
(17)   *This man is pregnant.

To summarize, we have shown how it is possible to subdivide portions of the vocabulary on the basis of semantic features. We have illustrated this with a small group of nouns. The assignment of features to these nouns is illustrated in Figure 4.9. This should not be confused with a PM.

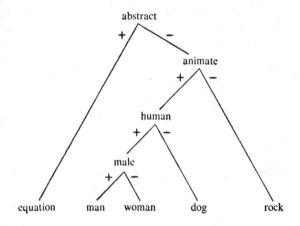

Figure 4.9

It is simply a graphic way of illustrating how the features divide up the classes of nouns.

We have also seen that these features can account for certain occurrence restrictions. That is, 'the rock' cannot occur as the subject of 'admire', 'the dog' cannot occur as the object of 'solve', and so on. In order to account for the strange character of the starred sentences in the above examples, we would need not only features such as we have described for the nouns above, but also features associated with verbs and adjectives that specify which classes of nouns may be selected to co-occur with them; these are known as **selectional restrictions.**

There has been a bit of debate in linguistic theory as to whether the kinds of linguistic facts that can be explained by appeal to selectional restrictions should be regarded as syntactic or semantic facts. In *Syntactic Structures* Chomsky coined the now-famous sentence, "Colorless green ideas sleep furiously" and claimed that it is syntactically correct but semantically anomalous. In *Aspects of the Theory of Syntax* (1965) he suggested that selectional restrictions should be represented as constraints on lexical insertion in the syntactic component of the grammar. He stated this as a tentative move that could be modified with the advent of a semantic theory adequate to account for such restrictions. The point here is that such facts are linguistically relevant and should be explained at some level in a theory of linguistic competence.

Before leaving the topic of semantic features, it is important to distinguish between **denotative** and **connotative** meanings. Traditionally this refers to the distinction made between the definitional aspects of the meaning of a word and its affective aspects, respectively. For example, a little boy and the parents of a little boy will have quite different connotative, or affective, meanings for the word 'boy', although the denotative features of young, male human will remain constant for all English speakers.

4.23 Analyticity and contradiction

An adequate semantic representation must account for the fact that (18) is an **analytic** statement.

(18) The bachelor is unmarried.

That is, the predicate of the sentence gives us no new information about the subject of the sentence. The predicate is implied by the semantic representation of the subject. This fact can be accounted for in terms of the semantic features associated with the subject. If the predicate makes a statement about the subject that is already stated in the lexicon as a semantic feature of the subject, then the sentence is analytic. In the case of (18) the feature [–married] is one of the semantic features of 'bachelor'; therefore (18) is analytic.

(19) The bachelor is married.

Conversely, (19) is a **contradiction** because the predicate makes a statement about the subject that is in direct contradiction to one of the defining features of the subject. The contradictory statement is to be distinguished from the anomalous sentence, in which selectional restrictions have been violated.

4.24 Focus and presupposition

In addition to the aspects of meaning described in the preceding few paragraphs a semantic representation of a sentence must contain information concerning its focus and presupposition. By **focus** we mean information contained in a sentence that is to be conveyed from the speaker to the hearer; the speaker assumes that the hearer does not possess the focus information. **Presupposition,** on the other hand, refers to information in a sentence that the speaker presupposes to be part of the hearer's knowledge. Jackendoff (1972) defines these notions in the following way:

> As working definitions, we will use 'focus of a sentence' to denote the information in the sentence that is assumed by the speaker not to be shared by him and the hearer, and 'presupposition of a sentence' to denote the information in the sentence that is assumed by the speaker to be shared by him and the hearer. (p. 230)

These distinctions can be made clear by considering pairs of sentences, such as (20) and (21).

(20) Was it Margaret that Paul married?
(21) No, it was Maxine.

These sentences share the presupposition that 'Paul married someone'. 'Margaret' is the focus in (20) and thus may be corrected by the hearer, since it does not represent presumably shared information. On the other hand, (22) is an inappropriate or anomalous response to (20) because it violates the presupposition expressed there.

(22) No, he killed her.

In (23) the presupposition is that Paul did something to Margaret, and *marry* is the focus of the sentence. (The italics in (23) indicate emphasis.)

(23) Did Paul *marry* Margaret?

Therefore (22) is a perfectly reasonable response (if it's true, of course).

Another semantic dimension that must be distinguished from presupposition yet is superficially similar to it is the **implication** of a sentence.

(24) Betty remembered to take her medicine.

A presupposition of (24) is that Betty was supposed to take her medicine, but the implication of (24) is that she did in fact take her medicine. The test for distinguishing between the implications and the presuppositions of a sentence involves the effects of negating the sentence. Negating a sentence always negates the implications but never negates the presuppositions. Thus in (25) the presupposition that Betty was supposed to take her medicine still holds, but the implication of (25) is that she did not take the medicine, the opposite of the implication of (24).

(25) Betty did not remember to take her medicine.

Presupposition and implication are dimensions of semantic representation that are not directly represented in the sentence itself. However, both presuppositions and implications constitute information that is in an important sense contained in a sentence. Both the presupposition and implication of (24) are controlled by the semantics of the verb 'remember'. Sentence (26), on the other hand, contains no information beyond that stated in the body of the sentence itself.

(26) Betty wanted to take her medicine.

The hearer has received no information about whether Betty should have or actually did take her medicine.

Such aspects of semantic structure have important implications for linguistic descriptions as well as for psycholinguistics. It is clear that the relatively simple formal devices of features and selectional restrictions are inadequate to handle such complex semantic phenomena. From the point of view of psycholinguistics, studies (e.g., Just and Clark, 1973, Offir, 1973) have demonstrated that comprehension of a sentence also involves the receipt of presupposed and implied information. Not surprisingly the question, How must we characterize the meaning of a sentence? is closely related to the question, What does it mean to understand a sentence? Some of the most interesting research in the field of semantics involves such questions as these.

4.25 Three theories of semantics

Since historically the development of transformational-generative grammar centered around syntactic descriptions, the central question that has emerged is, What is the relationship between syntax and semantics? The answers divide roughly into two schools, the interpretive semanticists and the generative semanticists. Actually, however, interpretive semantics divides itself into two separate theories. In fact it was difficulties with the original version of interpretive semantics that spawned the development of the new interpretive semantics as well as generative semantics. There are, then, three theories.

4.251 The early interpretive semantics. In the early 1960s Fodor and Katz (1964) and Katz and Postal (1964) put forward the hypothesis that the deep structure of a sentence contained all the information necessary to interpret it semantically. A semantic theory evolved that contained rules (known as **projection rules**) to map deep-structure PMs into semantic representations, much like the phonological rules map surface-structure PMs into phonetic representations. The syntactic component of the grammar, and in particular the PS rules and lexical insertion rules, were considered to be the only creative components of the grammar. Semantic rules interpreted deep structures; T rules converted them into surface-structure PMs, which were in turn interpreted by phonological rules.

This hypothesis (sometimes known as the **deep structure-hypothesis**) was a very good one because it provided an elegant description of an enormous number of linguistic facts and because it made very precise predictions that could be tested rigorously—put differently, it was sufficiently explicit that it could be disproved easily by empirical observation. And it was. There were two independent assumptions at the heart of the theory: (1) that the syntactic component of the grammar was the only creative component, and (2) that deep structures contained all the information necessary for a semantic interpretation, i.e., that transformations do not change meaning. Research clearly disproved the latter assumption. Two kinds of examples show this. First, consider sentences with quantifiers, such as (27). The passive version of that sentence, (28), is obviously not a paraphrase of (27) in the same sense that (30) is a paraphrase of (29).

(27) All the arrows did not hit the target.
(28) The target was not hit by all the arrows.
(29) The boy did not answer the question.
(30) The question was not answered by the boy.

The difference between (29) and (30) is at the most a stylistic variation in emphasis; the two sentences would both be true simultaneously under the same set of conditions. Put differently, (29) and (30) have similar truth conditions, but (27) and (28) do not. This is clear when you consider that (31) is a paraphrase of (27) and (32) is a paraphrase of (28).

(31) None of the arrows hit the target.
(32) Not all of the arrows hit the target.

Another kind of difficulty the deep-structure hypothesis ran into involved grammatical relations. Consider in (33) and (34) that 'the glass' functions as the subject of the sentence in (33), the object in (34), yet 'the glass' clearly has the same semantic function in both. The same problem is illustrated by (35) and (36).

(33) The glass broke.
(34) Peter broke the glass.
(35) John sold the car to Bill.
(36) Bill bought the car from John.

In this pair of sentences subject and object are reversed, yet it is obvious that the same semantic relationship holds between John and Bill in both sentences. A semantic theory that operates solely on deep structures and the syntactically defined grammatical relations available at that level of analysis cannot adequately account for the semantic facts illustrated in these two examples. For this reason (and other similar ones) few linguists still maintain the deep-structure hypothesis. Nevertheless, it is important to consider the hypothesis and the reasons for its demise, because in solving the problems that it revealed linguists have gone in two different theoretical directions.

4.252 The new interpretive semantics. The linguistic theory that incorporated the early interpretive semantics is often called the **standard theory.** By analogy the theory that incorporates the new interpretive semantics is frequently referred to as the **extended standard theory.** This theory retains one assumption of the deep-structure hypothesis—namely that the syntactic component is the only generative, or creative, component of the grammar. It also holds to the importance of deep structure as a significant level of linguistic description. It differs from the early interpretive semantics in that semantic interpretation operates at all levels of the grammar—on deep structures, surface structures, and derived structures in between. The rules of interpretation themselves are considerably richer in incorporating facts such as found in the similarity of sentences (33) and (34). After contrasting this view with that of generative semantics, we will show how the two theories account for the relationship between (33) and (34).

4.253 Generative semantics. The generative semanticists reject the first assumption of the deep-structure hypothesis, that the syntactic component of the grammar is the only creative component, as well as the obviously false second assumption. In generative semantics semantic representations are considered primary and are mapped onto surface structures by a series of transformational rules. There is no linguistic level of deep structure. Transformations operate on semantic structures, then on structures that are partly semantic and partly syntactic, and so on until a surface structure is achieved.

It may help clarify the distinction between these two kinds of theories by an example. Consider again the sentences in (33) and (34), reproduced here for convenience.

(33) The glass broke.
(34) Peter broke the glass.

A generative semantics analysis of (33) and (34) these sentences would involve initial semantic structures of the form in Figure 4.10. These structures would be converted into appropriate surface structures by a series of T rules. Notice that the verb "cause" in these examples is not a real verb inserted by a lexical insertion rule, because the underlying structure

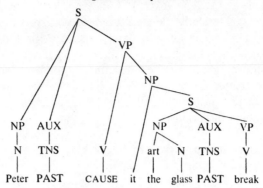

Figure 4.10   Peter PAST   CAUSE   it   the   glass PAST   break

is a semantic representation, not a deep structure. Instead "cause" should be thought of as a semantic marker expressing the semantic relationship that holds between an unknown someone or something (which gets deleted by T rules) and the glass in (33) and between Peter and the glass in (34).

A solution to the same problem in interpretive semantics (suggested by Jackendoff, 1972, p. 29, based on an analysis by Gruber and similar to the case interpretation of Fillmore, 1968) involves traditional deep-structure PMs, as illustrated in Figure 4-11, plus a new and very general interpretive convention in which a theme noun phrase is identified for each sentence. Selection of the theme is dependent on the semantic function of the verb. For verbs of motion such as 'break' the theme is the NP that undergoes the motion. 'The glass', then, is interpreted as the theme in each of the above sentences even though it functions as the grammatical subject in (33) and the grammatical object in (34). Notice that the distinction between grammatical subject and object is explicitly ignored in the generative semantics analysis.

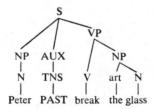

Peter PAST break the glass

Figure 4.11

4.254 Choosing between the two theories. The best way to choose between two theories in any scientific discipline is to see which of the two can explain or predict more data. In this case one would like to find examples in which interpretive semantics and generative semantics make different predictions about the meaning of sentences in some natural language. Then we could investigate to ascertain which of the two theories did a better job of predicting the facts. Unfortunately there do not seem to be clear instances of the two theories yielding different predictions about meaning, ambiguity, grammaticality, or paraphrase. The two theories seem to compete in their analysis of existing facts, but they seem to be equivalent in their empirical predictions.

It is a frequent misconception that generative semantics is preferable to interpretive semantics because it seems to mirror more directly the actual processes of language production. Since people begin with an idea when they use language, the argument goes, a linguistic theory that presents semantic structures as more basic is better. Such an argument confuses the concepts of competence and performance. Linguistic theory describes the organization of particular grammars; these are, in turn, theories of linguistic competence, not theories of performance. A theory of speech production would certainly make reference to the theory of competence, but they remain totally different theories, evaluated by different kinds of data. In the following chapters of this book we shall present the kinds of data by which performance theories can be tested—basically, data generated in experimental investigations of psycholinguistic abilities. Theories of competence, on the other hand, make predictions about, and are tested by, the judgments of native speakers of particular languages about the grammaticality, ambiguity, and paraphrase relations of sentences in their language. It is this kind of empirical linguistic data that is required if we are to choose among competing grammars and, ultimately, metatheories.

As further research produces more explicit analyses, it should become possible to decide between the two theories on empirical grounds. But what if we cannot? What if we are faced with two theories that make essentially the same empirical predictions but differ in their metatheoretical formulations? In the first place it should be borne in mind that the two metatheories are very similar in many ways. Both postulate underlying structures that are related to meanings and superficial structures that are related to sound. Both theories represent linguistic structures in terms of phrase markers, both effect derivations by transformational rules, and both claim to represent the form of Language of which each particular language is an instance. There are more similarities than differences between them.

Observing that the two metatheories are very similar does not save us from the initial question: How shall we choose between them if they make similar empirical predictions? This is a very complex question, similar to those that have been debated by philosophers of science for decades, and we do not pretend to give the answer here. We can state a general principle, however, although to justify it would take us beyond the scope of this book. In linguistics the most desirable metatheory is the one that will describe the smallest class of grammars for individual languages. Just as the theory of a particular language must generate (predict, describe) all and only the possible grammatical sentences of that language, so a metatheory must generate all and only the possible human languages. Many possible human languages, like many possible sentences in a particular human language, may of course never exist. But a theory of a language—

say, English—must present a formal definition of what it means to be a grammatical sentence of English. In just this sense the metatheory must present a formal definition of what it means to be a human language. Putting it a different way, the perfect metatheory would be one that would not allow us to write a particular grammar that could not be the description of a natural language.

It can be shown mathematically that the extended standard theory is not a sufficiently restrictive metatheory. "It "overgenerates" in that it describes too many possible grammars of particular languages. (See Bach, 1974, pg. 200–204, for a readable account of this problem.) Therefore a move from the extended standard theory should only be in the direction of a more restricted metatheory. Many linguists argue (Chomsky, 1972b) that generative semantics is in fact a less restricted theory and overgenerates to a much greater degree than does the extended standard theory. Such an argument provides a philosophical way of choosing between the two theories in the absence of decisive empirical evidence.

4.26

Summary of Semantics

In this section we presented a brief sketch of some of the main points of current semantic studies. Not all of this material is directly relevant to the psycholinguistic investigations reported in the following chapters; it cannot be denied, however, that an explication of a complete and formal theory of semantics will be of great importance to psycholinguistics. The concept of semantic features has already provided the basis for some psycholinguistic investigations, as has the notion of presupposition; these studies are reported in Part Two of this book.

SUGGESTIONS FOR FURTHER READING

The following books deal with general linguistics and broad theoretical issues:

Chomsky, N. *Language and Mind.* New York: Harcourt, Brace & World, 1972.

Fodor, J. A., and Katz, J. J. (eds.). *The Structure of Language: Readings in the Philosophy of Language.* Englewood Cliffs, N.J.: Prentice-Hall, 1964.

Fromkin, V., and Rodman, R. *An Introduction to Language.* New York: Holt, Rinehart and Winston, 1974.

Lenneberg, E. H. *Biological Foundations of Language.* New York: John Wiley & Sons, 1967.

Lyons, J. *Noam Chomsky.* New York: Viking Press, 1970.

Miller, G. A. (ed.). *Communication, Language, and Meaning.* New York: Basic Books, 1973.

The following books deal primarily with syntax:

Bach, E. *Syntactic Theory*. New York: Holt, Rinehart and Winston, 1974.

Chomsky, N. *Syntactic Structures*. Janua Linguarum 4, The Hague: Mouton, 1957.

Chomsky, N. *Aspects of the Theory of Syntax*. Cambridge, Mass.: M.I.T. Press, 1965.

Jacobs, R. A., and Rosenbaum, P. S. *English Transformational Grammar*. Waltham, Mass.: Blaisdell, 1968.

Reibel, D. A., and Schane, S. A. *Modern Studies in English: Readings in Transformational Grammar*. Englewood Cliffs, N.J.: Prentice-Hall, 1969.

The following books deal primarily with semantics:

Fillmore, C. J., and Langendoen, D. T. *Studies in Linguistic Semantics*. New York: Holt, Rinehart and Winston, 1971.

Jackendoff, R. S. *Semantic Interpretation in Generative Grammar*. Cambridge, Mass.: M.I.T. Press, 1972.

Katz, J. J. *Semantic Theory*. New York: Harper & Row, 1972.

Steinberg, D. D., and Jakobovits, L. A. *Semantics*. Cambridge, Mass.: Cambridge University Press, 1971.

The following books deal primarily with phonology:

Anderson, S. R. *The Organization of Phonology*. New York: Academic Press, 1974.

Chomsky, N., and Halle, M. *The Sound Pattern of English*. New York: Harper & Row, 1968.

Hyman, L. R., *Phonology: Theory and Analysis*. New York: Holt, Rinehart and Winston, 1975.

Postal, P. M. *Aspects of Phonological Theory*. New York: Harper & Row, 1968.

Schane, S. *Generative Phonology*. Englewood Cliffs, N. J.: Prentice-Hall, 1973.

The following journals publish reports of linguistic research:

Foundations of Language
Journal of Linguistics
Language
Linguistic Analysis
Linguistic Inquiry

PART 2

LINGUISTIC PERFORMANCE

Linguistic Performance

In the following chapters we turn to investigations of linguistic performance. As linguistics is the academic discipline concerned with linguistic competence, so is psycholinguistics the discipline that concerns itself with linguistic performance. Psycholinguistics is a branch of human cognitive psychology, so we begin our presentation of psycholinguistics by showing how it relates to the discipline of psychology. Later chapters will provide introductions to the basic ideas and research methodologies in the three primary areas of linguistic performance—phonological performance, grammatical performance, and children's acquisition of their native language. One of the principal themes of this book is that linguistic competence and linguistic performance are inseparable when one considers the total linguistic activities of human beings. In the following chapters, then, we attempt to demonstrate the mutual dependence of performance and competence. At the same time we hope to alert the reader to the myriad of unanswered questions about the relationships between the two.

Psycholinguistics as a Psychological Discipline

5

The subtitle of this book is *A Cognitive View of Language*. In psycholinguistics this distinguishes the authors' view from a behaviorist view of language, which has been held by a number of psychologists and linguists. A behaviorist would call Part Two of this book "linguistic behavior," whereas we insist on the term "linguistic performance." As we explain in this chapter, there is more at stake here than an arbitrary choice of words.

To understand the distinction between the cognitive and the behaviorist approach to language, it is necessary to look briefly into the history of psychology and linguistics (especially in the United States) during the twentieth century. In this chapter we describe the intellectual atmosphere in which psycholinguistics developed and continues to exist, sketching the main features of opposing schools of thought.

5.1
Behaviorist Psychology

5.11 Introspectionism.
At the beginning of this century psychology as an experimental discipline was just getting under way. Psychologists such as Wundt in Germany and Titchener in the United States described psychology as a "science of the mind" and were interested in investigating the state of human consciousness (Blumenthal, 1970). This worthy goal was reduced in the laboratory to a study of the details of perception of color, form, auditory signals, and so on. The method of study was introspection. This meant that an introspectionist would concentrate very hard on some stimulus and report in great detail his internal states and the images elicited by the stimulus. An impressive example of this activity is to be found in Titchener's image for the word 'meaning': "the blue-gray tip of a kind of scoop which has a bit of yellow about it (probably a part of the handle) and which is just digging

into a dark mass of what appears to be plastic material (reported in Brown, 1958, p. 90).

Psychology was getting nowhere fast, as you can imagine. The biggest problem was that even among highly trained introspectionists there was very little agreement about the internal sensations associated with particular stimuli. Another problem was that if an introspectionist was joking and really felt that the tip of the scoop was red, rather than blue-gray, no one would ever know. There were no objective criteria for the investigation of phenomena. Everything was completely subjective, so there could be no verification or agreement among members of the scientific community. Psychology was ripe for revolution.

5.12 The behaviorist revolution

The revolution came in the 1920s, led by John Watson in the United States. The followers of Watson, known as behaviorists, took as their philosophical ancestors the radical empiricists, such philosophers as John Locke and David Hume. The radical empiricists held that the only way of knowing anything was by experiencing it physically. It followed, then, that the only kind of data considered valid by the radical behaviorists was that obtained by objective, observable test. One had to *observe* the results of an experiment rather than have someone report on his unobservable internal states.

To the extent that the behaviorist revolution saved psychology from introspectionism, it allowed psychology to become a scientific discipline. To the extent that it limited psychological *explanation,* however, it prevented the development of psychology as a mature science. Another assertion of the radical empiricists and the behaviorists was that in accounting for physical phenomena one could use only other observable physical phenomena. Thus, not only did psychology become the science of behavior in that only observable aspects of organic functioning were admitted as data, but the behavior that psychology was to account for had to be explained in terms of other observables.

In this spirit gross behaviors were analyzed as chains of smaller units of behavior, linked by general principles of association (which had also been accepted by the introspectionists). An important cause of two events (or units of behavior) being associated in this way is their contiguous occurrence in space or time, stronger associations being formed when two actions occur together frequently (habitually). Motor sequences provide a perfect, if simple, example of this sort of association—the old horse pulling the milk wagon follows a habitual path unerringly, not because it has a mental map of its route, but because units of walking, stopping, turning have been associated in a particular sequence over the years.

Experimental investigations of the origins of associational linkages between units of behavior led to the discovery that associations can in fact be formed between previously unpaired units of behavior through a process known as conditioning. Actually there are two distinct kinds of condition-ing, **classical** and **operant** (or **instrumental**). Since many behaviorist theories are closely related to these processes, we will take a moment to present a basic overview of them. The brief sketch presented below is just sufficient to show how conditioning—or "learning"—theory has been applied to the analysis of linguistic "behavior." There have been and are still far more complicated learning theories than are presented here. (See Hilgard and Marquis, 1961, for one of many excellent reviews of learning theory.)

5.121 Classical conditioning. Classical conditioning is associated with the twentieth-century Russian physiologist Pavlov. In his famous experi-ments (Pavlov, 1902) he rang a bell and then immediately squirted meat powder in the mouths of dogs, making them salivate. He then found that the dogs would salivate upon hearing the bell even before the meat powder was introduced. Thus through classical conditioning an association was in-troduced between the hearing of the bell and salivation which had not existed previously. The bell is called the **conditioned stimulus,** while the meat powder (associated with salivation without training) is called the **unconditioned stimulus.** Salivation is a **conditioned response** to the bell and an **unconditioned response** to the meat powder.

The association formed by classical conditioning has a number of in-teresting properties. In order to produce the desired association, the bell must immediately precede the introduction of the meat powder. If it ar-rives too far in advance or if it follows the meat powder, the procedure does not work. Once formed, the association will continue for some time without the introduction of meat powder. That is, the dog will salivate upon hearing the bell for a number of times, but salivation will gradually de-crease in intensity until the response vanishes; this is known as **extinction** of the response.

Before extinction one may observe **stimulus generalization,** which means that a different bell, similar in tone to the conditioned stimulus, will pro-duce some salivation (although not as much as the original bell). The more dissimilar the bell, the less the salivation. The classical conditioning paradigm has provided behaviorist psychology with its basic orientation as stimulus-response (S-R) psychology, a description of units of behavior and their antecedents.

5.122 Operant conditioning. Operant (or instrumental) conditioning, developed in the first half of the twentieth century by B. F. Skinner, empha-sizes not so much the association of two units of behavior as the increased frequency and intensity of a particular unit of behavior. If an organism produces a type of behavior and is rewarded, it will tend to produce that behavior with greater frequency and intensity that it originally did. A con-crete example from the animal laboratory is a hungry rat in a small cage with a steel bar. Although bar-pressing is not something rats normally do (the behaviorist would say that the bar-pressing response is not naturally in the rat's response repertoire), he will probably push the bar by accident while exploring his cage. If the bar-push is followed immediately by food, and if each subsequent bar-push is followed by food, the rat will gradually increase his bar-pressing behavior.

The statement that reward will increase the intensity and frequency of a response is called the **law of effect.** There are several new terms associated with operant conditioning. The response is said to be an instance of **operant,** or instrumental, behavior. The food pellet is called **positive reinforcement** and is contrasted with another conditioning device, **negative reinforcement,** a noxious stimulus that an animal will learn to avoid. If the floor of the rat's cage is electrified, delivering a painful shock to the animal, and the bar-press turns off the electricity, the animal learns to press the bar. The painful shock in this case would be an instance of negative reinforcement.

If one wanted to extinguish the bar-pressing response after, say, food pellet training, one could shock the rat every time it pressed the bar. The painful shock in this case is called **punishment** and is used to extinguish, rather than to condition, a response. As in classical conditioning extinction of the response may also be achieved by ceasing to pair the operant response with the accustomed reward.

A great deal of research has been done to discover exactly how conditioning procedures relate to the development of operant behavior. It has been found, for instance, that it is not necessary to reward each response. In fact a response that has been rewarded only intermittently will take longer to extinguish than one that has been reinforced each time it is emitted. The crucial aspect of conditioning is **selective reward.** This means that if you are trying to condition a particular response, you never reward the opposite of that response. If you want to condition a rat to press a bar, you never give it a reward if it has not pressed the bar. If you want to teach a pigeon to peck at a red dot, given a choice between red and blue, then you give it a bit of seed every time (or perhaps every second or third time) it pecks the red dot. You never reward it for pecking the blue dot. (In fact a combination of punishment for negative responses and reward for positive ones produces very fast learning.)

5.123 Mediation. Another principle of associative chaining that was developed considerably later in this century than conditioning is the principle of **mediation.** In simple terms this is a transitive principle that says that two things associated with a third thing will tend to be in association with each other (via the common element). An example of list learning in humans will clarify this principle. A number of psychologists have spent a great deal of time attempting to discover general principles in human learning by investigating the manner in which people learn various kinds of lists—words, nonsense syllables, digits, and so forth. One such list is the **paired associate list,** the learning of which gives us an excellent example of mediation.

A paired associate list is a set of, say, twenty (usually unrelated) word pairs, such as 'cow–picture', 'book–mushroom', and so on. The subject's task in this experiment is to respond with the second element of each pair upon seeing (or hearing) the first member, which serves as stimulus. If you were a subject in such an experiment, you would learn to respond 'picture' every time you saw the word 'cow'. Research into this sort of learning has demonstrated that if you learn a second list in which there is a pair 'picture–broom', then you will learn the pair 'cow–broom' very quickly on a third list. The principle of mediation accounts for this by saying that the association between 'cow' and 'broom' is mediated by the word 'picture' even though 'picture' is not present in the third list. The real associative chain is 'cow–picture–broom', but the response 'picture' is an internal link established through previous learning.

For the twentieth-century behaviorist psychologist the observable responses (behavior) of an organism constituted the data to be accounted for, and associative chains constituted the basic theoretical device for explaining them. Such theorizing has had a pronounced effect on psycholinguistics. We will be more specific later about just how these general associative principles have been adduced to account for psycholinguistic abilities and their development, but first let us look a bit more deeply into the philosophical motivation for the behaviorist's view of the world.

5.13 Philosophical foundations of behaviorism

Epistemology is the philosophical term for "theory of knowledge," and behaviorists adopt the epistemology of the empiricists before them. This epistemology says that nothing can be known that is not experienced. For mankind as a group this means that scientific knowledge is limited to what scientists have directly observed. For individuals it means that all personal knowledge must be the direct result of the experience of that individual. Under this theory of knowledge the scientist and the individual alike are passive recipients of knowledge bestowed on them by their environment. The scientist must be clever and set up experiences (experiments, etc.) in such a way that he will observe the kinds of phenomena he wants to observe; the average individual, on the other hand, is at the mercy of the environment.

The empiricism of the behaviorist psychologists, then, is twofold: first, they are empiricists as scientists, who allow themselves to explain physical phenomena only in terms of other directly observable physical events; secondly, they are empiricists as they view the individual organisms they study—that is, they view the behaviors that they reveal as components of associative chains imposed on the organism by the environment.

5.131 Radical behaviorism. Some distinction should perhaps be made here between radical and nonradical behaviorists, although we will end up arguing that from the point of view of empiricist epistemology the distinction is not important. Radical behaviorism, which has been called black box psychology, is well-known to many laymen because of the work of B. F. Skinner. Skinner has attempted to relate principles of operant conditioning discovered in the animal laboratory to human language (Skinner, 1957) and more recently to the social development of man (Skinner, 1973).

The basic tenet of radical behaviorism is that since you cannot look inside a living organism, you cannot observe its internal states. Since you cannot observe the internal states, you cannot know anything about them. Since you cannot know anything about them, any statements you make about internal states or processes are ipso facto meaningless. Each organism should be regarded, then, as a black box that cannot be opened for observation. The only meaningful statements one can make about the organism concern what goes into it (stimuli) and what comes out of it (responses). Explanation for a particular set of behaviors is to be found in the pattern of rewards and punishments associated with those behaviors. We explain the rat's pressing the bar with great frequency and intensity by describing the circumstances of reward that have been associated with this particular response. No internal states of the rat are mentioned in this explanation of its behavior. The goal of the radical behaviorist, then, is to discover and create predictable (probabalistic) relationships between stimuli and responses.

It is worth noting that behaviorist psychology is frequently characterized as being concerned with the control of behavior. This terminology is accurate only in a very narrow, technical sense. It has, however, been seized on by many intellectuals of humanistic moral persuasion who object to radical behaviorism because they believe it to be authoritarian and fascistic. In point of fact radical behaviorism is no more or less authoritarian than any other area of psychology. When radical behaviorists are said to be concerned with the "control" of behavior, it simply means that the goal of research in that discipline is to discover functional relationships between stimuli and responses by altering observable stimulus-response relationships. Such alteration is usually achieved by operant (or related) conditioning techniques. When one goes beyond the basic philosophical and methodological foundations of radical behaviorism and begins to think about applications of its techniques in a context such as "human engineering," then it is clear that the techniques can be applied in either a humane or inhumane manner.

The authors know of humane attempts to apply operant conditioning in various types of therapy and of inhumane applications such as those conducted currently in American prisons and in the past by the U.S. Army in an attempt to control the behavior of understandably recalcitrant draftees. The major problem with radical behaviorism is not that it is inhumane but that it is not conceptually rich enough to account for any significant aspects of human behavior.

5.132 Nonradical behaviorism. Inasmuch as the traditional goals of scientific investigation have revolved around explanation of more depth than that allowed by the radical behaviorist, it is not at all surprising that many psychologists began to try to fill the "black box" with postulated internal psychological structures and processes in order to account for the observed behavior of organisms. It is difficult to postulate internal states and continue to believe wholeheartedly in empiricist epistemology, since the epistemology holds that only observable elements can be known. In order to resolve this problem, the nonradical behaviorists considered the postulated internal structures to be reduced replications of overt stimuli and responses. This brings us back to mediating responses, mentioned a few paragraphs back.

Recall the paired-associate list in which the association between 'cow' and 'broom' was mediated by an internal representation of the word 'picture'. The principle of mediated association is in fact a principle developed by nonradical behaviorists, and the mediating response is considered to be an internal replication of a "real" response. Thus the internal response 'picture' has many but not all of the components of the external response 'picture'. Such internal responses are called **fractional responses** or **internal mediating responses.** Most psychologists who are behaviorists are of the nonradical type and are concerned with developing theories about the internal states of the organisms they study. Their explanatory devices, however, are strictly limited to constructs that are shadows of overt behavior. For this reason the theories available to them are still tightly constrained by empiricist epistemology.

Now that we have outlined these basic positions in behaviorist psychology, let us examine how they relate to Language and psycholinguistics.

5.14 American linguistics in the early twentieth century

As the behaviorist revolution was sweeping the United States, American linguists were following the "taxonomic" school of linguistics, which was in turn superseded by transformational-generative linguistics. The taxonomists viewed language as a string of speech sounds that the trained linguist could faithfully reproduce in phonetic transcription. The data of primary importance consisted of sets of transcriptions of this type, presumably representing the exact linguistic behavior of the speaker. The primary task of the linguist was to segment and classify the individual speech sounds and thereby to discover the phonemic structure of the language being studied. This conception of Language fit nicely with the behaviorist view of psychological analysis. The psychologists were interested only in the overt behavior of their subjects (e.g., speech), and the linguists were concerned with the observable results of that behavior (e.g., speech sounds). The behaviorist approach to Language use took a number of forms, which we will outline briefly here.

5.15 Sentences as stimuli and responses

First, psychologists and linguists alike were concerned with Language use, i.e. with regarding utterances as holistic stimuli or responses in their own right. An example from a major taxonomic linguistics book (Bloomfield, 1933, p. 24), concerns a behaviorist account of the following incident:

> Suppose that Jack and Jill are walking down a lane, Jill is hungry. She sees an apple in a tree. She makes a noise with her larynx, tongue, and lips. Jack vaults the fence, climbs the tree, takes the apple, brings it to Jill, and places it in her hand. Jill eats the apple.

Following this description of the events Bloomfield presents an analysis of the chain of verbal stimuli and responses by which Jill succeeded in getting the apple. The analysis is followed by this (italicized) conclusion: *"Language enables one person to make a Reaction (R) when another person has the Stimulus (S)."* Bloomfield, a linguist, adopted the behaviorists' characterization of language in two senses: first, as a taxonomist linguist who studied the sounds people make with their mouths, and second, in the more traditionally psychological sense of examining the use, or function, of language.

Skinner (1957) argued that speaking should be considered a conditioned operant response (one for which the exact stimulus is not immediately apparent) to some internal or external stimuli. He developed a small set of categories of verbal responses that correspond roughly to the function of the utterances. A **mand** response was said to be a sort of request emitted under the stimulus of deprivation. An example Skinner gives is the thirsty person manding 'water'. Other verbal operants are the following: **tact,** a labeling response to things in the environment, such as saying 'cow' if one is stimulated by the sight of a cow; **echoic,** or imitative, responses, like echoing 'cow' if one is stimulated by someone else saying 'cow'; **textual** operant, reading the word 'cow'; and **interverbal** operant, an oft-produced response to some verbal stimuli, like saying 'Fine, thanks' when someone says 'How are you?'

Clearly analyses such as those of Bloomfield and Skinner do not address issues such as how linguistic knowledge is stored in the brain or how it is used in the encoding and decoding of messages. The approach taken by Skinner and other psychologists is instead a simplistic analysis of the function of human speech. Such an analysis might be interesting if it included more commonplace linguistic functions, such as conversation, persuasion, seduction, teaching, and so on.

5.16 The sentence as a chain of associations

Behaviorist psychologists described actual speech as a chain of associated events. Therefore a sentence was conceived of as a string of words, each of which served as the response to the preceding word and stimulus to the following one. In turn, sounds within words were regarded as stimulus-response chains. The origins of the chains were considered to be the various situations in which associations between stimuli and responses could form, including frequent co-occurrence in the environment. 'The boy' would occur frequently; thus an association would form between 'the' and 'boy', with 'the' considered a stimulus and 'boy' considered a response. Such an association would not form between 'the' and 'a' since 'the a' is not a frequent speech event. The claim that sentences should be viewed as associative chains constitutes the major psycholinguistic claim of the behaviorist. We will have a great deal more to say in Chapter 8 about the behaviorist's conception of how these associations arise in childhood. It is possible to view this conception as it relates to the adult, however, and see what sort of linguistic competence would be predicted by this approach.

We would expect that a behaviorist description of linguistic knowledge would consist of networks of words, with a specification of the response probabilities obtaining between them. The response probability would represent the degree of association between the word pairs. On a strict associationistic account such as we are outlining here the response probabilities would only obtain between individual words. Producing and understanding sentences (linguistic performance) would be fairly easy to account for in terms of response chaining and probability matching.

5.17 The sentence as a conditioning device

The classical conditioning paradigm has been evoked to account for the acquisition of meaning of individual words and, further, for the transfer of meaning to other words via language (Mowrer, 1954). It is instructive to examine this theory in some detail not only because it shows how classical conditioning was incorporated into a behaviorist description of language, but also because it illustrates a key concept of behaviorist psycholinguists—that of meaning as an internal replica of an external response.

According to Mowrer's theory a word is a conditioned stimulus (like the bell for Pavlov's dog), while the thing to which the word refers is the unconditioned stimulus (like the meat powder). The normal external response to the referent is the unconditioned response (like the salivation and eating responses of the dog), and the conditioned response—to the word, remember—is a fraction of the external (unconditioned) response, experienced internally (this has no real analog in the Pavlovian procedure).

Mowrer's examples are the conditioning of meanings to the words 'Tom' and 'thief'. By the hypothesized procedure the word 'Tom' becomes a conditioned stimulus that elicits in a hearer the conditioned response, the meaning of 'Tom', which is in turn a fraction of the complete Tom-response (the unconditioned response to the person called 'Tom', the unconditioned stimulus). Similarly 'thief' comes to evoke in the hearer part of the thief-response (distrust, apprehension) by " . . . being associated with actual thieves" (p. 15). These basic processes of acquiring meaning are called first-order conditioning experiences. The next step is that the sentence 'Tom is a thief' can become a conditioning device and trigger a "second-order" conditioning process by which the meaning of 'thief' becomes a conditioned response to the word 'Tom' and (by analogy) to the person Tom.

Mowrer suggests that the understanding of a sentence should be defined as this transfer of meaning by way of classical conditioning.

5.18 The Chomskyan revolution

The publication of Chomsky's *Syntactic Structures* in 1957 ushered in a new age of linguistics. It was immediately apparent that the new linguistics was not compatible with behaviorist psychology, for both philosophical and empirical reasons. The data and methods of linguistic analysis underwent radical revision. Furthermore the new conceptions in linguistics had profound implications for psychology, partly because all the new linguistic constructs (deep structures, linguistic rules, levels of analysis, phrase markers, and others) are abstract and, in principle, not of a form identical to any structures subject to *direct* observation. Beyond that, transformational-generative linguists claimed that these unobservable constructs represented the linguistic knowledge of the language user. Such a claim was completely contrary to behaviorist epistemology: That which is unobservable cannot be known, either by the individual or by the scientist. The new linguistics committed epistemological heresy on two levels: It was claimed simultaneously that the individual knew unobservable things and that furthermore the linguist (as scientist) could discover those things. In terms of language acquisition the philosophical heresy became even worse, since the new linguists would have children actually learning unobservable things—but more about this later.

From a theoretical point of view the analysis of language as hierarchically ordered sets of constituents that may be moved around, as it were, in rule-governed ways is a falsification of the hypothesis that the sentence is a chain of associated events. Consider the behaviorist hypothesis that in a sentence such as 'George picked up the baby' an association exists between 'picked' and 'up' (a verb and particle, repsectively). This hypothesis is considerably weakened by the observation that there exists a paraphrase 'George picked the baby up'. Discontinuous constituents that break up like this are troublesome for associationist hypothesis, but the linguistic process of embedding is disastrous. What are we to say about the association between 'the man' and 'picked' if an entire sentence (in the form, say, of a relative clause) is embedded between them as in 'The man who just returned from a long business trip happily picked the baby up'? We must conclude either that it is incorrect to characterize the relationship between 'the man' and 'picked' in traditional associationist terms or we must agree that an association is allowed to bend and stretch over an indefinitely long embedded sentence, while contiguous words such as 'man' and 'who' are not as closely associated. Such a concession weakens the theoretical power of the construct and renders the concept of association devoid of explanatory value. (See Bever, Fodor, and Garrett, 1968, for an elegant formal account of these difficulties.) Either way, it was clear that new psychological principles had to be developed to deal with the new linguistics.

5.181 The behaviorists' response. There have been two major kinds of attempts to develop the required new principles. The first comes from within the behaviorist tradition in psychology and is, essentially, nonradical behaviorist psycholinguistics. The second is what this book is about—explicitly nonbehavioristic, cognitive psycholinguistics.

Nonradical behaviorists attempted to reconcile transformational-generative linguistics with mediational accounts of linguistic representations. While such attempts were common during the 1960s, we will focus on two such theoretical accounts, one by Osgood (1963) and another by Jenkins (1964). We chose these because they are characteristic of mediational accounts of psycholinguistic processes and because they are among the better known theories of the sixties.

Osgood's **Three-Stage Mediational Model** postulates the chaining of stimuli and responses on three different levels—sensory (dealing with involuntary responses), integrational, and representational. It is the latter two levels that are critical for psycholinguistics. At the integrational level associations between individual words are replaced by associations between higher-ordered constituents, like noun phrase and verb phrase. Osgood suggests that phrase-structure–like rules describe the various ordering of associations at levels within the integrational level. At the representational level fractional internal responses (such as Mowrer's internal responses) represent meanings, and there is a separate system of associations between individual meaning representations.

Essentially Osgood tried to solve the problem of associationism, but his theory is at once too powerful and too weak. It is too powerful because it allows for virtually anything to be associated to anything else without being constrained by the basic tenet of associationism—in order to be associated, things must occur in the physical world. No stretch of the theoretical imagination can make noun phrases, verb phrases, or plural morphemes into representations of observable phenomena. His theory is too weak because it does not even attempt to handle the concept of the transformation as a linguistic device. Put differently, his scheme does not save associationism from the difficulties created for it by embedding transformations.

As Osgood's theory is an attempt to reconcile associationism with the principles of generative grammar, Jenkins' is an attempt to account for the phenomenon of linguistic creativity (in the sense of the ability to deal with

Linguistic Performance

novel sentences) within a behaviorist framework. He does this by appeal to the kinds of mediational processes we discussed earlier in connection with verbal learning research.

Recall our example (section 5:123) of an association between 'cow' and 'broom' being mediated by the word 'picture'. This sort of mediation is called **response chaining** by Jenkins. For convenience we will assign letters to the stimuli and responses; in the above example 'cow' is assigned the letter A, 'picture' the letter B, and 'broom' the letter C. We can then represent the response chaining in the following way: If we learn A–B and then B–C, the learning of A–C will be facilitated because it will be mediated by B.

Stimulus equivalence is the association between two things that are themselves related to a third. If we learn A–B and C–B, for example, the learning of A–C will be facilitated because they each previously served as a stimulus for B. **Response equivalence,** similarly, is the facilitation of A–C after prior learning of B–A and B–C. Jenkins suggested that words that belong to the same grammatical class are grouped together in this manner. In addition he postulated a principle of association that allows any member of the stimulus class to be chained with any member of the response class. Thus knowledge of the following sequence (1)–(5) will account for production of the novel sentence (6).

	A	B	
(1)	The ball is red.		'Ball' and 'dress' become members of a stimulus class by stimulus equivalence.
	C	B	
(2)	The dress is red.		

	A	D	
(3)	The ball is new.		'Red' and 'new' become members of a response class by response equivalence.
	C	D	
(4)	The dress is new.		

	E	B	
(5)	The car is red		'Car' joins the stimulus class.

(6)	The car is new.	A novel sentence is formed by the chaining of a member of the stimulus class with a member of the response class.

The inadequacy of this system to account for the enormous creativity in language is surely obvious. This simple paradigm would not begin to account for the richness of structure of human language; even the simplest transformational operations are too complex to be admitted to this system.

The difficulties with behaviorist psycholinguistics in general and the mediational paradigm in particular were not lost on Jenkins, who is now one of the leading cognitive psycholinguists in the United States.

5.182 The rejection of behaviorist psycholinguistics. A classic article by Miller published in the *American Psychologist* in 1965, pointed out to psycholinguists the utter failure of behaviorist principles to account for the linguistic behavior of humans. He discussed seven commonplace, unremarkable aspects of human language that render a behaviorist account untenable. Greatly abbreviated, Miller's seven points are:

1. "Not all physical features of speech are significant for vocal communication, and not all significant features of speech have a physical representation." This aspect of language shows that observability is neither necessary nor sufficient for linguistic significance.

2. "The meaning of an utterance should not be confused with its reference." Meanings are highly complex interrelationships of symbols; a fractional response is far too simplistic a construct to account for the richness of meaning.

3. "The meaning of an utterance is not the linear sum of the meanings of the words that comprise it." This point exemplifies the inadequacy of a corollary of an associationist account of language—that the meaning of a sentence is a simple sum of the meanings of its words. A moment's reflection on language shows that sentential meaning is crucially determined by such complex syntactic devices as hierarchical structure, grammatical relationships, and relationships among atomic sentences.

4. "The syntactic structure of a sentence imposes groupings that govern the interactions between the meanings of the words in that sentence." Not only does syntax govern the expression of the meaning of a sentence (see number 3 above), but syntactic organization is abstract and unobservable, yet demonstrably used unconsciously in the daily life of every normal human.

5. "There is no limit to the number of sentences or the number of meanings that can be expressed." Miller makes reference here to the infinite capacity to produce language possessed by every human. The recognition of such an infinite capacity demands the simultaneous recognition of a finite system of principles underlying that capacity. Thus we are led to join the linguist in postulating an abstract, unobservable rule system that is part of each human's mental machinery.

6. "A description of a language and a description of a language user must be kept distinct." Here Miller states his belief that cognitive psycholinguists should observe the competence/performance distinction in all of its theoretical implications.

7. "There is a large biological component to the human capacity for articulate speech." As we shall see when we discuss language acquisition, an epistemology that is an alternative to empiricism must admit knowledge from sources other than the environment. One other source is the innate

information-processing capabilities of the human brain itself, which appear to render it uniquely suited for the learning—or reconstruction—of human language.

Near the conclusion of Miller's article, he described the then new field of cognitive psycholinguistics:

> If we accept a realistic statement of the problem, I believe we will also be forced to accept a more cognitive approach to it; to talk about hypothesis testing instead of discrimination learning, about the evaluation of hypotheses instead of the reinforcement of responses, about rules instead of habits, about productivity instead of generalization, about innate and universal human capacities instead of special methods of teaching vocal responses, about symbols instead of conditioned stimuli, about sentences instead of words or vocal noises, about linguistic structure instead of chains of responses—in short, about language instead of learning theory.

5.2
Cognitive Psycholinguistics

In the years since Miller wrote these words many psychologists have attempted to do just what he suggested—to talk about language instead of learning theory. The remainder of this book will be devoted to showing just how they have gone about trying to do that.

As we have seen, transformational-generative linguistics provided the primary impetus for the development of nonbehaviorist psycholinguistics. This is true because the new linguistics made claims about the nature and complexity of Language and hence of the Language user, that had never been recognized before. Chomsky has said repeatedly that his theory of Language transformed linguistics into a branch of cognitive psychology. This information came as something of a surprise to a whole generation of cognitive psychologists who had never heard of a transformational rule or a deep structure. Under the intellectual leadership of Miller many such psychologists began to devote large portions of their lives to assimilating the new linguistics and to devising ways to test its claims in the laboratory under controlled conditions—thus the new science of psycholinguistics had its inception.

Recall that we have made an important distinction between the theory of linguistic competence and the theory of linguistic performance. The former is considered the linguist's theory of linguistic knowledge. Psycholinguistic theory, on the other hand, is a theory that psychologists hope to develop in order to account for the actual linguistic-processing abilities of the individual. The distinction between competence and performance has played an important role since the beginning of generative linguistics. Since it has been the belief of generative linguists that a theory of competence is logically prior to a theory of performance, it is easy to understand why developments in linguistic theory have preceded developments in psycholinguistics for roughly a decade. Linguistics has been considered, for better or worse, the mother science.

As we shall see in Chapter 7, early experiments in psycholinguistics were primarily concerned with testing what psychologists believed to be the psychological claims of Chomskyan linguistics. The experiments of that period investigated variables that were defined in linguistic theory. They began with the working hypothesis that theories of competence and theories of performance were very similar and employed many of the same hypothetical constructs in the form of levels and units of analysis. As psycholinguistics developed, three important changes occurred in parallel. Psychologists discovered that there was a great deal of difference between competence theory and performance theory; linguistically defined variables began to be replaced by cognitive variables in psycholinguistic theory and experimentation; and psycholinguistics resigned its filial stance relative to linguistics.

.In the early days of cognitive psycholinguistics, following the publication of *Syntactic Structures* in 1957, psychologists began by asking quite simply: Do the constructs of linguistic theory—deep structures, transformational rules, surface structures—have psychological reality? We shall see that the answer to this question is equivocal; psycholinguistic research answered simultaneously 'yes' and 'no'. It was clear almost immediately that linguistic constructs are not the fundamental components of performance theory. As research progressed, it became apparent that when we talk about encoding and decoding languages, we must talk about information processing. We are interested in describing the kinds of information available to the language user at various levels of processing. Furthermore we want to be able to specify the relevant levels of processing and the cognitive operations that intervene between them.

The emphasis on the information-processing aspects of linguistic performance by no means denigrates the importance of linguistic constructs in psycholinguistics. It simply demonstrates that while the psycholinguistic activities of the language user must certainly be based on his internalized linguistic knowledge, it is based on many other things as well. There is always the hope and expectation that as we progress with linguistic and psycholinguistic theories, they will once again converge, and we will discover that the information levels, units, and processes of psycholinguistics can be shown to interact predictably with the descriptive levels, constituents, and rules of linguistics.

In his *Psychological Explanation* (1968) Fodor observes that "an important goal of psychological inquiry is the discovery of *new kinds of mental events*" (p. 43, italics his). It is just this that cognitive psycholinguists are attempting to do. We are trying to discover the kinds of mental operations available to language users as they perceive speech, as they produce and understand spoken messages, and as they develop their linguistic systems in childhood. You will see that while we have been successful in discovering some new mental processes, we have not yet developed a comprehensive theory that will incorporate all of them in a systematic way. For this reason it cannot be said that a cognitive revolution, analogous to the behaviorist revolution of the thirties, has been effected. A great deal of progress has been made, however, and there is every reason to be optimistic about the future of theoretical cognitive psycholinguistics.

5.21 Philosophical foundations of cognitive psycholinguistics

As behaviorism has its philosophical roots in the empiricism of Hume and Locke, so cognitive psycholinguistics has its philosophical roots among such rational philosophers as Plato and Descartes. The major distinction is in the rationalist versus the empiricist epistemology. While the empiricists believe that only sense data is knowable, the rationalists believe that the human intellect incorporates many abstract principles of organization and processes of cognition that are qualitatively different from events that occur in the observable world. Rationalists believe, in fact, that it is by means of such abstract cognitive principles and processes that individuals are able to organize and deal with observable events in their environment. In the realm of Language the cognitive psycholinguist considers it eminently plausible that abstract linguistic structures and processes underlie the production and comprehension of utterances.

The hypotheses advanced by cognitive psycholinguists always assume that there are underlying principles of linguistic organization by which the language user construes and operates on his linguistic environment. Thus language users' perception and comprehension of utterances are considered to be the result of a complex interaction between external and internal events—the external acoustic signal and the internal perceptual and comprehension processes.

While cognitive psycholinguistics is rationalistic in the sense outlined above, it is important to note that theories of the perception and comprehension processes are *materialistic* theories. By this we mean that the cognitive processes that are postulated are believed to be affected by physical activity within the human brain. That is, the postulated operations, while clearly unobservable, are all considered to have a physical basis.

The initial response of the reader might be to wonder why we are saying all this—how could cognitive processes fail to have a neurological origin? The reason this is an important distinction is that Descartes, one of the most influential rationalists, believed that body and mind were of separate substances and that the mind did in fact have a nonphysical (metaphysical) substance qualitatively different from that of the body. This concept is known as **dualism** and is discounted by all scientists who do not wish to assume the existence of supernatural or metaphysical phenomena. Because the Cartesian concept of dualism was related to the mind/body dichotomy, it has been frequently equated with mentalism or a theory of mental processes. Some mentalistic theories are in fact dualistic, but that is not necessarily the case. Cognitive psycholinguistics and transformational-generative grammar are mentalistic in the sense that cognitive (mental) processes are believed to exist that are unobservable and unlike any observable phenomena. Mental processes are conceived of as qualitatively different from the observable behavior they underlie. Thus psycholinguistic processes are mental as opposed to behavioral, but they are certainly not metaphysical. This is an important distinction because cognitive psycholinguists are frequently referred to as mentalists, and this confuses some people who equate mentalism with dualism.

It is also important to understand that cognitive psycholinguists reject the theoretical formulations of the behaviorists although they agree with them in using rigorous experimental methodology. Cognitive psycholinguistics is an experimental science. As will be evident in the chapters dealing with phonological and grammatical performance, cognitive psycholinguists use precise, rigid experimental techniques to test hypotheses and to evaluate theories. There is no return to introspectionism in the methodology of cognitive psycholinguists.

From our hypotheses we derive predictions about observable, quantifiable aspects of behavior that can be experimentally induced in a laboratory environment. For example, a particular hypothesis about the process of understanding sentences may lead us to predict that one type of sentence will be understood more quickly than another. We can test this hypothesis by setting up an appropriate experiment in which we select a time measure that we believe will reflect comprehension speed and compare comprehension time for the two sentence types of interest. While the hypothesis is about an unobservable cognitive process, the test of the hypothesis is by means of a measurable, objective human response.

5.22 Conclusion

We hope that we have succeeded in explaining that the use of "linguistic performance" rather than "linguistic behavior" is far from an arbitrary choice of words. The two concepts rest on qualitatively different epistemologies and imply entirely distinct conceptions of what the study of language in the individual should be like.

SUGGESTIONS FOR FURTHER READING

The following books contain articles relevant to the transition in psycholinguistics from the behaviorist to the cognitive mode of theorizing:

Dixon, T. R., and Horton, D. L. (eds.). *Verbal Behavior and General Behavior Theory*. Englewood Cliffs, N. J.: Prentice-Hall, 1968.

Jakobovits, L. A., and Miron, M. S. *Readings in the Psychology of Language*. Englewood Cliffs, N. J.: Prentice-Hall, 1967.

Phonological Performance

In this chapter we will investigate the performance dimension of phonology. Chapter 4 presented some of the linguist's conclusions about what a person *knows* about the sound structure of his language; in this chapter we will explore what the person *does* about it. The essential argument of this chapter (and of the entire book, for that matter) is that there is an intimate relation between what a person knows about his language and his psycholinguistic activity—that is, linguistic competence and linguistic performance are mutually dependent. Unfortunately we do not as yet have a theory that explains how the two are related. We can, however, show whenever possible the psychological reality of linguistic constructs and demonstrate psycholinguistic activities that appear to depend on linguistic knowledge for their successful execution.

6.1
Phonological Activities

People who use a spoken language are performing phonologically every time they utter a string of speech sounds and every time they hear someone else speak and identify these sounds as speech. In order to encode an idea into sound, speakers must, among other activities, translate the surface structure of a syntactically appropriate sentence into a phonetic representation, then activate their vocal apparatus (there are about 100 muscles that must act in synchrony to produce one speech sound) to translate the phonetic representation into an acoustical signal. In the analogous situation of receiving another's idea by way of an acoustic signal, the hearers must first decode the sound into a phonetic representation. Only then are they in a position to perform the relevant phonological and syntactic decoding operations necessary to recover the meaning being communicated. The psycholinguist, then, is interested in the cognitive activities that are involved in both the production and perception of speech.

We can ask two kinds of questions as we investigate phonological activity. First, we can ask whether the linguistic constructs of feature, phoneme, and phonological rule have any psychological reality. Second, we can ask what the purely performance aspects of phonological activity are, and if they seem to be related in any way to competence theory.

In this chapter we will first examine evidence that phonological rules, derivational levels, phonemes, and features have psychological reality. Then we shall move to an exploration of theory and research in speech production and perception. Since the anatomy of the speech mechanism has been sketched in Chapter 4, our consideration of speech production will be concerned primarily with the organization of speech. A great deal more is known about speech perception than about speech production. It is generally true in psycholinguistics that receptive skills have been studied more thoroughly and with more success than expressive skills (an exception to this generalization is language-acquisition research).

6.11 The psychological reality of linguistic rules

In a classic study Berko (1958) investigated the ability of preschool, first-, second-, and third-grade children to use many of the phonological rules of English productively. Her experimental format involved showing the child a line drawing of a cute little nonsense animal (such as the creature below), with a nonsense syllable for a name (such as "wug," for the creature in the diagram). The child would be told "This is a wug."

Then a picture of two animals would be produced and Berko would say, "Now there is another one. There are two of them. There are two _____." As her voice trailed off, the child would be induced to finish the sentence with the correct plual form, wug/-z/. Another little creature was a bik, which induced the plural /-s/ (the reader will recall the linguistic description of the plural formation rules given in Chapter 4). Other inflections that Berko tested were the possessive endings on nouns; past tense, third person present, and progressive on verbs and comparative and superlatives on adjectives. Even very young children demonstrated their ability to use these rules productively. The Berko style test has since been used widely in language research and also in tests designed to assess the linguistic skills of children and adults. It is possible to observe the creative use of phonological rules naturalistically in very young children first learning their language. They tend to overgeneralize the new rules to produce deviant forms such as mouse /-əz/ and eat /-əd/. This phenomenon will be discussed in more detail in Chapter 8.

6.12 The psychological reality of a level of phonology

In Chapter 4 we illustrated the phonological rules that relate such pairs of words as 'permit'/'permissive' and 'intrude'/'intrusive'. Recall that there is a level in the derivation of 'intrusive' from 'intrude' at which the /d/ has been changed to a [z] by the spirantization rule which changes to an [s] by the devoicing rule. No such level is postulated for the /t/-final verbs, such as 'permit', however. In these forms the /t/ changes to [s] by spirantization and there is no intermediate [z] level in the derivation.

Anisfeld (1969) reasoned that the postulated derivation should predict that the intermediate form 'intruzive' would be more readily acceptable to English-speaking subjects than would 'permizive'. This prediction is made in spite of the fact that neither are English words. To test this hypothesis Anisfeld developed a set of nonsense verbs ending in /t/ (e.g., 'yermit') and a set ending in /d/ (e.g., 'garlude'). For each nonsense verb he has constructed a correct adjective form (e.g., 'yermissive' and 'garlusive'). Subjects never heard the correct adjective form, however. They heard the nonsense verbs and a set of 'wrong' adjectives constructed by replacing the [s] in the correct adjective form by either [z], [š], [ð], or [f]. Each subject, then, was asked which of the set of "wrong" adjectives would be the best adjective for the original verb. Thus a subject would choose among 'yermizive', 'yermishive', 'yermithive', and 'yermifive' as the preferred adjective form of 'yermit'. They would choose among 'garluzive', 'garlushive', 'garluthive', and 'garlufive' for the preferred adjective form of 'garlude'. Anisfeld's derivational reality hypothesis, which predicted that 'garluzive' would be selected more often than would 'yermizive', was confirmed. (There were control forms included in the experiment that demonstrated that [z] is not generally preferred for words ending in a voiced segment.) Anisfeld argues that the best way to account for these results is to state that ". . . subjects made their judgments not on the basis of sound similarities but by reference to . . . [phonological] rules" (p. 194).

Another interesting aspect of this study was that the order of preference for the four phones substituted for [s] was [z], [š], [ð], and [f] in all conditions. Why is [z] always the substitution of choice in spite of the fact that each of the substitute phones differs from [s] by only one feature (voice, anterior, strident, and coronal, respectively)? Anisfeld suggests that the reason for this is that [s] and [z] frequently alternate in morphophonemic alternations (such as possessive and plural of nouns and third person singular forms of verbs) in English. Thus they are felt to be more "similar" for the English speaker than are other pairs the same distance apart in terms of features.

We do not believe speakers mentally go through each stage of each derivation between the surface structure and the systematic phonetic level of representation described by the phonological component of the grammar in speaking and understanding. Anisfeld doesn't make the claim that derivational levels represent psychological states in any physical sense. To make such claims would confuse the concepts of competence and performance. The claim being made—by us and, we believe, by Anisfeld—is that the language user has access to all the information incorporated in the grammar or derivable from it. If it can be demonstrated that this information is used productively and systematically by language users, then we may claim that the theoretical device describing that information (the grammar) has psychological reality. An informational claim about the reality of grammatical devices must be kept sharply distinct, however, from physical claims. We shall see in Chapter 7 that the failure to maintain this distinction with regard to syntactic processing has sent some psycholinguists off on a wild-goose chase in terms of both theory and research.

6.13 The psychological reality of features, phonemes, and words: evidence from speech errors

For many years a linguist at UCLA named Fromkin has been collecting speech errors, or slips of the tongue. These errors turn out to be far from random and demonstrate a number of interesting aspects of phonological performance. Of more than 6,000 speech errors involving the substitution and permutation of various segments of sound, an error never produced a string that violated any segmental or sequential constraints of English. Never, for instance, did anyone produce a high front rounded vowel ([ü]); it is not a phoneme of English and its production would be a violation of a segment structure rule (see section 4.13 for a discussion of these rules). Slips did not violate sequential constraints either, so non-English strings of sounds were not produced. As Fromkin puts it in her article "Slips of the Tongue" (1973), someone might mispronounce the title of the article as "Stips of the Lung" but not as "Tlips of the Sung" because a word initial cluster of [tl] is disallowed by the sequential constraints of English (see section 4.13). The implication in all this is that the phonetic output of a speaker is somehow constrained by information about the allowable segments and sequences in his language and that this information constrains even deviant phonetic output. Put differently, the constraints of the phonology set a limit on the kinds of speech errors fluent speakers will produce.

Another interesting aspect of Fromkin's error data involves the type of speech units that are affected. Entire words may be exchanged, as in 'Seymour sliced the knife with the salami' instead of 'Seymour sliced the salami with the knife'. Individual phonemes may move, as in 'Yew Nork' for 'New York'. Even individual features may be exchanged, as in 'glear plue sky' for 'clear blue sky'. Notice that the voicing values of the initial segments of 'clear' and 'blue' change places in this error, as does the feature nasality in the slip 'Cedars of Lemadon' instead of 'Cedars of Lebanon'. In this latter case the nasality of the [n] moves to the left and attaches to the [b]. The resulting phoneme retains the [b] place of articulation with the nasality of the [n], which results in an [m]. The [n], having lost its nasality, becomes a [d] (you may verify these feature switches by referring back to the feature chart in Figure 4.5). The point Fromkin makes is that such errors demonstrate that the units of language developed by linguists are "... real units ... which ... have an independent existence in the mental grammar." The fact that errors may involve units as small as the feature and as large as the word indicates that speech is hierarchically organized, with elements at a number of different levels being organized simultaneously.

The scope of speech organization is another issue that may be illuminated by looking at speech errors. For example, Fromkin reports transposition errors, such as 'Yew Nork', in which two phonemes are transposed, and anticipation errors, such as 'taddle tennis' instead of 'paddle tennis'. Notice that in both types of error the initial phoneme was not destined to occur until later in the utterance. This shows that the speech organizing system must have some look-ahead capacity—the cognitive system that plans and directs actual speech must be able to know in advance of the speech event what that event is going to be.

There is even more compelling evidence for the existence of some kind of speech-control system, but many fundamental questions about the actual properties of such a system remain unanswered. It is to this evidence and these unanswered questions that we now turn.

6.2
The Systematic Phonetic Level of Linguistic Representation and the Articulation of Speech Sounds

At first thought it seems trivially obvious to say that the systematic phonetic representation of an utterance is related to the physical production of that utterance. When we attempt to make explicit just what the relationship might be, however, we see that it is not a trivial claim but a meaningful assertion. Consider for a moment the hypothesis that each segment at the systematic phonetic level is related to a specific set of articulatory gestures. (We shall see that this is an untenable position, but we should explore it because it is logically the simplest kind of relation that could exist between the systematic phonetic representation and the articulation of an utterance. Also, it turns out that the reasons why it is wrong lead us to further insights about the nature of the relationship.)

To cite a concrete example, consider a word such as [spun] ('spoon'). If it were the case that each phone were hooked up with a unique set of articulatory gestures, then the [s] would activate the muscle commands that produce the [s] articulatory gestures; the [p] would activate the set of [p] gestures; the [u], the [u] gestures; and the [n], the [n] gestures. On this hypothesis each phone would activate a unique set of muscle commands that are directly related to a unique set of articulatory gestures. Thus the relationship between the phones and their articulation would be very direct.

It turns out that there are many things wrong with the account given above. One problem is that all commands for a particular phone cannot be sent out simultaneously from the brain because the neural impulses that take the commands from the brain to the individual muscles travel at different speeds. If all the commands for one phone are to reach the muscles at the same time, they can't all leave the brain at the same time. Let us take [spún] as an example. The production of the [u] involves, among other things, the rounding of the lips and the lowering of the larynx. Apparently this happens because it is necessary for the entire vocal tract to be elongated for the production of this sound—but whatever the reason, it is known that the production of [u] involves the operation of two distinct sets of muscles—those that round the lips and those that lower the larynx. It happens that impulses travel from the brain to the lips faster than those from the brain to the muscles that raise and lower the larynx. If they were both activated by a unique and simultaneous set of [u] commands, then the lip rounding and the larynx lowering would not occur simultaneously and an [u] would not result. This example illustrates the general fact that speech production must be organized—or planned. The relationship between the systematic phonetic representation and the actual articulation of an utterance is not direct and must be mediated by a very complicated organizing system that directs the articulatory gestures necessary for speech production.

Further evidence of the complexity of the relationship between the systematic phonetic and articulatory aspects of an utterance is the fact that speech sounds are not articulated in strict linear order, although they occur in linear order in systematic phonetic representations of utterances. Furthermore phones do not occur in linear order in the sound waves that result from the articulatory gestures.

Consider the word [tʰu] ('two'). Say it to yourself and then say the word [tʰi] ('tea'). Notice the behavior of your lips during the production of the initial [tʰ]. In [tʰu] the lips are already beginning to round in anticipation of the vowel [u]. In [tʰi] the lips are already beginning to spread in anticipation of the vowel [i], which is produced with lips spread. This phenomenon is called **coarticulation,** and it occurs whenever some of the articulatory gestures for one speech sound overlap with those of another speech sound. This is what we mean when we say that speech sounds do not occur in strict linear order at the level of articulation: coarticulation effaces the boundaries between speech sounds. This is not an isolated, rare phenomenon, but is a fact about almost every phase of speech production. It is extremely important for a theory of speech production because it demonstrates that the organizing system that plans speech must be able to plan out an entire utterance at one time, since the production of phones overlap each other. The organizing system must somehow be able to "read" the systematic phonetic representation of an utterance and make plans in advance for the production of segments of the utterance.

In anticipation of later parts of this chapter we should point out that coarticulation is also an important phenomenon from the point of view of speech perception. Since the phones are not articulated in linear order, they cannot occur in linear order in the sound wave that is speech; hence they cannot occur in linear order when they impinge on the eardrums of the hearer. Speech sounds are, however, perceived as occurring one right after another in spite of the fact that they literally do not occur in this manner anywhere except at abstract linguistic levels of representation.

The simplest hypothesis stating the relationship between phones and articulatory gestures—that each phone is directly related to a particular muscular command—turns out to be too simplistic. Even without considering the complicating phenomenon of coarticulation, it is easy to see that the muscular commands and related muscular movements will be different for the same phone depending on its phonetic environment, i.e., the phones that precede and follow it. Contrast the final [t] in [sit] ('seat') to that of [sut] ('suit'). In 'seat' the vowel before the final [t] is pronounced in the front part of the mouth, so the tongue does not have to travel far to be in the correct position for the alveolar closure of the [t]. The final [t] of 'suit', however, is preceded by a vowel pronounced in the back part of the mouth, and the muscles of the tongue must carry the tongue farther (hence, at a greater rate) to achieve the alveolar closure at the appropriate moment. Clearly the muscular commands and gestures are different for the two different [t] sounds. What seems to be the same for all [t] sounds is that closure is made somewhere in the alveolar area of the mouth. It seems that, all occurrences of the [t] phone share a common target, regardless of the environment in which they may occur.

6.21 The articulatory target hypothesis

The most widely accepted current hypothesis concerning the relationship between phones and articulatory gestures is the **articulatory target hypothesis,** which says that all manifestations of a single phone share a common target in terms of the spatial coordinates in the mouth. Many different sets of muscular commands may lead to the same target, in which case that set of muscular gestures is said to have "motor equivalence" because, while they emanate from different sets of commands, they have an equivalent goal or target. The articulatory target hypothesis is compatible with the process of coarticulation, since the articulations can be in target position for one phone, while unused muscles are anticipating a following phone. The example of coarticulation given above, with 'two' and 'tea', illustrates this.

Sometimes coarticulation may prevent the articulators from actually achieving the target intended. It has been shown, for instance, that in pronouncing the nonsense syllable [ikʰi] the closure for the [k] is actually produced farther forward in the mouth than in the production of the nonsense syllable [ukʰu]. In [ikʰi] the tongue not only has to move back rapidly after the production of the front vowel, it also has to move forward immediately after the [k] closure for the following front vowel. It is not surprising that in this situation the tongue does not move as far back for the [k] in [ikʰi] as it does for the [k] in [ukʰu]. This does not mean, however, that the two [kʰ] sounds necessarily have different targets. According to the articulatory target hypothesis both sounds have the same target, although it is not quite achieved by the articulators because of the effects of coarticulation. When an articulatory target is narrowly missed, it is called **undershoot.** Rapid speech may also result in undershoot. (For a fuller discussion of these and related issues see Harris, 1974, and MacNeilage, 1972.)

An important question addressed by contemporary research in speech production regards the role of feedback in the speech production process. Is there constant information being sent from the speech articulators to the area in the brain that organizes and plans speech? Does the organizing system wait for information about the position of the articulatory gestures? The answer to the first question seems to be that the oral cavity has the feedback capabilities to accomplish this. We have **tactile** feedback, which relies on pressure variations as parts of the mouth touch each other, and **proprioceptive** feedback, which relies on the amount and direction in which muscles are stretched and can deliver information about the position of parts of the mouth (such as the tongue) even if they are not touching anything.

The second question is essentially one about how the mechanisms of speech production use the feedback capabilities of the mouth. Since this is an open question from a theoretical point of view, we can do little but speculate about the question. On the one hand, it seems that the area of the brain that organizes speech does not need moment-to-moment knowledge about the position of the articulators. We know by the very existence of coarticulation phenomena that sequences of phones are planned and executed together, not one right after another.

Consider again the positioning of the lips in the words 'tea' and 'two'. The fact that the lips round during the production of the [tʰ] in the word 'two' is strong evidence for the claim that the speech organization mechanisms "know" that an [u] is going to be produced before the occurrence of full articulation of the [u]. Therefore, the organizing system "knew" what the articulators were about to do. If such knowledge is available, the question is: Why is feedback necessary? As we pointed out, answers to this question are very tentative. There is definite evidence that feedback is necessary to provide recognition of an error if one occurs and also to provide information necessary to bring the articulators to a position appropriate to begin an utterance. The question remains as to how feedback is actually utilized in the moment-to-moment planning and execution of articulation. It is probably the case that units larger than phones (perhaps as large as syllables) are planned and executed with little or no appeal to information derived from feedback.

6.22 The acoustic target hypothesis

The articulatory target hypothesis is inadequate to account for some speech situations. Consider the fact that it is possible to speak intelligibly when one has food in one's mouth or a pipe clenched between the teeth. (For an extensive discussion of this issue see MacNeilage, 1970.) In these situations the articulatory targets must be completely readjusted. This is more than simple undershoot; the whole plan must be changed in many cases. Consider the production of the vowel [a] if, for instance, you have your teeth clenched. Try saying the word 'honor', first in the normal way, then with your teeth clenched. One of the primary articulatory gestures associated with the normal production of [a] is a lowering of the jaw. With your teeth clenched you cannot make the [a] in the usual way. It seems to be done by pushing the tongue down and back in the oral cavity, since the jaw is fixed. The point is that even with your teeth clenched it still sounds like an [a]. Your voice may be muffled, but the string of speech sounds is clearly recognizable. Here we have a situation that demonstrates that perceptible speech can take place even when the targets associated with the particular phones and phonemes are qualitatively altered.

The state of affairs described above suggests that the speech-organizing mechanisms are able to represent acoustically the sound that will be produced by a particular articulatory gesture. Thus we could see the **articulatory target hypothesis** replaced by an **acoustic target hypothesis.** If so, we would have to say that the systematic phonetic level of representation is a linear sequence of acoustic, rather than articulatory, targets. Alternatively, we could assume that the speech-organization system is capable of representing the systematic phonetic level in terms of acoustic targets and of planning articulatory gestures such that the acoustic output of the vocal apparatus matches the desired acoustic targets. A great deal of research —both theoretical and empirical—will be required before these questions can be answered with any degree of certainty.

Although the processes are obviously not well understood, it is a fact that, when people speak, other people usually perceive and understand their speech with surprisingly little error.

6.3
Speech Perception

We shall define speech perception as the process that takes the sensation produced by the sound wave in the auditory system and produces a perceptual representation of the linguistic characteristics of the utterance. The most basic task of this process is that of interpreting the speech signal as a linear string of phones, occurring one after another, each a distinct entity. It is very important to note that such a representation is an abstraction. Although physical speech sounds do not occur one after another in the acoustic signal, they are perceived that way by the hearer. Furthermore, this abstraction may be symbolized as linguistic units as defined at the systematic phonetic level of the grammar.

In this section we will not deal with such important aspects of speech perception as the perception of stress and intonation. The major thesis of this section is that the perception of speech exemplifies the crucial interaction between linguistic knowledge and the physical aspects of language that permeate every aspect of language use.

The process of speech perception relates a concrete physical event (the speech signal) to an abstract linguistic one (the perceptual representation of the speech signal). This relationship is very complex, and the perceptual process is therefore very difficult to account for theoretically.

6.31 The speech signal

A complete specification of the speech signal is beyond the scope of this book. The following characterization must be regarded, therefore, as minimal. The speech signal consists of variations in air pressure that come out of a speaker's mouth (and nose) as the result of the activity of his articulatory mechanisms. The speaker selects a message (a meaning), encodes it according to the rules of his language and the constraints of his physiology, and sends it out in the form of variations in air pressure that impinge on the ear drum of the hearer. There are, essentially, two major sources of sound that contribute to the speech signal, phonation and supraglottal sources, as in obstruents.

6.311 Phonation. The primary sound source of sonorants is phonation (voicing, section 4.111). Bursts of air pass through the glottis (the opening between the vocal cords) and out into the vocal tract at a frequency for an adult male of approximately 120 puffs per second. The frequency of emission of these glottal pulses is referred to as the **fundamental frequency** of the speech signal and is perceived by the hearer as pitch. The fundamental frequency and perceived pitch of a woman's voice are higher than those of a man, and those of a child are higher still.

Phonation produces a repetitive, complex sound wave that is composed of many tones of many different frequencies. The component tones are called **harmonics,** and their frequencies are integral multiples of the fundamental frequency. Thus, if the complex laryngeal wave has a fundamental frequency of 120 Hz. (Hz. means 'Herz', or 'cycles per second'), then there will be harmonics at 120 Hz. (1 × 120); 240 Hz. (2 × 120), 360 Hz., and so on.

A complex sound (such as is produced by phonation) can be transformed by a resonating system. This simply means that when the complex wave is introduced into an enclosed area, some of the harmonics of the complex wave will be reinforced and some will be weakened. The phenomenon of resonance is the reinforcement of certain frequencies. Just which frequencies will be reinforced and which will be weakened depends on many properties of the resonating system, such as its size and shape. If you blow a stream of air across the open mouth of a partially filled soft drink bottle, you will hear a sound of a particular pitch. If you take a swallow of the liquid and blow into it again, the pitch lowers. The sound from your mouth has remained the same, but the resonating properties of the soft drink bottle have changed as the size of its resonating cavity is enlarged by eliminating some of the liquid. Different frequencies of the original sound are reinforced in each case, so the sound wave you hear is different each time.

The vocal tract works in a very similar manner. As the articulatory organs assume the various configurations corresponding to the different speech sounds, the size and shape of the vocal tract varies, thus changing its resonating characteristics. For different speech sounds, then, different frequencies will be reinforced and canceled. The reinforced frequencies tend to be in groups, or bands, or neighboring harmonics. These frequency bands that are formed by a resonating system are called the **formants** of that system. We shall see later that each sonorant sound is characterizable by the frequency bands that are reinforced during its production.

When the velum is open, the nasal cavity also acts as a resonating cavity, in addition to the vocal tract. It does not change shape, of course, as the vocal cavity does, but it does give rise to nasal resonance, or formants.

6.32 Supraglottal sound sources

Other sources of sound in speech come from areas of the vocal tract above the glottis. There is the hissing sound produced when air is forced through a constriction. Such sound is not generally characterizable as periodic since it does not consist of a repetitive wave form. It does not possess a harmonic structure, although it does consist of energy at many frequencies. Another supraglottal sound source is the slight explosion of air that results when a constriction is released.

6.33 The sound spectrograph

Research in speech perception accelerated greatly upon the development of an instrument sophisticated enough to measure the acoustic detail of the speech signal. The sound spectrograph is such an instrument. A description of the actual mechanisms involved in the spectrograph is beyond the scope of this book, but it is important that the reader understand the type of information it provides. The sound spectrograph analyzes an ongoing speech signal according to three dimensions, graphically depicting each. It produces dark lines that correspond to the frequencies in the speech signal. The intensity of the frequencies is indicated by the darkness of the lines, and the duration of each acoustic event is indicated by the length of the darkened area. Figure 6.1 shows the output of a spectrographic analysis of an adult male producing the vowels [i], [a], and [u].

The dark bands represent the bands of reinforced frequencies, revealing the formants of the system. By convention we refer to the lowest frequency band as the first formant (F1), the second lowest as the second formant (F2), and so on. Formants are conventionally specified by their center frequencies, representing the areas of greatest reinforcement. In Figure 6.1, for instance, we see that the vowel [i] has an F1 with a center frequency of about 270 Hz, an F2 of 2500 Hz., and an F3 of around 3000 Hz. The vowel [u] has an F1 of about 270 Hz., an F2 of 700 Hz., and an F3 of about 2600 Hz. Thus we are able to observe the composition of the acoustic signal that underlies our perception of speech as a string of linguistic segments. Let us now turn to a discussion of the types of relationships that exist between acoustic and linguistic segments.

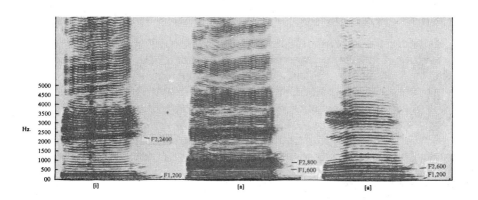

Figure 6.1

The simplest relationship that could exist between an acoustic and a linguistic segment is that of **invariance,** or **isomorphism.** This is the case when every acoustic event of particular type is perceived as a particular linguistic segment and every perception of that particular linguistic segment is based on an acoustic event of a particular type. If all linguistic segments and acoustic events were related in this simple way, we would not say that the relationship between physical event and abstract perception was a complex code—it would in fact be a very simple one-to-one mapping. Very few linguistic segments, however, are related invariably to one acoustic cue. The sounds [s] and [š] come close to bearing this simple relationship to the acoustic signal that underlies their perception. In general an [s] is perceived when there is a concentration of noise energy around 4,000–6,000 Hz. and above, [š] when there is a concentration of noise energy in the area of 2,000 to 3,000 Hz.

Let us consider for a moment the characteristics of a perceptual system that could carry out the perception of linguistic segments invariably related to a particular acoustic stimulus. A very simple system, indeed, could do the job—some simple filter that would produce the percept of [s] when it received a high-frequency fricative stimulus and of [š] when it received one of lower frequency. Such a device would be completely **passive.** For a passive perceptual device to produce the correct linguistic perceptions based on acoustic signals, the relationship between the linguistic percept and the acoustic stimulus must be one of invariance.

As we examine speech perception further, we shall see that since most linguistic segments and acoustic signals do not bear this sort of relation to each other, the human perceptual system cannot be a passive system. In fact we shall see that the perceptual system is instead **constructive** and makes use of a great deal of information about language stored inside the brain as well as information from outside that is brought in by the acoustic signal. If there were an invariant relationship between each linguistic segment and each acoustic segment, however, it would be unnecessary to postulate a constructive perceptual system.

Consider the perception of vowels. As discussed above, the acoustic properties of vowels are determined by the shape of the vocal tract, which acts as a resonating system, reinforcing some harmonics produced by phonation, canceling others. Thus the vowel formants represent concentrations of acoustic energy corresponding to the frequencies reinforced by the vocal tract as it produces the sound.

Two articulatory gestures affect the first formant of the vocal tract: jaw opening and area of tongue constriction. In general, the more open the jaw, the higher the first formant. Furthermore, a constriction far back in the pharyngeal area of the oral cavity will produce a high F1. The second formant will be high if a vowel is produced with a constriction near the alveolar ridge. General shortening of the vocal tract also raises F2. Lowering of F2 takes place when a vocal tract is lengthened and also when there is a constriction at either the lips or the velar area.

It has been known for many years that the various vowels are identified by reference to their formants, but it was not until the development of the sound spectrograph and a related instrument, the Pattern Playback, that the perceptual role of vowel formants could be investigated quantitatively. The Pattern Playback was designed by Franklin Cooper of Haskins Laboratories in the United States in the late 1940s. It is a device for producing synthetic speech from painted patterns similar to those produced by the sound spectrograph. Conceptually it is the "opposite" of the spectrograph. While the latter takes a speech signal and displays the intensity and duration of each component as marks on paper, the Pattern Playback takes these marks, which have been copied onto a special acetate belt, and reconverts them into sounds. If the painted copy has preserved every detail of the original spectrogram, the output of the Pattern Playback sounds like speech relayed over a loudspeaker. However, production of natural-sounding speech is not the goal of the Pattern Playback.[1] What researchers want to know is just how much acoustic information is necessary to produce the perception of particular linguistic segments.

Consider the spectrographic display of the vowel [i] in Figure 6.1. Recall that the darker areas represent concentrations of energy (formants) at frequencies corresponding to the resonant frequencies of the vocal tract as the vowel is produced. There are, in addition, gray areas corresponding to harmonics that are partially but not completely canceled by the vocal tract. Work with the Pattern Playback has demonstrated, however, that the human perceptual system does not require nearly this much acoustic detail in order to perceive an acoustic signal as an [i]. In fact it turns out that a synthetic signal including only the first two formants of a vowel is all that is necessary for its perception. Apart from certain detailed exceptions, which are beyond our present scope, we may say in general that the first two formants are sufficient acoustic cues for the identification of most vowels.

The most perceptually distinct vowels are [i], [u], and [a]. By this we mean that these vowels occupy the limits of the acoustic space defined by the first two formants. Figure 6.2 is a schematic representation of the first two formants for these three (and other) vowels. Consider first the F1's for [a], [i], and [u]. The vowel [a] has the highest F1 of any vowel. This is because production of the vowel [a] involves a tongue constriction very far

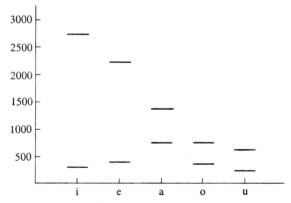

Figure 6.2 These formant values are approximations based on average values of several productions of Charles Cairns' vowels.

[1] The Pattern Playback has been superseded now by a computer that carries out logically equivalent operations as the Pattern Playback.

back in the pharyngeal area of the vocal tract, posterior to the velum. Also, [a] is produced with the jaw maximally lowered, which also contributes to the raising of F1. This configuration of the vocal tract produces a high F1. Both [i] and [u] have low F1's—lower than any of the other vowels, with [u] having the lowest F1 of all. It is primarily the second formant (F2) that differentiates [i] from [u], however; [i] has the highest F2. This is because during the production of [i] the lips are spread and the larynx is raised, effecting an over-all shortening of the vocal tract; also, there is a constriction at the alveolar ridge in the oral cavity. Each of these articulatory gestures results in a raising of F2. Since the production of [i] involves both, [i] has a high F2. On the other hand, [u] has a low F2. In production of the [u] the lips are rounded and protruded, while the larynx is lowered, resulting in an overall lengthening of the vocal tract. In addition, constrictions at the lips and velar area all contribute to the lowering of F2; therefore, [u] has a maximally low F2, the lowest of all vowels.

Figure 6.2 also shows F1 and F2 for two more vowels of English, [e] and [o]. You can see that F2 for [o] is low but not quite as low as that of [u]. This is because [o] is produced with slightly less lip-rounding and with the entire body of the tongue a little less retracted. By the same token [e] has a high F2, but not quite as high as [i] because the constriction for [e] is slightly back of the alveolar ridge and the lips are not spread as much for [e] as for [i]. Notice that the F1's of [e] and [o] are neither as high as that of [a] nor as low as those of [i] and [u].

Figure 6.3 graphically depicts the acoustic properties of the five vowels of English. The vertical axis represents the second formant, and the horizontal axis represents the first formant. The point for each vowel is defined by both its F1 and its F2 values simultaneously. (For more extensive but still elementary discussions of acoustic phonetics we recommend Ladefoged, 1962, and Williams, 1972.) In Figure 6.3 the dotted line encloses the full range of possible F1 and F2 combinations. The three vowels [i], [u], and [a], sometimes referred to as point vowels, play a special role in that they represent the extremes of acoustic variation (in terms of the first two formants) of which the human vocal tract is capable. Since the first two formants are known to constitute the primary perceptual cue for the quality of vowels, we can also say that the point vowels represent the extremes of human vowel perception.

The vowels [i], [u], and [a], representing the extremes of articulatory, acoustic, and perceptual space, are the most perceptually distinct vowels. It is not surprising, then, to discover that these vowels also play a special role in universal phonological theory, as they are the only universal vowels. By this we mean that no human language has other vowels unless it also has these three (except that some languages substitute /o/ for /u/.) There are a few human languages that have only one or two but not all three point vowels; there are a number of languages that have only the point vowels; most languages have [i], [u], [a], and a number of other vowels. The point is that a language is not free to have vowels of lesser perceptual distinc-

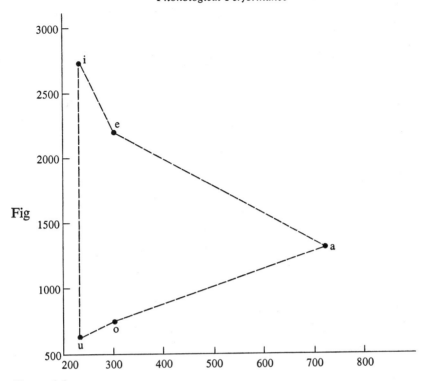

Fig

Figure 6.3

tiveness (i.e., with less extreme F1 and F2 combinations) unless it first has the vowels that represent the acoustic extremes imposed by human anatomy. In the case of vowel systems, then, we have clear evidence that the development of abstract linguistic systems has been shaped by the biological properties of the language-using species. (For an extensive discussion of biological and linguistic interaction see Lieberman, Crelin, and Klatt, 1972, and Lieberman, 1973.)

6.34 The perception of vowels

To understand the perception of vowels we must make a distinction between vowels produced in isolation (steady-state vowels) and those produced in context—within a syllable, a word, a sentence, or an entire conversation. In the case of vowels produced in isolation by one speaker the relationship between acoustic signal and linguistic percept is essentially invariant. If the vowels shown in Figure 6.2, with formants at exactly the frequencies specified there, are presented to hearers for identification, we can predict with a high degree of accuracy that they will be perceived as the labeled linguistic segments [u], [o], [a], [e], and [i], respectively.

In speech, however, the formants associated with vowels do not have the same absolute values as those depicted in Figure 6.2, although the acoustic relationships among the vowels remain generally the same. For example, it is known that the formant frequencies of vowels produced by female speakers may be from 10 to 20 percent higher than those of a perceptually identical vowel produced by male speakers. (In the speech of children the upward shift is even greater.) Moreover, there is a great deal of individual variation within male groups and female groups. Thus a female voice with very high formants might produce a phonetic [e] with an F2 above 2,000 Hz. In isolation an F2 this high would probably be associated with the vowel [i], but the female in question would produce her [i] with still higher F2. If such a woman produced her [e] in isolation, it might be perceived as an [i], but not if it were heard in conjunction with a sample of her speech sufficient to reveal to the hearer that the formants of all her vowels tend to be higher than average.

Vowel perception of day-to-day running speech does not involve the invariant pairing of an absolute acoustic cue with a particular linguistic percept. The challenge for a theory of speech perception is to account for the manner in which the perceptual system selects the correct linguistic percept for individual acoustic events, given that the latter vary within a phonetic category.

An experiment by Ladefoged and Broadbent (1957) may give us a clue to some of the principles on which the perceptual system might be operating in the perception of segments that vary acoustically between speakers. Since a great deal of interspeaker variation involves formant differences because of different vocal tract sizes, this experiment simulated such differences using synthetic speech and showed that the phonetic perception of an individual acoustic segment in a linguistic context may be determined by the *relative* formant values of the contextual vowels.

The description of one condition from the Ladefoged–Broadbent ex-

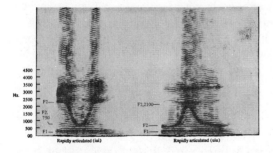

periment illustrates the findings of the entire study. A synthesized syllable was prepared, beginning with [b], ending with [t], and having a medial vowel segment with an F1 of 375 Hz. and an F2 of 1,700 Hz. The synthesized syllable could thus be perceived as either [bɪt] or [bɛt], depending on whether the 375 Hz. first formants were considered by the perceptual system to be quite low (in which case the higher vowel [ɪ] would be perceived) or slightly higher (in which case the vowel would be perceived as [ɛ]). Several different experimental tapes were prepared in which the synthesized syllable [bVt] (where V stands for vowel) followed the synthesized sentence "Please say what this word is." The same [bVt] syllable was used on each tape, but the vowels of the sentence were synthesized with varying F1 values. One version of the sentence, for instance, had vowels with F1's ranging between 275 and 500; another had F1's at a lower range, between 200 and 380 Hz. The finding from Ladefoged and Broadbent's experiment was that the subjects who heard the sentence with high F1's perceived the syllable as [bɪt], whereas those who heard the sentence with low F1's perceived the syllable as [bɛt].

The acoustic dimension of interest here is the first formant of the synthesized syllable. Typically, [ɪ] has a lower F1 than does [ɛ]. The 375 Hz. F1 is perceived as low (hence, the perception of [bɪt]) when it is perceived as low relative to higher F1's in the lead sentence. It is perceived as high (hence the perception of [bɛt]) when it is perceived high as relative to lower F1's in the lead sentence. Other conditions of this experiment provided similar data, so we are led to speculate that the perceptual system has the ability to compute the range of variation for an individual speaker by hearing a number of vowels in his repertoire, then interpreting new acoustic signals from that individual with reference to the vowel system so established. This may be one reason why we sometimes find an unfamiliar speaker difficult to perceive at first, but things become much easier after half an hour of conversation. Perception improves as our perceptual system gathers data about other vowels in the speaker's system, their interrelationships, and their use in familiar lexical contexts.

Another important source of variation in the acoustic characteristic of vowels is the intraspeaker variation produced by the immediate phonetic context of the vowel, i.e., the segments that immediately precede and follow the vowel itself. Lindblom and Studdert-Kennedy (1967), in an experiment we shall discuss shortly, illustrate rather elegantly that the perceptual system must use knowledge about the production dynamics of strings of speech sounds. Their experiment suggests that the perceptual system is in a sense able to predict the acoustic effects of coarticulation phenomena and base its phonetic decisions on those predictions.

Before we present the Lindblom and Studdert-Kennedy study, we must introduce the phenomenon of **formant transitions.** We have seen that a formant is a band of reinforced harmonics determined by the shape of the vocal tract at any given moment in time. If sounds are produced in isolation, then the vocal tract remains fixed in one position and the formants do not change. The sound thus produced is referred to as a steady-state speech sound. In normal speech, of course, the vocal tract is constantly changing shape, so the formants are constantly changing from those associated with one vocal tract configuration to those of the next. A formant transition, then, is simply the rapidly changing bands of reinforced frequencies that intervene between the relatively steady-state formant patterns of the individual segments. (This is actually something of an oversimplification—in rapid speech sounds usually do not last long enough to reach steady state.)

Figure 6.4a is a spectogram of an adult male producing the nonsense strings [iui] and [uiu] slowly and carefully. In the former you can observe the F2's moving down (from the high [i] to the low [u]) and back up again. In the latter the opposite directions are observed, with the F2 beginning low, then moving up and back down again. The area of change, where the formant is moving up or down, is of course the formant transition.

Figure 6.4b shows the same syllables produced more rapidly. Notice that F2 for the rapidly produced medial [u] does not dip quite as low as does the one that is spoken slowly. Similarly, F2 for the rapidly produced medial [i] does not reach as high as does that of the one spoken slowly. Both the rapid and slow [u]'s, however, sound like [u]'s and both the [i]'s sound like [i]'s. While the target frequencies for F2 are slightly missed in rapid speech (recall that this is called undershoot), producing nonoptimal vowel segments, our perceptual system seems able to cope with that bit of variation and still assign the appropriate phonetic label. The experiment by Lindblom and Studdert-Kennedy investigated exactly this ability of the perceptual system.

In this study twenty vowels were synthesized. All had F1's of 350 Hz., which is low enough that the vowel would be perceived as a fairly high vowel, either an [ɪ] or [ʊ], depending on the F2 with which it was paired. Each of the twenty vowels had a different F2, varying in equal intervals from 1,000 Hz. to 2,000 Hz. In isolation, vowels with F2 higher than 1,700 Hz. were perceived as [ɪ]. Those with an F2 lower than 1,700 Hz. were perceived as [ʊ]. The perceptions changed, however, when the same twenty stimuli were embedded in syllables.

The syllables used were [wVw] and [yVy]. These syllabic frames were selected because [w] and [y] have approximately identical F1's but vastly differing F2's. F2 for [w] starts very low, while F2 for [y] starts very high. Each of the twenty vowels, then, was used as the vowel in the [wVw] syllable and also in the [yVy] syllable. The results are very interesting. The vowels with very low F2's (from 1,000 to 1,450 Hz.) were perceived as [ʊ] in both the [wVw] syllable and in the [yVy] syllable. The vowels with very high F2's (from 1,750 to 2,000 Hz.) were perceived as [ɪ] in both syllables. But the vowels with F2's between 1,450 Hz. and 1,750 Hz. were perceived differently according to the syllable in which they appeared; we will refer to these as the "ambiguous vowels". When these vowels appeared in the [wVw] syllable, they were perceived as [ɪ]; when they appeared in the [yVy] context, they were perceived as [ʊ]. This means that when the sounds preceding and following an ambiguous vowel started with a low F2, the ambiguous vowel was perceived as an [ɪ] which has a high F2. If, however, the ambiguous vowel was embedded in sounds starting with a high F2, it was perceived as an [ʊ], which has a lower 2. Thus the ambiguous vowels in this experiment demonstrate that the same acoustic signal may be perceived as a different linguistic segment under certain circumstances; again, the relationship of invariance between acoustic signal and linguistic segment does not hold.

We can account for the results of this experiment by postulating a perceptual system with certain characteristics. When the vowel is embedded between two [w]'s, the perceptual system "knows" that the F2 of the entire syllable must begin low for the initial [w], rise for the vowel, then dip down again for the second [w]. Since the vocalic interval is very brief, the perceptual system calculates that there was not enough time for the vowel to reach its intended, or target, F2. That is, the F2 of the vowel is perceived as falling short of its ideal F2. Thus the vowel is perceived as one with a higher ideal F2 than is actually represented in the speech signal.

It appears that in connected speech the perceptual system predicts that the articulators will always undershoot their phonetic targets because of the speed with which they must move. Now let us see how this explanation fits the perception of the ambiguous stimuli as [ʊ] in the [y] context. In this case the F2 of the syllable begins high, dips down for the vowel, then immediately up again for the second [y]. The vowel is perceived as having undershot the lower target F2 of [ʊ]. This explanation illustrates the constructive character of the perceptual system. It uses the knowledge stored in the central nervous system to compute the rate of change of the articulators and thus to predict configurations of the vocal tract (and the resulting acoustic signal) under specifiable circumstances. Then it bases its percepts on the predictions it has constructed. The system must, on this view, have access both to the acoustic ideal (or target) and also to information about how that ideal may fail to be realized in real time. The predictions and percepts generated by the perceptual system depend on the simultaneous analysis of both kinds of information.

6.35 The perception of pure stops

The perception of the pure stops ([p, t, k, b, d, g]) illustrates the most striking examples of the lack of invariance between acoustic stimulus and linguistic percept. As we shall see below, it is actually impossible for a stop to exist in isolation, as a vowel can. That is, there is no such thing as a steady-state stop. Furthermore, a number of greatly divergent acoustic signals will be perceived as the same stop consonant, while two quite similar acoustic signals will be perceived as different stop consonants. This seemingly paradoxical state of affairs will be explained in detail below. We shall also see that the interpretation of facts such as these gives us a great deal of insight into the speech perception system.

First, consider that there are only two distinctions among the English stop consonants (excluding affricates) that must be made by the perceptual system—place of articulation and voicing. In English the stops arise from three points of articulation: [p] and [b], bilabial; [t] and [d], alveolar; [k] and [g], velar. Each pair is further distinguished by voicing differences. In order to explain how the perceptual system distinguishes the stop consonants, then, we must understand the acoustic bases of the linguistic dimensions of point of articulation and voicing.

Research done at Haskins Labs has shown that the primary cue to place of articulation for a stop consonant followed by a vowel is in the transition into the second formant of the vowel. Figure 6.5 shows synthetic spectrograms which are perceived as the indicated sequence of vowels preceded by the consonants [b], [d], and [g] (Delattre, Liberman, and Cooper, 1955). The little hook at the beginning of each vowel formant is the formant transition. It reflects the rapidly changing resonant properties of the vocal tract as the articulators move from the position associated with the initial stop to the position associated with the following vowel.

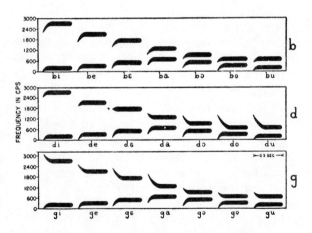

Figure 6.5 From Pierre Delattre, Alvin Liberman, and Franklin Cooper, *Journal of the Acoustical Society of America,* 1955, with permission.

Formant transitions associated with the voiceless counterparts of these three stops point in the same direction but are a bit shorter, simply because in the voiceless stops voicing does not take place immediately on release of closure. Notice that the transitions into the first formants are essentially similar for all initial stops. There is wide variability, however, among the second formant transitions, and experiments with synthesized speech have shown that it is the transition into the second formant that is the primary cue for place of articulation. If the transition is changed, then the perception of the initial segment is changed.

It is important to note that all syllables depicted in the middle diagram of Figure 6.5 are perceived as beginning with the consonant [d]. Although there is a striking dissimilarity among the physical signals associated with [d], all the [d]'s so produced are reported by subjects to sound exactly the same. This is an example of an extreme degree of variance between physical signal and linguistic percept. The acoustic signal associated with [d] of [di] is a rapidly rising formant transition, while that associated with [da] is a rapidly falling one. Yet to the hearer there is absolutely no perceptible difference among [d]'s preceding different vowels.

Conversely, note that the formant transitions for the [g] of [ga] and for the [d] of [du] are actually more similar than, say, the [d] of [di] and the [d] of [du]. At least the transitions of both [gu] and [du] are falling. These two acoustic stimuli are perceived as completely distinct, however. This phenomenon, then, demonstrates the other type of variability—that which occurs when similar acoustic signals are perceived as quite different linguistic segments.

Another cue for the place of articulation of voiceless stops is the frequency of the little burst of air (associated with aspiration) that occurs just as the stop is released. Again, research has shown that this cue is ambiguous and lacks invariant association with linguistic percepts. This information comes from experiments in which stop + vowel syllables were synthesized without formant transitions. The syllables were produced by synthesizing a burst of energy at varying frequencies followed by formants characteristic of different vowels. It was found that one burst would be perceived as different stops, according to which vowel it was paired with. For example, a burst at 1,440 Hz. is perceived as a [p] if the following vowel is [i] or [u], as a [k] if the following vowel is [a]. This is of course yet another instance in which similar (in this case identical) acoustic cues are perceived as different linguistic segments (Cooper, Delattre, Liberman, Borst, and Gerstman, 1952).

We have here what appears to be an almost arbitrary pairing of acoustic signal and linguistic segment, but this impression is erroneous. The pairing, though not invariant, is explicable if we examine abstract characteristics of the stimuli in question. Look closely at Figure 6.5. Notice that all the second formant transitions for [d] seem to point toward the same frequency; so do the transitions for all the [g]'s and all the [b]'s. By extending the transitions with a constant slope until all intersect, it is possible to calculate the frequency to which each set of transitions is pointing. That frequency is known as the **locus** for its stop consonant. The locus frequency for [g] (and also [k]) is about 3,000 Hz.; for [d] (and also [t]), about 1,800 Hz.; and for [b] (and also [p]), about 720 Hz. We have already said that a formant transition "is simply the rapidly changing bands of reinforced frequencies that intervene between the relatively steady-state formant patterns of the individual segments." The loci for the formant transitions into the stops can be understood in this same framework because the locus for a stop consonant reflects the resonating frequencies of the vocal tract closed at the point of articulation for the stop in question. Of course, at the moment of closure there is no energy, hence no speech signal for a brief moment. As soon as the occlusion opens sufficiently for sound to be produced, the second formant moves rapidly from that occluded frequency to the vowel formant.

The idea that certain invariant loci exist for the second formant transitions of the stop consonants in initial position led to what was once called the Locus Theory of Speech Perception. It was hoped that the locus could somehow be viewed as an invariant acoustic cue associated with the various stops. However, there are two reasons why it is impossible to view loci in this manner. First, and most important, research in coarticulation phenomena has shown that the loci for stops in medial and final positions are obliterated in the dynamics of ongoing articulation. Second, even in initial position the locus could not be computed by the perceptual system for an individual stop-vowel sequence; the locus for one stop is in fact defined over many instances of that stop. It seems that the most reasonable theoretical statement is that the locus may be thought of as the frequency associated with an ideal, or target, place of articulation, which is often missed in running speech, as are the vowel targets.

The issues we have been discussing—with reference to strident fricatives, vowels, and pure stops—may be characterized as the **classification** (or identification) of particular speech sounds by the perceptual system. We shall return to this subject when we discuss the perception of the voice/voiceless distinction in the stop consonants. We must not leave Figure 6.5, however, without mentioning the other dimension of perception with which we must be concerned. That is the **segmentation** of speech sounds.

As mentioned earlier, speech is perceived as a linear string of sounds, similar to the string of sounds represented at the systematic phonetic level of the grammar. We pointed out that the systematic phonetic representation and the perception of speech as discrete sounds occurring one after another is an abstraction. The acoustic signal does not contain discrete physical signals occurring one after another. When we say that the perceptual system must segment the speech signal, we mean that the perception of a string of discrete sounds is constructed by the perceptual system on the basis of the nondiscrete physical stimulus. This phenomenon will be discussed at more length below, but it should be noted that our consonant–vowel syllables represented in Figure 6.5 provide evidence that the acoustic signal itself does not contain discrete sounds in linear order.

The demonstration goes like this. If you take, for example, the signal that is perceived as [di] and, using a gating procedure, "cut off" little pieces of the signal beginning at the left and moving toward the right, you will at first continue to hear the entire syllable [di]; after a great deal of the formant transition has been eliminated, you will hear only the vowel [i]. It appears, then, that the signal consists of a [d] segment (which you gradually eliminated) and an [i] segment (which remains). This turns out to be false, however, when you work back the other way. If the vowel segment is eliminated gradually from the right, it turns out that there is no signal created that will be perceived as "just" a [d]. In fact, under these circumstances you would hear the syllable [di] again and again, with a vowel of increasingly shorter duration. Then suddenly you would hear a little chirp—not a [d] at all, and not even a speechlike sound. Thus it appears that the acoustic information leading to the perception of the consonant is literally part of the vowel itself. Information about the consonant and about the vowel is entering the perceptual system simultaneously because they occur simultaneously in the acoustic signal. A major task of the perceptual system is to analyze the acoustic signal (with simultaneously occurring information) as two discrete, linearly ordered (segmented) sounds.

6.351 The perception of the voiced/voiceless distinction in stop consonants.

The second perceptual dimension that distinguishes the stop consonants is voicing. There are a number of acoustic differences between a voiced and voiceless stop. In a consonant–vowel sequence, for instance, a voiceless pure stop will be aspirated in English while its voiced counterpart will not. This aspiration is associated with a little burst of air accompanying the release of closure for the voiceless, but not in the voiced, sound. On a spectrogram, transition of the first formant into the vowel has less energy if the stop is voiceless than if it is voiced.

In general we think of the primary difference between voiced and voiceless sounds as the presence versus the absence of phonation. Research at Haskins Labs by Lisker and Abramson (1964) has made the difference more explicit. Underlying the acoustic differences between voiced and voiceless sounds is not simply the presence against absence of voicing, but the time at which voicing begins, relative to other features of the speech sound, especially the release of the oral closure. This is referred to as **Voice Onset Time** (VOT).

It is, then, not the case that voiceless stops are never accompanied by vocal cord vibration, but it is the case that for these sounds phonation is delayed several milliseconds beyond the release of the closure. This is referred to as **voicing lag. Simultaneous voicing** occurs when phonation begins at the moment the closure is released, and **voicing lead** occurs when voicing begins before the closure is released. In English voiceless stops usually occur with some voicing lag (around 25 msecs. for [p] and [t], a bit longer for [k]), and voiced stops are produced with either simultaneous voicing, a slight voicing lead, or even a very slight voicing lag in the case of [g], but never as much lag as the voiceless counterpart.

To summarize, in English we have two classes of stops with reference to voicing, and one member of each class appears at each of the three points of articulation. For each voiced/voiceless pair the primary difference between the members is that voicing begins later in the voiceless segment than it does in the voiced segment. As was discussed in some detail in Chapter 4, voicing is phonemic in English. Thus we can show that the feature [voice] can keep meaningful words distinct from each other. There are other languages, however, such as Thai that have three categories of phonemic distinctions among apical stops in the phonology of the language: voiced, /d/; voiceless, /t/; and voiceless aspirated, /tʰ/.

An aspirated stop is characterized in speech by even more VOT lag than the unaspirated stop. To test the perceptual consequences of varying VOT and no other parameter of the speech event, Abramson and Lisker (1965) constructed a series of synthetic speech stimuli that were nonsense syllables with the first segment constructed with the formant transition typical of an apical stop. The first segments of the series of stimuli varied only in VOT; there were stimuli with a voicing lead of 150 msec, stimuli with a voicing lag of 150 msec, and stimuli corresponding to VOT of each 10 msec. increment between these two extremes.

These tape-recorded stimuli were played to speakers of English and to speakers of Thai, all of whom were asked to identify the first segment of each nonsense word. The results of this experiment illustrate two very important aspects of speech perception: First, a hearer's perception of a speech signal depends to a large extent on the structure of the language he has internalized. This is another important instance of an aspect of linguistic performance, speech perception, interacting with linguistic competence, or the structure of one's native language. Second, we tend to perceive many speech sounds categorically—that is, we tend to perceive all sounds of the same type as the same, even though they vary acoustically. We shall take up these two points one by one, turning first to the degree one's percepts depend on the nature of one's internalized linguistic knowledge.

The English speakers in the Abramson and Lisker study perceived all stimuli with voicing lead, with simultaneous voicing, and with a voicing lag of up to 25 msecs. as /d/. All signals with a VOT lag of greater than 25 msec. (even 30 msec.) were perceived as /t/. The Thai speakers, on the other hand, perceived only those signals with voicing lead as /d/. Those with simultaneous voicing and lags up to 40 msec. were perceived as /t/, while those stimuli with lag of greater than 40 msec. were perceived as /tʰ/. Remember that all subjects heard exactly the same acoustic signals. Their perceptions differed only because they speak different languages. The English speakers have two perceptual categories associated with apical stops, /d/ and /t/. English speakers do produce aspirated [tʰ] (as in the first segment of 'tin' and in hundreds of other English words), and, as we discussed in Chapter 4, the rules of English can predict just when aspiration will occur. However, the feature of aspiration does not distinguish meaningful English words from each other, and the aspirated stop does not define a perceptual category for the English speaker.

The Thai speaker divides the same acoustic sequence into three perceptual categories, depending on the phonemes of his language. He perceives stimuli with a long VOT lag as /tʰ/, while the English speaker perceives it as only /t/. What is even more arresting is that the stimuli between a VOT lag of 0 msec. (simultaneous voicing) and 25 msec. are perceived by the English speakers as /d/, but by the Thai speakers as /t/. Thus we see that the two language communities have different perceptual categories, rather than simply different linguistic labels for speech sounds. Such a phenomenon illustrates yet another example of variance between acoustic signal and perceptual event—another circumstance under which the same acoustic signal will be perceived as two different linguistic events. Again, the theoretical importance of this finding is that it leads us to postulate a constructive perceptual device—one that is not totally dependent upon acoustic information but that uses information from within as well as from without.

6.352 The categorical nature of speech perception. The Abramson and Lisker study is also an example of the categorical nature of the perception of speech sounds—in this case pure stops. Hearers perceive differences between acoustic signals separated by category (phoneme) boundaries but not between signals that vary within phonemic categories. An example of this phenomenon emerges from the Abramson and Lisker study. For their English-speaking subjects, the perceptual boundary between the /d/ category and the /t/ category occurs at almost exactly 25 msec. VOT lag. Thus almost 100 percent of the subjects identified the stimulus with 10 msec. lag as /d/ and almost 100 percent of the subjects identified the stimulus with 40 msec. lag as /t/. These two stimuli differ by only 30 msec. of VOT, yet they are perceived as completely different phonemes because they are separated by a phoneme boundary. Pairs of stimuli which were actually more different acoustically were, however, perceived as the same phonemes. For example, both the stimulus with 100 msc. lag and the one with 150 msec. lag were perceived as /t/. Not only were they both identified as the same phoneme, even though there was a 50 msec. VOT difference between them, but subjects could not *discriminate* between them. That is, within phoneme categories, stimuli sound exactly the same to subjects. This feature of perception is unique to speech stimuli. Variation in almost every physical dimension produces perceptual differences in non-speech sounds. Fine differences in pitch and intensity can be perceived by people who suffer from no auditory pathology, but acoustic features that define phoneme categories do not work this way. Small variations in the acoustic stimulus will produce no perceptible difference as long as they occur within a phoneme category, but they will produce the perception of completely different phonemes if they occur across a category boundary.

When we speak of the categorical nature of speech perception, we are in fact speaking of perceptual processing as distinct from initial auditory processing. We would expect the auditory system to distinguish between all discriminable acoustic signals. That is, we would not expect categorical distinctions to arise at the auditory level. Tash and Pisoni (1973) in fact demonstrated a probable auditory processing difference between acoustic signals in the same phoneme category by a clever experimental technique. Usually an experiment investigating categorical perception involves asking subjects for their judgments about the similarity between two acoustic signals—say two versions of the syllable /pa/. One pair might consist of two /pa/'s each of which has an initial segment with 100 msec. voicing lag; another such pair might have one /pa/ with a lag of 75 msec. and another with a lag of 125 msec. Experiments show that in each pair the members will be judged to be identical.

Tash and Pisoni (1973) not only asked subjects for a judgment of sameness, they also timed their judgments. They found that it takes subjects longer to judge that two acoustically different segments are the same (such as the second /pa/ pair mentioned in the above example) than it does to judge that two identical acoustical segments are the same (such as the first /pa/ pair mentioned in the above example). Tash and Pisoni take these data as support for the hypothesis that the different pairs are identified as different at an auditory level, then recoded and perceived as the same segment at a level of phonetic processing (speech perception).

We do not want to leave the impression that the perception of voicing is the only instance of categorical perception of speech sounds. In other experiments at Haskins categorical perception according to point of articulation has been demonstrated through the use of stimuli that vary according to the slope of the second formant transition. It has generally been assumed that vowels are not perceived categorically, as are consonants (particularly stops), but continuously, as are nonspeech sounds. Some work at the Royal Institute in Stockholm, Sweden (reported by Studdert-Kennedy, 1974), has demonstrated that in certain experimental situations speakers can be induced to perceive vowels categorically. The theoretical importance of the phenomenon of categorical perception of speech sounds is that this phenomenon demonstrates that there is a speech mode of perception that operates at a higher level than that of the raw acoustic signal. Speech sounds are analyzed by the perceptual system in terms of linguistic rather than acoustic categories. The perceptual system analyzes a particular signal as a /d/. Once the analysis has been made, it no longer matters whether the perception was based on an acoustic stimulus with a simultaneous voicing or with a slight VOT lead. In fact, that useless information is not even retained by the perceptual system; therefore, discriminations cannot be made on the basis of that information. Chistovich and her colleagues (1966) were able to produce categorical perception of vowels by inducing the subjects to pay attention to their phonetic (or speech) qualities rather than to their acoustic properties. Pisoni (1971) was able to induce the categorical perception of vowels by decreasing the duration of the stimuli. (For an extensive discussion of these issues in particular as well as the field of speech perception in general, we recommend Studdert-Kennedy, 1974.)

A question of great importance for our understanding of the structure of the human perceptual and cognitive processes is, Where do the phonemic categories come from? Are we born with them or do we learn them? To some extent they must be learned, of course, since Thai speakers and English speakers (for example) are certainly not born with different types of brains.

If tiny children must learn all the perceptual categories in the brief period before they begin processing speech, they are faced with an enormous learning task. (In fact, it is not at all clear that it would be possible to learn the categories without first being able to process the speech.) We will explore this question in the chapter dealing with language acquisition, although effective research in this area has only recently begun. Answers to the question are unclear, but it does appear that human babies are born with some perceptual categories (Eimas et al., 1971; this research will be discussed in Chapter 8). If true, this is extremely important because it shows the relationship between innate structural features of the human brain and purely linguistic characteristics of human language. Thus we see that an individual's performance seems to be based on competence, while in the species it is possible that constraints on competence are set by the performance capabilities of the individual members of the species. In Chapter 7 we shall argue that similar constraints operate in the syntax of natural languages.

6.36 Coarticulation in connected speech

The information we have examined deals with very simple speech events—usually single syllables made up of a consonant followed by a vowel. It is generally considered necessary to understand how people perceive small segments of speech before theorists can begin to develop explanations of speech perception in running discourse. We have seen that a most important characteristic of even simple speech events is that there is a lack of invariance between the acoustic signal and the hearer's percept. As we look at longer segments of naturally occurring speech, we find that the lack of invariance between signal and percept becomes greater and greater; the code becomes more and more complex. This is true primarily because of the phenomenon of coarticulation, which arises in speech production and, of course, has acoustic consequences.

Forward coarticulation was introduced in section 6.2, when it was pointed out that the lips are spread during pronunciation of the [t] in 'tea' but rounded during the [t] in 'two'. A related phenomenon is backward coarticulation, in which a set of muscles is completing a previous speech gesture during the production of a sound for which it is not needed. Consider the difference in the position of your articulators during production of the [t] in 'spurt' versus that in 'spent'. The former [t] is produced with the tip of the tongue curled back and contacting the roof of the mouth just behind the alveolar ridge. This articulation is due to the preceding [r], which involves this shape of the tongue, but in a lower position. The [t] in 'spent' does not involve any such influence from a preceding phone; it is pronounced with the corona of the tongue pressed against the alveolar ridge. The point is that when the muscles work together to convert the systematic phonetic representation into an acoustic signal, the articulating organs frequently adopt features of preceding, as well as following, sounds. In so doing, the linearity of the phonetic representation is destroyed. Speech sounds do not come out of the speech apparatus one after another.

Recall that the acoustic signal is determined by the shape of the vocal tract at any particular moment. Coarticulation means that the acoustic signal associated with any particular speech sound will vary according to the speech sounds preceding it and following it. This is yet another source of invariance. A spectrogram of your pronunciation of 'spurt' and 'spent' would indicate that the formant transitions into the [t] would be quite different in each instance.

A Swedish phonetician (Öhman, 1966) has studied coarticulation phenomena extensively. Figures 6.6a and 6.6b are schematic drawings of some of the spectrograms he collected in his investigations. In Figure 6.7a we see the second formants resulting from pronunciation of the syllable [ögü]. (These are Swedish vowels, of course.) The first, [ö], is a mid-front rounded vowel (like a rounded [e]), while [ü] is a high-front rounded vowel (see section 4.13). In Figure 6.7b the syllable is [öga], differing from the first syllable only in the last vowel, [a], which is a low, unrounded vowel. What you should look at particularly is the transition of the second formant into and out of the [g] in the two figures. Recall that one of the major acoustic cues to the identification of a stop consonant is its second formant transition. (There is, of course, silence for the brief period of closure for the [g].) Even though the first two segments are identical in these two syllables, the transitions associated with the [g] are different according to which final vowel is being anticipated by the vocal tract during the production of the [g]. This is an example of forward coarticulation. In both of these instances the hearer perceives a [g], which in both utterances sounds identical (remember categorical perception). This is another example of a phenomenon that occurs all the time in connected speech.

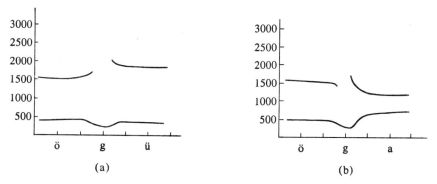

Figure 6.6   From Sven Öhman, *Journal of the Acoustical Society of America,* 1965, with permission.

6.4
Toward a Theory of Speech Perception

The facts about speech perception we have examined so far prove that the human speech-perception system cannot be a passive system that merely matches acoustic signals with phonemic percepts. We have been led to postulate instead an active, constructive perceptual system that is capable of using internalized information about language and the dynamics of articulation as well as information contained in the physical speech signal.

Theories of this type are called **analysis by synthesis** theories of speech perception (Halle and Stevens, 1964; Stevens, 1972). Such a theory postulates that the perceptual system forms an hypothesis about the phonemes and the systematic phonetic representation that underlies the analyzed signal. If the actual speech signal is sufficiently similar to that predicted by the perceptual system's hypothesis, then the system accepts its hypothesis as the percept. Theories of this sort are referred to as analysis by synthesis theories because the analysis of speech signals is accounted for by postulating the internal construction (synthesis) of hypothetical phonetic representations that are assumed to underlie the actual acoustic signal. This explains, among other things, why we perceive a linear string of speech sounds even though they do not occur this way in the acoustic signal. The utterance is represented by a linear string of symbols at the systematic phonetic level and at the systematic phonological level. It is these levels that are recaptured by the perceptual system as it decodes the complex acoustic signal.

It is important to note that no analysis by synthesis theory has yet been made sufficiently explicit to test directly. It is quite likely, however, that a theory of this general form will be necessary to account for the obviously constructive nature of speech perception.

It is necessary to postulate an active, constructive perceptual system to explain the day-to-day perception of spoken language, but our confidence in such a theory is strengthened when we examine perceptual illusions occurring in a speech context. The most startling illusions, of course, are hallucinations that consist of perceptions constructed by the perceptual system in the complete absence of physical signal.

Since hallucinations are not available to everyone, it is desirable to induce experimentally phonetic illusions which subjects perceive as a speech sound that does not occur in the physical signal. A group of Haskins workers recorded the word 'slit' and made a number of copies of the original tape (reported by Liberman et al., 1967). Then they made a cut between the [s] and the [l] and spliced in segments of blank tape of increasing lengths. When the segment of silence was less than 50 msec. long, subjects perceive the word as 'slit', but when the silent interval exceeded 50 msecs., the percept became 'split'. People who have listened to these tapes report that the effect is very striking. The perceptual system inserts a [p] that is indistinguishable from any old ordinary [p] that you hear all the time. What happened? When the silent interval became too long for the perceptual system to ignore, it was analyzed as part of the speech signal, since it was preceded and followed by speech. The perceptual system hypothesized that the moment of silence was produced by the closure for a [p]; the acoustic signal confirmed that hypothesis; thus the hypothesis was accepted and became the percept. Such a [p] is indistinguishable from "normal" [p]'s simply because "normal" [p]'s are also perceived in this manner. It is significant that subjects do not perceive any other voiceless stop in this experiment—neither [t] nor [k]—only [p]. According to our constructive perceptual theory this is easy to explain. Both [stlɪt] and [sklɪt] violate sequential constraints on initial consonant clusters in English. Hypotheses advanced by the perceptual system are constrained by the phonological rules of the hearer's language.

Another very interesting illusion is reported by Warren & Warren (1970) (see also Obusek and Warren, 1973). To simulate the after-dinner speaker effect, they recorded a sentence that included the word 'legislature' and then removed the [s], replacing it by a cough. They then played the resulting sentence to subjects, who perceived the [s] just as though it were present in the signal. In fact they were unable to identify which speech sound was missing when they were told that one was absent. They were also unable to identify the exact location of the cough. It was frequently perceived as occurring before or after the [s] (which was, you recall, perceived as a perfectly good [s]). Warren reports that even the investigators who prepared the tapes found it difficult to fail to perceive the [s]. Apparently the percepts (hypotheses) generated by the speech perception are very compelling, indeed.

6.41 Feature detectors

In section 6.352 we mentioned Eimas' theory that human infants are born with certain perceptual categories by which they organize speech. In particular Eimas postulates that babies—and also adults—are equipped with specialized neurons that are activated by special features of the acoustic signal. Such specialized neurons are known to exist in other animals. For example, Lettvin, Maturana, McCulloch, and Pitts (1959) have shown that there is a receptor neuron in the brain of the frog that is activated only when a small, dark, moving object crosses the frog's visual field. Such a system is obviously convenient for a creature whose life depends on its ability to catch flies. It is Eimas' claim that the human speech-processing system contains similar neural systems, sensitive only to particular features of the acoustic signal that are of potential linguistic relevance, such as voice onset time and acoustic characteristics associated with different points of articulation.

Research into the existence and properties of neurological feature detectors is in its infancy, but there is every reason to believe that such investigations will constitute a significant portion of speech-perception research in the future. In the course of these investigations it is imperative that the distinction between the phonetic features and acoustic features be maintained. An acoustic feature detector is a neurological device that is sensitive to various critical aspects of the speech signal. As such, it provides to the speech-perception system a specialized kind of information about the acoustic signal. Further processing, probably in an analysis by synthesis routine, would produce as output the phonetic percept. If the detectors are, instead, thought of as phonetic feature detectors, the claim would seem to be that the detector represents a passive device that mechanically matches features of the acoustic signal with linguistic features of the phonetic percept. Since it is known that a passive perceptual system simply cannot work, it would seem unwise to conceptualize the feature detectors as part of the perceptual system itself. It seems much more plausible to conceive of the detectors as being part of the auditory system, whose job it is to deliver preprocessed auditory information to the perceptual system.

6.5
Conclusion

Communication between two speakers can be characterized as the exchange of an idea. One person has an idea, encodes it into a systematic phonetic representation, sends instructions to his vocal apparatus, which creates a speech signal—a sound wave—that impinges on the ears of the hearer. The hearer first decodes the signal to ascertain what systematic phonetic and phonological representations the speaker encoded. He then uses that information to form further hypotheses about what the speaker meant—the idea he originally encoded. This process happens in a fraction of a second and is completely unconscious. The only physical contact between speaker and hearer (ignoring nonverbal cues) is the sound wave that passes between them. It must carry all of the information. The first step, then, in converting sound to meaning is to analyze the phonological and phonetic representations that underlie the speech event. We have seen that this process, as well as the relationships that obtain between physical and linguistic phonetics, is extremely complex.

We now move to a consideration of the syntactic processes involved in linguistic performance.

SUGGESTIONS FOR FURTHER READING

The following books deal with research in acoustic phonetics and speech perception.

Horton, D. L., and Jenkins, J. J. *The Perception of Language*. Columbus, Ohio: Charles E. Merrill, 1971.

Kavanagh, J. F., and Mattingly, I. G. (eds.). *Language by Ear and by Eye: The Relations Between Speech and Reading*. Cambridge, Mass.: M.I.T. Press, 1972.

Ladefoged, P. *Elements of Acoustic Phonetics*. Chicago: University of Chicago Press, 1962.

Ladefoged, P. *Three Areas of Experimental Phonetics*. London: Oxford University Press, 1967.

Lehiste, I. (ed.). *Readings in Acoustic Phonetics*. Cambridge, Mass.: M.I.T. Press, 1967.

Wathen-Dunn, W. (Ed.). *Models for the Perception of Speech and Visual Form*. Cambridge, Mass.: M.I.T. Press, 1967.

The following journals publish reports of research in the areas of speech production, speech perception, and acoustic phonetics:

Brain and Language
Journal of the Acoustical Society of America
Journal of Speech and Hearing Research
Language and Speech
Perception and Psychophysics

Grammatical Performance

7

When people use a language to communicate, they pair sounds with meanings. In language production meanings are encoded into sounds; in language comprehension sounds are decoded into meaning. Since the grammar of a language provides a formal system for relating sound and meaning, we have decided to refer to the activity of encoding and decoding messages as **grammatical performance.** This chapter presents a summary of theory and research dealing with this aspect of linguistic performance.

First, we will present the three major areas of grammatical performance with which psycholinguistic theory must deal: production of speech, comprehension of spoken language, and memory for linguistic events. Research and theory in language comprehension will, however, comprise the major portion of this chapter. This is true because there has been little research in language production for methodological reasons and research in memory for linguistic events is just beginning on a large scale. The purpose of this chapter is to present the goals, theory, and methodology of contemporary cognitive psycholinguistics and to show how it has developed, in a very short period of time, into an important area of experimental psychology.

7.1
The Production of Speech

When an utterance is produced, an idea is transformed into a sequence of sound waves. In Chapter 6 we dealt with the problem of how information is transmitted to the articulatory muscles after the utterance is planned. The question we want to deal with here is how the idea is transformed into a syntactically appropriate configuration of lexical items. Put differently, once a person decides what he wants to say, what cognitive operations must intervene to encode that idea into a sentence? Clearly, those operations must make reference to the speaker's internalized grammar if he is to produce a syntactically correct utterance. Schlesinger (1971) refers to such operations—those that turn ideas into utterances—as realization rules.

It is only fair to state that well-formulated hypotheses about encoding operations simply do not exist. However, two kinds of questions about production at this level have yielded some rather interesting research. One question concerns the encoding units of speech, which we have already discussed in Chapter 6 in connection with Fromkin's work with slips of the tongue. The other question concerns the types of decisions made by the speaker and the points during the production of a sentence at which these decisions seem to be made.

7.11 Decision processes during speech production

Studies of hesitations (pauses) in spontaneous speech illustrate the distinction between lexical and syntactic processing. Martin (1971) reports that there are two major locations for hesitations in running speech—those at constituent boundaries (by which he means phrases or clauses but not individual words) and those that occur within phrases, immediately preceding lexical morphemes. This is certainly not to suggest that there are always pauses before lexical morphemes or that speakers regularly punctuate their sentences with pauses. The claim is that when pauses do appear, these are the most likely places for them. Clark (1971) has labeled these two kinds of pauses conventional and idiosyncratic, respectively.

It seems reasonable to hypothesize that the conventional pauses (those between constituents) mark points of syntactic planning by the speaker or perhaps a deliberate attempt to punctuate a difficult sentence for the hearer. At any rate conventional pauses demarcate abstract, linguistically defined segments of surface structure. Idiosyncratic pauses, on the other hand, are assumed to reflect word-finding difficulty on the part of the speaker, which is of no decoding value for the hearer and of no deep psycholinguistic significance. Martin (1971) was able virtually to eliminate idiosyncratic pauses from subjects' speech by providing them in advance with a list of words to use in experimental utterances. Subjects reading aloud (hence avoiding word-finding delay) are said to produce conventional, not idiosyncratic pauses (Clark, 1971).

Martin (1971), investigating encoding hesitations, produced results that are of interest regarding the perception, as well as the production, of speech. Comparing the pauses produced by speakers with those perceived by hearers in the same speech event, Martin found that hearers (decoders) do three very interesting things: First, they always hear the conventional pauses of the encoder; second, they usually fail to perceive the idiosyncratic pauses, apparently editing them out of perception since they are of no value to them as decoders; third, they perceive conventional pauses where they do not in fact exist. As the hearers decoded the sentences syntactically, they perceptually inserted short periods of silence that were in fact not there in the speech signal. This should not surprise us, since we have developed a conception of the perceptual system as an active, constructive system that makes use of internal as well as external information.

The experiment described above calls into question two assumptions about encoding and decoding speech. One is that conventional pauses reflect a planning period for the speaker. Since speakers produced conventional pauses at some, but not at all, constituent boundaries, we can hardly conclude that speech production is dependent on organizing pauses. Perhaps the speaker only pauses because he needs to breathe and does so at linguistically defined points that will be at least distracting to the hearer. The other assumption this experiment calls into question relates to the hearer. It has been assumed that intonation cues provide the decoder with valuable information about the surface structure of the sentence he must comprehend. On the contrary, according to this study, perception of the intonation breaks followed from the syntactic analysis rather than the other way around.

Research in speech production at a semantic and syntactic (rather than a physiological) level is likely to flourish in the next decade. We eagerly await the first viable theory of the information processing that takes place between idea and muscle commands. Now let us turn to language comprehension, which provides us with more research, more questions, more hypotheses, and perhaps one or two tentative answers.

7.2
The Goals of a Theory of Language Comprehension

In order to understand how language comprehension takes place, we must be able to specify the cognitive operations that intervene between perception of sound and assignment of meaning. We can think of a theory of comprehension as a specification of all the decoding operations that take place between sound and meaning. For convenience we refer to the whole set of these decoding operations as the **language comprehension system** (LCS).

We want to make it clear that the LCS is not located in one area of the brain. You could not dissect a brain and say, "Come here and look at the Language Comprehension System; it's lying out on the table." The LCS is a set of cognitive operations that may take place in more than one area of the brain but that have one thing in common: they enable humans to understand what is said to them. Someday neurological theory will be sufficiently advanced to describe in neurological terms those processes of the LCS that we now describe in cognitive terms only.

For example, the LCS must have access to some sort of stored representation of all the words one knows (a lexicon), plus a retrieval routine for finding the appropriate words and selecting an appropriate meaning for each as a sentence is understood or produced. It is not known how the set of all the words that an individual knows is actually represented in the brain. There is probably not one area in the brain that contains all the words. Some neurologists think the lexical items may be coded in individual cells scattered over a large area (Penfield and Roberts, 1966); others think perhaps the hormones of the neural system may code lexical information (Whitaker, 1971). Fortunately, we do not have to wait for neurological theory to make a final decision on these questions. In the meantime we can make the cognitive statement: The LCS incorporates, among other things, a representation of all the words the individual knows and certain phonological, syntactic, and semantic information about each.

When we say that we believe that neurological theory will eventually rephrase our cognitive statements in more nearly physical terms, we are expressing the belief that our theory of language comprehension will be reducible to neurological theory. This is an important concept in the philosophy of science because it means that even though we are now forced to use vague terms like "semantic information," we are talking about a materialistic theory for which each cognitive term will ultimately have a physical counterpart.[1] (You will recall from section 5.21 that it is these beliefs that prevent our mentalistic theories from being metaphysical.)

It is interesting to look at the analogies that exist between speech perception and language comprehension, as we have divided them here. Recall that the most difficult aspect of speech perception to account for theoretically is the lack of invariant correspondence between the physical speech signal and the perceived speech sound. It is clear that in order to perceive speech hearers rely on both the acoustic signal entering their ears and their internalized knowledge of the phonological patterns in the language. Since internalized knowledge must be used and the hearers cannot rely exclusively on the acoustic signal, we said that speech perception must be active, or constructive. We will present evidence below that all language-performance systems must be active and constructive—the comprehension system, the

---

[1] We explicitly reject the common philosophical assertion that the reduction of one science (e.g., psycholinguistics) by another (e.g., neurology) constitutes *true explanation* of the phenomena dealt with by the former. In point of fact the discovery of the physical "building blocks" of a system does not explain how the entire system is organized or how the various components of the system function relative to one another. To discover, say, that the basic memory unit is a neurochemical (such as DNA) constitutes reduction of psychological theories of memory to neurological theory *only* in the sense that the psychological theories have been shown to be physical, rather than metaphysical, entities. It would not constitute reduction of psychological theories of memory in the sense that we could then forget about psychological theories of memory because they had been superseded by neurological theories. We would still have just as much use for psychological theories of memory, because only those theories could explain the structure of memory and its relationship to such other psychological processes as learning and sentence comprehension. (For excellent discussions of reductionism in psychology, see Fodor, 1968, pg. 111, and Putnam, 1973.)

sentence-memory system, and even the language acquisition system by which the child constructs his linguistic knowledge.

The lack of invariance between perceived sound and meaning is even more obvious than that between perceived sound and acoustic signal. In fact the illustrations that demonstrate lack of sound to meaning invariance are exactly the illustrations that demonstrate that the description of a language must incorporate a level of deep structure (see Chapter 2). In no language are surface forms sufficient to represent directly the meaning of all sentences—nor is one meaning always uniquely representable by one surface form. Consider again the sentences in (1) and (2).

(1) The professor is easy to understand.
(2) The professor is anxious to understand.

We showed in Chapter 2 that in order to describe the structure of these sentences correctly, a theory of linguistic competence must contain a level of deep structure in which the different grammatical functions of 'the professor' in each sentence are described. By the same token, the individual who comprehends these sentences must construct a meaning for them, making those same distinctions that are clearly not revealed in the perceived speech signal. Since the sound–meaning correspondence is mediated by syntactic structure, the construction of a structural analysis by the LCS is a decoding operation of considerable importance.

Even very simple sentences such as (3) and (4) reveal the lack of invariance between sound patterns and structural descriptions.

(3) The river is flowing.
(4) Her hair is flowing.

In the case of (3) 'flowing' must be labeled a verb by the LCS, while in (4) it is labeled an adjective. Syntactic units, like phonetic ones, are not always unique at the surface level.

We believe that sentence comprehension is a constructive process in which the hearer uses "external" information from the speech-perception system as well as internal information, consisting of linguistic knowledge, facts about the world, lexical information, expectancies at many levels, and a set of strategies for inducing a meaning from a superficial form. Most research in language comprehension can be viewed as an attempt to discover and characterize the internal information available to the LCS and the manner in which it is used.

7.21 Types of decoding operations

It is possible to isolate three major categories of processes employed by the LCS: lexical processes, syntactic processes, and semantic processes. In order to understand an utterance, the hearer must perform operations in each of these categories. He must (1) retrieve each lexical item from his mental lexicon along with a great deal of information about the item, including its meaning; (2) construct a syntactic analysis of the utterance such that the grammatical relations that obtain between and among the lexical items are described; (3) assign a semantic reading (a meaning) to the syntactic analysis.

While we suggest that lexical, syntactic, and semantic processes represent qualitatively different kinds of decoding operations, it is a matter of considerable theoretical importance to ascertain whether these operations are carried out simultaneously or one after another and just how much and what kinds of information are available from one set of operations for use by another. Intuitively we anticipate that the relationships will differ depending on the levels in question. It seems necessary in principle for semantic operations to use information from both lexical and syntactic analyses. It is not obvious, however, whether lexical retrieval must use information from structural analyses or vice versa.

Let us begin our investigation of research in lexical, syntactic, and semantic processing with an examination of some of the early psycholinguistic experiments that emerged in response to the development of transformational-generative linguistics.

7.3
Early Psycholinguistic Research

The initial response of psychologists to transformational-generative linguistics was, properly, to see whether the constructs developed by that theory had any "psychological reality." It was reasoned that if these initial investigations supported the claims of linguistics, then psychologists would feel obligated to develop theories to actually account for the role of linguistic constructs in language processing. It must be borne in mind that these early studies were important because the results provided initial confirmation of the psychological relevance of linguistic theory, which, though weak, made many psychologists very interested in the philosophical and theoretical problems posed by transformational-generative grammar. While much of the early work seems naïve from our present perspective, we should not lose sight of the fact that had it not been done and had it not turned out as it did, there would probably not be a branch of cognitive psychology known as psycholinguistics today.

7.31 The psychological reality of deep structure

Experiments by Blumenthal (1967) purported to demonstrate the psychological reality of deep structure. He had subjects memorize lists of sentences of the form of (5) and (6) below.

(5) The letter was sent by John.
(6) The letter was sent by mail.

He did not allow them sufficient time to memorize the sentences perfectly, however, and during recall he presented words from the sentences to jog the subject's memory (referred to as "memory probe)." It turned out that in sentences such as those above 'letter' works equally well as a probe for both sentences, but 'John' is a more effective memory probe. Thus 'John' was more effective in assisting a subject to recall underlearned sentences such as (5) than was 'mail' for sentences such as (6). Blumenthal explained this effect by pointing out that while there are only minimal surface structure differences between 'John' and 'mail', the two words function quite differently at the level of deep structure. 'John' is in fact the subject of the deep-structure sentence 'John sent the letter', the underlying form of which also underlies (5). The fact that (5) has undergone the passive transformation accounts for the appearance of 'John' in last position; 'mail', on the other hand, is simply the head noun of an adverbial phrase, hardly as significant as the subject of the sentence. The word that is most salient in deep structure, then, acts as a more effective memory probe.

Further work by Blumenthal and Boakes (1967) provided more support for the psychological reality of deep structure. They demonstrated that in sentences of the form of (7) and (8) 'John' is a better memory probe for (8) than for (7).

(7) John is easy to please.
(8) John is eager to please.

This is explained by two assumptions: first, the subject of an underlying structure is somehow more "salient" than is its object; second, the memory for the sentence is somehow represented as a linguistic deep structure. Blumenthal, then, demonstrated the psychological reality of deep structure that was then the key issue. Virtually ignored at the time was the importance of this work for theories about storage and retrieval processes in memory.[2]

7.32 The psychological reality of transformational rules

A similar kind of experimental paradigm was developed by Jacques

---

[2] Recent work by Perfetti (1973) has shown that it is not generally true that underlying subjects are better memory probes than underlying objects. In experiments similar to Blumenthal's he shows that subjects that function as actors and objects that function as recipients of action are better probes than subjects that are recipients of action and objects that are actors. Thus it appears that the semantic function of a word determines its efficacy as a memory probe more strongly than does its syntactic function. These facts are quite consistent with recent hypotheses concerning the nature of memory for sentences.

Mehler (1963). He had subjects learn sentences that were either **kernel** sentences[3] (simple, active, affirmative declarative sentences) or similar sentences differing only in that they had undergone either the passive (P), negative (N), or question (Q) transformation, or some combination of the three. A kernel sentence may be viewed for our purposes as a sentence that has not been operated on by one or more of the following three T rules: T-NEG, T-Q, T-PASS. For one kernel sentence, K, seven sentences can be formed by these transformations. Sentences (9)–(16) form a set of eight sentences constructed in this manner.

(9) The man bought the house.   (K)
(10) The house was bought by the man.   (P)
(11) The man did not buy the house.   (N)
(12) Did the man buy the house?   (Q)
(13) Was the house bought by the man?   (PQ)
(14) The house was not bought by the man.   (PN)
(15) Didn't the man buy the house?   (NQ)
(16) Wasn't the house bought by the man?   (PNQ)

As subjects attempted to recall such sentences, Mehler was particularly interested in the kinds of errors they made. He found that the most prevalent kind of error was a syntactic error in which the subject recalled the content of a sentence correctly but produced a less transformed version of the original sentence. Thus (14) may have been recalled as (11), the passive transformation being omitted in recall. This led Mehler to advance the **coding hypothesis,** which says that when a sentence is memorized, a representation of its corresponding kernel sentence is stored, plus a "transformational tag" for each transformation that has applied to it. Thus the memory representation of (16) would be a kernel representation, i.e., a representation of (9), plus three transformational tags, one for each of the three transformations. The hypothesis states in addition that transformational tags are lost from memory more quickly than is kernel representation. Mehler's early work, then, can be construed as demonstrating the psychological reality of transformations in terms of memory coding.

In the version of transformational grammar that was then in vogue the kernel sentence was not a representation of a deep structure, but it was certainly more closely related to deep structure than a more transformed version of any given sentence. Thus, by stretching the interpretation of Mehler's work just a little bit, we can claim that it was compatible with Blumenthal's hypotheses that deep structures correspond to memory representations.

[3] The term "kernel" is taken from the 1957 version of transformational theory as formulated in Chomsky's *Syntactic Structures*. The precise theoretical definition of kernel sentence is irrelevant here, since in this experiment it is defined simply as a sentence that has not undergone one of the three transformations mentioned in the experiment.

Had Mehler's hypothesis been taken seriously as an hypothesis about sentence memory rather than as a demonstration of the psychological reality of transformational operations, people would have probably thought it highly counterintuitive to say that the memory representation of a sentence does not directly include the meaning of that sentence. The coding hypothesis did say this, however. The kernel analog of sentence (11) is sentence (9), which means exactly the opposite of (11). If it is stored as a kernel plus a negative transformational tag, there is no real representation in memory for the meaning of the sentence. Furthermore, if the negative tag is lost in memory, a crucial aspect of the sentence's meaning has been lost. On the other hand, if the negative tag is lost from the representation of sentence (15), part of the meaning is not lost because (15) means the same as does sentence (12). In fact Mehler reported that Q and NQ sentences were frequently confused in memory, as were PQ and NQP, while sentences like K and N, which differed in meaning, were not. Mehler certainly recognized (and stated) that these facts pointed to a semantic component in sentence memory that his coding hypothesis did not attempt to deal with; he and other psycholinguists were primarily concerned with the status accorded transformational rules by the coding hypothesis.

In early psycholinguistic research the distinction between memory processes and immediate sentence-comprehension processes was not sharp. In Mehler's work the implication is clear that the transformations that are stored in memory and are subsequently employed in the recoding of the recalled sentences are also employed individually to decode and encode sentences in normal ongoing sentence comprehension and production. Another series of studies during this period (Miller and McKean, 1964) investigated transformational operations in an experimental format which did not involve memory. They engaged subjects in a sentence-matching experiment which worked like this: In any one experimental episode subjects would be matching sentences of two types, such as passives with passive negatives. There would be two lists of sentences and each would contain one version of a particular sentence. For example, List 1 might include sentence (17) while List 2 would contain a sentence such as (18).

(17) The old woman was warned by Joe.   (P)
(18) The old woman was not warned by Joe.   (PN)

Each list contained eighteen sentences in all. The subject would know before he was shown the list just what constructions he would be matching. His task would be to read each sentence on List 1, mentally perform the appropriate transformation, then locate the new sentence on List 2. There were pairs of lists comparing all possible combinations of kernels, negatives, passives, and passive-negatives. By computing and factoring out a constant amount of time required to search List 2, Miller and McKean (reported in Miller, 1962) were able to obtain an estimate of the time it took to perform the grammatical transformations. They reached the conclusion that the negative transformation requires about 1.15 secs. and the passive 1.65 secs. The time required to match a kernel sentence with its passive-negative analog was found to be 2.7 secs., almost exactly the sum of the negative and passive times.

Two other important experiments of this period confirmed the psychological reality of transformational rules by other measures. Clifton and Odom (1966) studied confusions among sentences in a recognition task and found that sentences that differed by one transformation were more likely to be confused than those differing by two or more. They investigated the same transformational types that Mehler had used and found the same similarity among questions (Q) and negative questions (NQ) as he had (and, also, as one would expect, between passive questions and passive negative questions).

Savin and Perchonock (1965) attempted to go beyond the weak "psychological reality" claim for transformational rules with a demonstration that each transformation represented a unitary decoding operation in short-term memory (STM). Using the traditional set of transformations plus the two others, they required subjects to hold eight short words in STM while recalling sentences of varying degrees of transformation. Their results were perhaps the most impressive in the early psycholinguistic literature. The more transformed the sentence recalled by their subjects, the more words were lost from STM.

Savin and Perchonock developed a spatial metaphor for STM, arguing that Mehler's coding hypothesis was correct and that, in fact, each stored kernel and transformational tag occupied a measurable amount of space in STM. Therefore, if more transformations had to be stored, some of the words (those that were presented first) had to be bounced out of the limited-capacity STM. These results were so impressive that many similar experiments followed immediately (see, for instance, Epstein, 1969; Matthews, 1968; Glucksberg and Danks, 1969; Foss and Cairns, 1970). All such experiments rested on the assumption that the comprehension mechanism received a sentence as input and produced as output a kernel sentence and information about each transformation that had applied to the comprehended sentence.

Most of the psycholinguistic theorists around this time seemed to feel that the assumption underlying the Savin and Perchonock research implied that the transformations were themselves decoded individually in something like serial order. At any rate it was assumed that extra transformations would add extra decoding operations, which would result in increased complexity. It seemed reasonable to test this assumption experimentally in a task that did not confound immediate comprehension of sentences and memory for them. This Gough did in 1965.

In this important experiment Gough (1965) presented subjects with a sentence (in either its active or passive version) followed immediately by a picture that either correctly depicted the action of the sentence or failed to do so. The subject's task was to judge whether the picture was true or false according to the meaning of the sentence and to press a button indicating the decision. It took subjects longer to verify passive sentences than active ones. It seems reasonable to assume that a subject's response consists of at least two stages: in one he must process the sentence in order to derive its meaning; in the other he must compare the meaning of the sentence with the picture. If we make the additional assumption that the comparison time does not differ for active versus passive sentences after they have been processed, we can conclude that the active/passive difference affects the sentence-processing stage in that passive sentences take longer to process than their corresponding actives.

On the face of it, then, Gough's experiment would seem to provide strong support for the hypothesis that the passive transformation has psychological reality not only in memory processes but also in immediate-comprehension processes. Fortunately, it was possible to test the assumptions underlying this conclusion directly. If a sufficient delay were introduced between the offset of the sentence and the appearance of the picture, and if the time to push the button were measured from the appearance of the picture, then the active/passive difference should disappear because the sentence-processing stage would occur before timing began. Gough (1966) conducted a second experiment to test this prediction, introducing a 3-sec. delay between the offset of the sentence and the onset of the picture. Unfortunately, in this second experiment it still took longer to verify the passive sentences than it did the actives. We are forced to the conclusion, then, that the passive sentences were for some reason more difficult to compare with the pictures than were the actives. That fact might be of interest to someone, but it is difficult to see how it is of much interest to a psycholinguist who is anxious to figure out how people actually understand sentences in the first place.

It has frequently been argued that experiments such as these (except for Gough, 1966), which were carried out in the early and mid-1960s, did in fact support the theory that transformational grammar is used directly in the comprehension of sentences. Put differently, it has been claimed that these early studies demonstrated that competence and performance are very similar and that the psychologist's model of linguistic performance should correspond very closely to the linguist's model of linguistic competence. It is certainly true that many enthusiastic linguists and psycholinguists (these authors included) were anxious to impose such an interpretation on these and similar results. But if we think about the theoretical issues, it is really quite a leap from the claim that a construct of linguistic theory has some kind of psychological reality (which these studies do demonstrate) to the much stronger claim that these linguistic constructs directly *represent* production or comprehension processes.

Many of the experiments of that period involved memory tasks. The

Miller and McKean study and the Gough studies employed matching tasks. It is not at all obvious that these tasks were testing—even indirectly —production or comprehension processes. In fact the only experiment that provided evidence directly relevant to a theory of comprehension was Gough's second experiment, after which "a hypothesis of a transformational process in [sentence] decoding is less defensible" (Gough, 1966, p. 494).

7.33 Linguistic constructs that do not contribute to psycholinguistic complexity

As the Gough experiment called into question the role of transformations in actually decoding sentences, a number of nearly simultaneous investigations discovered other transformations that did not seem to increase complexity as did the passive, negative, and question transformations. Before we discuss such transformations, however, let us look at this notion of complexity and how it relates to research in psycholinguistics. We assume that if a mental operation takes place (say, while a sentence is being understood), it will have some measurable effect. Obviously, we cannot measure mental operations themselves, so we seek to measure what we believe to be an effect of increased mental processing. A simple kind of measure is time.

If you compare two sentences and one requires more mental operations for its comprehension, then we would predict that it will take longer for someone to understand it than the other sentence. You might also expect people who are asked to memorize or interpret the sentences to make more errors with the complicated sentence. There are many measures of psycholinguistic complexity—time measures of various sorts (Gough's experiments illustrate use of timing), paraphrase and recall accuracy, and other measures that we will come across throughout this chapter. The point is that if we cannot demonstrate that a linguistic feature causes greater psycholinguistic complexity, we cannot claim that the linguistic feature actually corresponds to a mental operation.

Gough was not the only one who shook people's faith in the increased complexity of a sentence due to the presence of the passive transformation. Slobin (1966) showed that only reversible passive sentences such as (20) were more complex, not irreversible ones, such as (19).

(19) The ice cream cone was eaten by the clown.
(20) The boy was hit by the girl.

Sentences such as (20) are reversible because semantically (according to facts about the world) the subject and object could be reversed and the sentence would still be sensible (boys do hit girls). Irreversible passives, on the other hand, are those in which the first noun could not be the actor (ice cream cones do not eat clowns). We will have more to say about reversible and irreversible passives later, but the point here is that both have undergone the passive transformation, but only one type creates increased complexity that is measurable under experimental conditions. It is clear that the strongest claim we can make is that the passive transformation increases complexity only under certain conditions.

If we believe that a linguistic performance model is a direct analog of a competence model, then we would expect every transformation to increase complexity, but there are many examples that fail to satisfy this prediction. In transformational-generative theory, for example, preposed adjectives are derived transformationally from relative clauses. Thus 'The red apple' is derived, by a number of rather complicated transformations, from 'The apple which is red'. Fodor and Garrett (1967) showed that the insertion of adjectives into a sentence does not affect subjects' ability to paraphrase it accurately (paraphrasing accuracy is taken here as an index of psycholinguistic complexity).

The same authors (1966, p. 150) cite an unpublished experiment demonstrating that a sentence that has undergone the particle movement transformation (see section 2.21), such as 'John phoned the girl up', is no more complex than its less transformed analog, 'John phoned up the girl'. Furthermore, there are transformations, such as some forms of extraposition (the transformation that produces a sentence like (23) from a deep structure that also underlies (22)), which seem to produce sentences that are less complex than their analogs. For example, (23) is actually easier to process than (22).

(22) That the baby was tired was evident.
(23) It was evident that the baby was tired.

What must we conclude from this early research in the field of psycholinguistics? Two things seem clear: First, many of the constructs of generative grammar seem to have psychological reality, and the study of linguistic performance within a cognitive rather than a behavioristic framework seems justified. Second, it appears that the relationship between the linguist's grammar and a model of linguistic performance is far from simple. Those who had hoped to discover that each transformational rule matched an independent cognitive operation were disappointed, but their hope had not really been justified in the first place. There was never any reason to believe that the linguist was writing a model of performance when he was writing a grammatical analysis of a language. The experiments we have just cited served to indicate that there was not a one-to-one correspondence between performance theory and competence theory and that developing a psycholinguistic theory of the language user was going to be more difficult than had once been believed.

7.4
Toward an Autonomous Performance Theory

In the late 1960s psycholinguistic research turned from experiments that attempted to relate linguistic processes directly to psychological processes and began to investigate more directly the cognitive operations that intervene between heard sound and perceived meaning in actual sentence processing. The hearer's task is to relate each utterance he hears to the deep structure that underlies it. Since transformational rules cannot, in principle, work backwards,[4] and since each transformational rule does not seem to correspond to a psychological operation, this move to consider extralinguistic, cognitive processes seemed the most promising. The attention of psycholinguists turned to the various strategies or heuristics that a hearer might use to infer a deep structure (and hence a meaning) from a string of speech sounds.

We will use the language-processing model of Figure 7.1 to organize the hypotheses and findings that have characterized more recent psychological investigations. The model is not meant to be a theory of language processing, but rather a schema within which we can organize our discussion of language comprehension. We assume that it contains all the

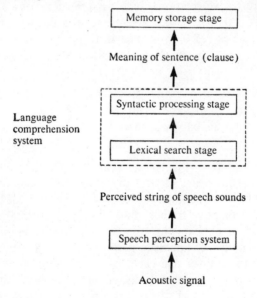

Figure 7.1

---

[4] If transformational rules worked backward, it would be possible to take a final derived phrase marker (a surface structure) and decompose it, transformation by transformation, until the initial phrase marker (deep structure) had been determined. Such a possibility demands that for every well-formed derived PM it should be possible by inspection to ascertain the shape of the derived PM immediately preceding it and the transformation that intervened between the two. This is not possible for every derived PM, nor is this a reasonable or desirable formal constraint in linguistic theory.

cognitive processes necessary to understand sentences, so we call it the language-comprehension system (LCS). It is described in terms of stages of processing a sentence undergoes as it is being understood.

The message is received as a perceived string of speech sounds roughly corresponding to the systematic phonetic and/or the systematic phonological representation of an utterance. We can think of it in this way: The speech-perception system operates on the sound waves that impinge on the ear and interprets them as a string of speech sounds (a process discussed at length in the preceding chapter); this string of speech sounds is the input to the language-comprehension system. It is necessary at this point to understand the difference between serial and parallel processing. In serial processing operations take place one after another—one operation is completed before the following one begins. In parallel processing, on the other hand, two or more operations are taking place at the same time.

We do not know whether comprehension operations take place in serial or parallel. It seems obvious that some parallel processing must be involved simply because of the incredible speed with which the comprehension process takes place. On the other hand, there are operations that cannot take place until information is received from earlier levels of analysis, so some serial processing must also take place during the comprehension process. In the discussion that follows we shall make the simplifying assumption that many relevant operations proceed in a serial fashion. Thus we shall look at each individual process as though it were occurring by itself. Even so, we must remember that it is an important future task for psycholinguistic theory to discover just which operations take place in serial and which take place in parallel.

7.41 The lexical-search stage

The first stage of processing is labeled the **lexical-search stage** (LSS). It is during this stage that individual words are paired with their meanings. Operations at this stage refer to the individual's mental lexicon, the huge store of words that the hearer knows. Questions that have been asked relative to this very low-level stage of processing are: (1) How are the lexical items coded and organized within a person's mental lexicon? (2) How are the lexical items that are received by the LCS retrieved from the lexicon, and how much information about each lexical item is immediately available? We shall discuss below experimental research that has attempted to deal with these questions.

7.42 The syntactic-processing stage

As words leave the LSS, they enter the SPS, which begins to project hypotheses about the structural relationships among the lexical items. Based on its structural analysis, the SPS produces as output a semantic interpretation of a chunk (or segment) of the sentence being operated on. For reasons we will discuss below it is currently believed that these chunks are probably pieces of the input sentence that correspond to underlying simple (atomic) sentences in its deep structure. These underlying sentences usually correspond to a clause in the surface structure of the sentence. All surface-structure clauses have their origin in underlying simple sentences, but the converse is not true—every underlying simple sentence does not emerge as an autonomous clause in surface structure. Psycholinguists tend to agree that the surface-structure clause (and hence the underlying simple sentence it represents) is probably the primary unit of language processing. The status of the underlying sentence that does not appear as a surface structure clause (i.e., one that is not dominated by an S-node in surface structure) is, however, questionable.

When we say that the clause is the primary unit of language processing, we mean that the SPS level of analysis takes individual clauses, performs a finer-grained syntactic analysis of the internal organization of the clause, combines the meanings of individual lexical items with the information from the syntactic analysis, and finally assigns all grammatical relations within the clause. It is this processing stage to which the vast majority of research in psycholinguistics relates. We need to know, first, how the LCS breaks the incoming message into clausal units; second, what aspects of an utterance facilitate processing at this level and why; and third, to what extent operations at this stage of processing rely on linguistic knowledge and to what extent the operations are independent of the hearer's explicit grammatical knowledge of the language.

Just as the LSS must have access to the hearer's mental lexicon, the SPS must have access to the hearer's internalized grammar (or knowledge of his language). This is not to claim that the grammar is represented in the brain in the same way that it is represented on paper by the linguist. The linguist represents the general principles of linguistic organization by writing rules in standard notation, with brackets, symbols, and arrows. It may be decades before we have any understanding of how linguistic knowledge is actually represented in the brain, but it seems quite certain that the general principles governing the well-formedness of sentences in the language must be represented in the brain of the language user and must furthermore be available to the language-comprehension system. Of equal importance to the language-comprehension system are operations that do not rely on formal principles of linguistic organization but that are purely cognitive processes developed by the system to decode messages as quickly as possible. Bever (1970) refers to such operations as "perceptual strategies," and we shall have a great deal to say about them later in this chapter.

7.43 The memory-storage stage

After the grammatical relations have been assigned and a meaning has been derived for a clausal unit, the SPS sends the coded meaning into the memory-storage stage (MSS). Gough (1972) has cleverly called this stage PWSGWTAU (the place where sentences go when they are understood). There is ample evidence that meanings are stored independent of information about the syntactic structure by which they were encoded, but exactly what happens to the meaning after it is sent to the MSS depends on what task the hearer is engaged in. If one is studying for an exam, one hopes the meaning will be stored securely in long-term memory. If the person is carrying on a conversation, the meaning will be used as the basis of an appropriate reply. If the person is performing as a subject in a psycholinguistic experiment, he will perform the appropriate experimental task after he has computed the meaning of the clause. By the MSS, then, we refer to a sort of staging area from which the abstractly coded, syntax-free meaning of a clausal unit can be channeled for any appropriate task. Of course, most of the sentences we encounter are composed of a number of clauses. A key function of the MSS is probably to combine the meanings of individual clauses in order to derive a unified meaning for a complex sentence.

There is compelling evidence (which we will consider in some detail in section 7.55) that further modifications of meaning take place at the level of sentence memory. We can think of the output of the SPS as the basic meaning of the sentence, which we shall define as the meanings of the individual lexical items plus the grammatical relations that relate them. There are further aspects of meaning that may be inferred from a sentence, however. This additional meaning, which goes beyond the information explicitly available in the sentence itself, is added to the basic meaning of the sentence as it is stored in memory.

7.5
Recent Psycholinguistic Research

We shall now present some of the findings of psycholinguistic research in the late 1960s and early 1970s. When possible, we will relate the experimental task and the findings to the model of the LCS outlined above.

7.51 The segmentation of the speech signal into clausal units

Over a period of several years a series of experiments was carried out by T. G. Bever, Jerry Fodor, Merrill Garrett, and several of their colleagues, all using the same basic experimental paradigm. In this paradigm an English sentence consisting of two or more underlying simple sentences encoded into two surface structure clauses is recorded on tape. Sentence (23) (from Fodor and Bever, 1965) is a typical example of an experimental sentence. A slash (/) separates the clauses.

(23) Because it rained yesterday / the picnic will be canceled.

Superimposed on the sentence is a click, located at any one of a number of places within the sentence. In (23) the click occurs during either 'yesterday' or 'picnic'. Immediately after hearing the sentence over headphones, the subject is given a typed copy of the sentence (or is sometimes requested to write the sentence) and is asked to indicate with a mark the point in the sentence at which he heard the click. That is, the subject is asked to reconstruct his auditory experience upon hearing the sentence and report it. The basic finding in all of these studies (Fodor and Bever, 1965; Garrett, Bever, and Fodor, 1966; Bever, Lackner, and Kirk, 1969) is that clicks are perceptually displaced into major clause boundaries. A click actually located in 'yesterday' would be reported as occurring later, between 'yesterday' and 'the'. Similarly, a click located in 'picnic' would be perceived as occurring earlier, also in the clausal break between 'yesterday' and 'the'. One might suspect that this effect is due to an intonational pause (see section 7.2) between the clauses which attracts the clicks. However, Garrett, Bever, and Fodor (1966) demonstrated that the phenomenon of subjective click displacement is not a result of acoustic cues. They recorded segments of speech, such as "...hope of marrying Anna was surely impractical" and made two copies, splicing the words "In her..." onto the beginning of one copy and "Your..." onto the beginning of the other, producing sentences (24) and (25), which are physically identical from the word 'hope' to the end.

(24) In her hope of marrying / Anna was surely impractical.
(25) Your hope of marrying Anna / was surely impractical.

The linguistic structures of the two physically identical segments are vastly different, however. Note that the clause break occurs between 'marrying' and 'Anna' in (24) and between 'Anna' and 'was' in (25). In fact clicks located in 'Anna' are displaced in opposite directions in the two sentences; in each case the click is perceived as having occurred in the clause boundary. In these experiments, then, an abstract syntactic organization produces the differential perception of identical physical signals.

The significance of these findings can hardly be overemphasized, for they support two very important hypotheses about sentence comprehension. First, the language-comprehension system must be an active constructive device, just as the speech-perception system is. Neither of these systems bases its analyses solely on the signals that come into it. If this were so, there would be no difference in the perception of the click located in the word 'Anna' in sentences (24) and (25). Instead, there is a complex interaction within the SPS between internalized knowledge about linguistic structures and the acoustic signals it receives. In the case of the language-comprehension system the segmentation of utterances into clauses is imposed upon the speech signal, but it is not determined by the speech signal (recall section 7.2, in which this phenomenon is related to pause perception). Thus we have a great deal of confidence in the hypothesis that the language-comprehension system receives a speech signal and actively assigns a structural analysis to it.

The second important hypothesis that this research confirms is that the surface-structure clause, which signals the existence of a simple sentence in deep structure, is the unit of comprehension. In other words, the LCS initially segments the speech signal into units corresponding to underlying simple sentences. Clause boundaries attract clicks even if the clause is embedded within another clause. Thus in sentence (26) clicks will be displaced into the clausal breaks between 'man' and 'who' and between 'likes' and 'is'.[5]

(26) The man who nobody likes is leaving soon.

In terms of our processing model we suggest that in accordance with the hypothesis that the clause is the primary unit of sentence processing, clause-sized units are in fact sent into the syntactic-processing stage for further syntactic analysis and, ultimately, assignment of basic meaning. If this is the case, as sentence (26) is received by the LCS, analysis of the words 'the man' must be delayed until the remainder of the clause, 'is leaving soon', is received.

Evidence of this sort demonstrates that the LCS must have access to some sort of temporary memory system during the early stages of processing in order to store incompletely analyzed material. Following Gough, perhaps this storage should be nicknamed PWSGBTAU (the place where sentences go *before* they are understood). Psycholinguists usually call this memory system short-term memory, primary memory, or short-term storage. All these names refer to the same thing, but no one is really sure what they are referring to. There does seem to be a memory system with a relatively small capacity from which material is quickly lost unless something is done with it. So if someone gives you a list of, say, eight digits, you can probably recall them unerringly if you have been allowed to say them over and over again to yourself prior to recall (this is called rehearsal). On the other hand, if you aren't allowed to rehearse them, forgetting will take

---

[5] There is some question about whether perceptual segmentation (demonstrated by click displacement) also takes place at constituent boundaries within clauses. Bever et al. argue that within-clause boundaries do not attract clicks at all. Chapin, Smith, and Abrahamson (1972) offer data that indicate that the major subject/predicate within-clause constituent break attracts clicks as well as do clause boundaries. It certainly seems intuitively plausible that major constituent breaks within clauses would attract clicks, and that fact in no way diminishes the importance of the findings that the clause boundary never fails to attract clicks and is in fact the strongest "click attractor" of all boundaries investigated. (For an alternative, although not mutually exclusive interpretation of experiments of this type, see Reber and Anderson, 1970, and Reber, 1973.)

Linguistic Performance

place very quickly. STM, then, is regarded as an unstable temporary store-house for incoming information. It is also usually regarded as the gateway to long-term memory (LTM), so that anything stored in LTM first passed through STM. Memory for digits and individual words has been studied extensively by psychologists through the years. A classic article is one by Miller (1956), in which he presents a theory about information processing that takes place prior to the storage of chunks of information in STM. In terms of the LCS it is probably reasonable to say that the STM has two primary functions: first, as a storage buffer for unanalyzed information; second, as a "working memory" during the syntactic-processing stage. Some psychologists might want to refer to the latter function as taking place in a separate memory system, but that question is irrelevant to the present discussion. The point is that the LCS must have access to a number of different kinds of memory with a number of different kinds of function to store and operate on different types of information. (For a discussion of the various types of memory used in the comprehension process see Norman, 1972.)

Let us return to the hypothesis that the clause is the primary unit of language comprehension and to recent evidence that information-recoding takes place after a clause is processed. Caplan (1972) studied the ability of subjects to recognize words that were taken from sentences they had just heard. The experimental paradigm is the following: The subject hears a tape-recorded sentence; 100 msecs. after the conclusion of the sentence, he hears a word and is required to indicate by pushing a lever indicating whether or not the word was in the sentence he just heard. The time elapsed between hearing the probe word and pushing the lever is recorded. This is the recognition time. The consistent finding in a series of such experiments was that recognition time is significantly shorter if the probe word is from the most recently processed clause. Caplan compared recognition times for two identical words in identical contexts, located at equal distances from the end of a sentence, which differed only in that one word was part of the last clause of its sentence and the other was part of the next-to-last clause. He found that recognition time for the former was shorter than for the latter. Consider, for example, the pair of sentences (27) and (28).

(27) When the sun warms the earth after the *rain* / clouds soon disappear.
(28) When a high-pressure front approaches / *rain* clouds soon disappear.

In (28) the word 'rain' is part of the last clause; in (27) it is part of the next-to-last clause. Recognition time for the word 'rain' was recorded and compared. Caplan controlled for intonation differences by preparing two identical recordings of the identical part of the sentences '. . . rain clouds soon disappear' and splicing them onto the initial parts of the sentences.

Recognition time for 'rain' was significantly faster in sentences like (28) than in sentences like (27). Notice that in (28) the probe word is in the final clause, while in (27) it is in the preceding clause. Since we believe that clauses are analyzed as syntactic units, Caplan's data are not too surprising. After a clause is assigned a semantic analysis, apparently, detailed information about the clause (such as the individual lexical items that occurred in it) is no longer as readily available as when it is being processed. With reference to our processing model it is tempting to speculate that the lexical item from the more recently heard clause is more available because that clause is still at the syntactic-processing stage, while the earlier clause has already been assigned a meaning and has progressed to the memory-storage stage. Since the assignment of meaning represents a recoding of information, the clause must be returned to an earlier processing stage before lexical recognition can take place.

Recent findings (Cairns and Blank, 1974) support this hypothesis. When recognition latencies for words from final clauses are compared, it is found that words from more psycholinguistically complex final clauses are monitored more quickly than are words from less psycholinguistically complex final clauses. Presumably the more difficult clauses, taking longer to process, remain at the SPS for a longer time than do the more easily processed clauses; therefore, their lexical information is available for the recognition task for a longer period of time.

Research by Jarvella (1971), together with Caplan's findings, suggests a three-stage recoding of information, with clause boundaries that are also sentence boundaries as well as within-sentence boundaries assuming a key role in the comprehension process. While Caplan compared a word in a final clause with the same word in a penultimate (next-to-last) clause, Jarvella compared penultimate clauses that varied as to whether they formed a sentence with the final clause or with an initial clause. Compare examples (29) and (30).

(29) The tone of the document was threatening//
     Having failed to disprove the charges/
     Taylor was later fired by the President.
(30) The document had also blamed him/for
     having failed to disprove the charges//
     Taylor was later fired by the President.

Initial, penultimate, and final clauses are set apart. A slash (/) indicates a clause boundary that is not also a sentence boundary. A double slash (//) indicates a break that is both a sentence boundary and a clause boundary. The clause of interest here is the middle (penultimate) one, 'having failed to disprove the charges'. In (29) it is part of the same sentence with the final clause, while in (30) it is part of the same sentence with the initial clause. In a recall task Jarvella's subjects recalled the middle clause far better if it was part of the last sentence, as in (29), than if it was part of the preceding sentence, as in (30). In both cases the final clause was remembered best, of course; the important point is that the availability of information from the penultimate clause apparently varies according to whether there is a sentence boundary preceding it, just as in Caplan's experiment the availability of information varied according to whether there was a clause boundary preceding it.

Another very interesting aspect of Jarvella's experiment was that if the penultimate clause was a subordinate clause that formed a sentence with the final clause—as in (29)—it was recalled better than if the two clauses were in the order main clause–complement clause, as in sentence (31).

(31) He and others were labeled as Communists//
    McDonald and his top advisers hoped/
    this would keep Rarick off the ballot.

Put differently, Jarvella's results suggest that subordinate clauses are not recoded as completely or as quickly. This is a reasonable finding because assigning a semantic interpretation to a subordinate clause, as in (29), must await the semantic interpretation of the main clause.[6] In a sentence such as (31), however, the main clause "McDonald and his top advisors hoped . . ." can be assigned a semantic interpretation before the complement clause is received. The SPS, then, may incorporate more than one level of processing, with clauses moving through the levels as units.

There is abundant evidence that lexical and syntactic information is lost to the hearer after it has been used to assign a semantic interpretation to an utterance. An early study by Sachs (1967) demonstrated that 27 seconds after reading a passage, the meanings of the sentences are retained, but syntactic detail is not retained independent of meaning. This study caused something of a stir in psycholinguistic circles at the time because it appeared when syntactic variables were being investigated almost exclusively, and it seemed to call into question both the truth and significance of hypotheses such as Mehler's coding hypothesis. Later, when we present the sentence memory studies of Bransford and Franks, Barclay, and Jenkins, we will see more evidence of information recoding that results in the loss of lexical and syntactic information. Before we leave the syntactic-processing stage of the language-comprehension device, however, we should examine the linguistic properties of clauses that either facilitate or impede comprehension.

7.52 The cue-deletion hypothesis

The assumption that a basic task of the language-comprehension system is to infer a deep structure from the speech signal leads to what is known

---

[6] An experiment by Kornfeld (1973) demonstrates that Caplan's effect is not attributable to a subordinate/main clause difference.

as the **cue-deletion hypothesis.** It is obvious that the only external information available to the LCS is contained in the input signal. Therefore, the more similar the input string of morphemes is to the deep structure, the easier an utterance will be to understand. Therefore, the application of a T rule that deletes a cue to the deep structure should result in a sentence that increases the processing load for the LCS. This hypothesis was initially put forth by Fodor and Garrett (1967), who argued that the application of a transformation to a deep structure would not make the resulting sentence more psycholinguistically complex unless it also destroyed surface-structure information that could serve as a cue to deep structure. Thus, although sentence (32) is more transformed than sentence (33) (since it includes an adjective), it is no more psycholinguistically complex because no cues to deep structure are obscured.

(32) The tired soldier fired the shot.
(33) The soldier fired the shot.

Consider, however, the deletion of a relative pronoun from a relative clause. Compare sentences (34) and (35); they differ only in the presence or absence of the underlined relative pronoun.

(34) The man whom the dog bit died.
(35) The man the dog bit died.

In (34) the relative pronoun signals the LCS that there is a clause boundary followed by an embedded sentence modifying 'man' and that in fact 'the man' is simultaneously subject of the main clause and object of the embedded sentence. Therefore, the relative pronoun allows the LCS to begin assigning structure to the input string early in the utterance. In (35), however, the cue to the deep-structure configuration is missing (having been deleted by the relative clause reduction transformation) and thus—according to the cue-deletion hypothesis—should be more difficult to process, that is, more psycholinguistically complex.

   The cue-deletion hypothesis is based on another more general hypothesis about psycholinguistic processing: As the LCS receives a string of words, it begins making guesses about the probable underlying structure of the utterance. In our model this would take place at the syntactic-processing stage. These guesses are constrained by the grammar of the language and are guided by a set of heuristics that Bever (1970) refers to as "perceptual strategies." In keeping with our distinction between speech perception and language comprehension, we will rename these **comprehension strategies.** One way of understanding the cue-deletion hypothesis, then, is to say that the LCS has a comprehension strategy that scans the input utterance for clause boundaries, indicating the beginning and end of component simple sentences in deep structure. Cues such as relative pronouns and complementizers signal such boundaries. In a sentence with such cues deleted, however, the LCS is unable to take advantage of this comprehension strategy and processing is delayed. Put differently, if cues are missing from the input to the LCS, more material must be processed before the clause boundary is located.

A general problem in psycholinguistic research involves how to test the hypothesis that one utterance is more psycholinguistically complex than another. What kind of behavioral measure can we devise that will reveal psycholinguistic differences among sentences? As we present the various experiments that have tested hypotheses about the relative complexity of various structures, we will consider the various kinds of complexity measures that have been used. It is very difficult to compare experiments that use different complexity indices unless we have evidence that the indices are actually measuring the same thing. Unfortunately, evidence of this sort is often difficult to come by.

Returning to Fodor and Garrett's cue-deletion hypothesis in general and the relative pronoun deletion hypothesis in particular, we see that they used paraphrase accuracy as an index of processing complexity. That is, they would give a subject a sentence (usually tape-recorded) and require the subject to rephrase the sentence without in any way changing the meaning. If sentence (35) were the experimental sentence, either sentence (36) or (37) would be perfect paraphrases.

(35) The man the dog bit died.
(36) The dog bit the man and the man died.
(37) The dog bit the man, who died.

The unfortunate thing about this measure is that subjects are so good at it. The LCS works very fast and very accurately, but for the paraphrase task to measure relative psycholinguistic complexity, some errors in paraphrasing must be made. The measurement of the errors made are, after all, the only indication of complexity in this task. Therefore, if all the sentences are of such a low degree of complexity that no errors are made, then they are inadequate for testing the hypothesis. The experimenter who wants to use paraphrase accuracy as a measure must construct sentences that are of sufficient difficulty to cause subjects to make mistakes. For this reason many experimenters have used double-center-embedded sentences, such as (38), which is a sentence used by Fodor and Garrett (1967), paraphrased in (39).

(38) The pen which the author whom the editor liked used was new.
(39) The editor liked the author, who used the pen, which was new.

In order to test the cue-deletion hypothesis as it relates to relative pronouns, they compared subjects' paraphrasing accuracy when presented with sentences such as (38) as opposed to identical sentences with the relative pronouns deleted, such as (40).

(40) The pen the author the editor liked used was new.

They found that sentences containing the relative pronouns were paraphrased much more accurately, thus confirming the cue-deletion hypothesis.

Using the same sentences that Fodor and Garrett (1967) used, Hakes and Cairns (1970) tested the cue-deletion hypothesis with yet another measure of psycholinguistic complexity, the phoneme-monitoring task, developed by Foss (1969; Foss and Lynch, 1969). In this task the subjects are required to listen for a word beginning with a specified phoneme in the experimental sentence and to push a button as quickly as they hear one. The time intervening between the target phoneme and the subject's button push is the subject's monitor latency. The rationale for this technique as a measure of psycholinguistic complexity is that monitor latency will be longer (more time will intervene between target phoneme and response) if higher-level language-processing activity is taking place. The phoneme-monitoring task has been used as an index of psycholinguistic complexity in a number of experiments that will be discussed in this chapter, so it is comforting to know that experiments using this task have also confirmed the relative-pronoun-deletion hypothesis, as well as replicating the paraphrasing effects found by Fodor and Garrett. In Hakes and Cairns (1970) (see also Hakes and Foss, 1970) the monitor phoneme was the first phoneme of the second verb u in sentence (40)—and monitor latencies associated with sentences such as (40) were significantly longer than those associated with sentences such as (38), indicating increased processing activity associated with the former sentence type.

Since the phoneme-monitoring task is much more sensitive than the paraphrase-accuracy task, Hakes (1972) was able to test another specific hypothesis derived from the general cue-deletion hypothesis with much more natural sentences than the double-center-embedded ones. The cue that Hakes investigated was the complementizer 'that' (see section 3.62 for a description of this structure). He used sentences of the form of (41) in which 'that' introduces a clause that in its entirety is the object of the verb 'see'.

(41) Everyone who was at the party saw (that) Ann's date had made a complete fool of himself.

Hakes used the phoneme-monitoring task to evaluate the psycholinguistic complexity of the sentence with and without the complementizer 'that'. He found that latency to monitor the d in 'date' was longer if the complementizer was deleted, thus indicating that the deletion of 'that' produces a more psycholinguistically complex sentence. There are three possible hypotheses for this effect. First is Hakes' suggestion that monitor latency is increased when 'that' is not present because no structure assignment can be made and a great deal of unanalyzed material must be held in short-term memory ("the place sentences go before they are understood). On this account the presence of 'that' allows the LCS to assign structure to "Everyone who was at the party saw . . ." and begin processing a new clause.[7] This explanation assumes a very different account of the source of the phoneme-monitoring latency effect than was previously suggested by Hakes and Cairns (1970) and Foss (1969; and Foss and Lynch, 1969). They had previously assumed that increased monitoring latency reflected decision processes during sentence comprehension.

A second hypothesis to explain the source of increased complexity when 'that' is deleted is one that we shall call the **exhaustive computation hypothesis.** The reduced version of sentence (41) is difficult to process on this hypothesis because after the LCS has received the words 'Everyone who was at the party saw Ann's date . . .' it projects two initial structural analyses of the potential deep structure of the utterance. One analysis (the correct one) is that the words 'Ann's date' begin a complement clause and constitute the subject of a deep-structure sentence, the entirety of which is the object of the verb 'see.' The other (incorrect) structural analysis is that the received words 'Ann's date' constitute the direct object of 'see'. The exhaustive computation hypothesis also attributes the monitor effect to an increased load on STM, the source of the increased memory load being the generation and storage of the two structural analyses projected by the LCS.

A third hypothesis to explain the relative difficulty of the reduced forms is that only one structure assignment is made by the LCS in the absence of 'that', and it is incorrect. On this suggestion the LCS might initially analyze 'Ann's date' incorrectly as the direct object of 'see'. On the receipt of 'had' the LCS would have to revise its initial hypothesis and reanalyze 'Ann's date' as the subject of the new clause. This hypothesis is quite reasonable because the monitor response occurs well after (around a third of a second) the target word has been heard by the subject. This hypothesis, which we shall call the **initial segmentation hypothesis,** is also consistent with the assumption that the phoneme-monitor task is affected by decision processes. The initial segmentation hypothesis, as well as Hakes' hypothesis, suggests that some mechanism in the LCS is constantly on the alert for major constituent breaks and responds every time an apparent break appears. Evidence for this hypothesis can be found in syntactic illusions such as sentence (42), which is a perfectly grammatical sentence produced by deletion of the relative pronoun from (43).

(42) The horse raced past the barn fell.
(43) The horse (who was) raced past the barn fell.

---

[7] An important paper by Kimball (1973), which presents a theory of surface-structure analysis, supports this hypothesis for this and all cue-deletion effects.

Most people perceive the sentence as strange, however, because they have initially analyzed "The horse raced past the barn . . ." as an autonomous clause. That is, in this case one's LCS does not hold two possible analyses of the initial six words of sentence (43). When 'fell' arrives, the sentence is either rejected as ill-formed or consciously and laboriously reprocessed. This sentence is a good illustration precisely because the single analysis is so compelling. The illusion (from Bever, 1970) certainly does not prove that the immediate-segmentation hypothesis is always correct and the exhaustive-computation hypothesis always wrong. In fact, since there is evidence for both hypotheses, it is quite probable that both operate in sentence processing in varying degrees, depending on the semantic and structural properties of individual sentences. In the case of complement deletion it would probably be impossible to determine which hypothesis accounts for the relative difficulty of the sentences with deleted complementizers because some subjects may use one comprehension strategy, some another. Or, alternatively, the sentences might trigger differing comprehension strategies depending on their semantic and structural properties.

Next we shall investigate a special case of the exhaustive-computation hypothesis, which has produced some disturbingly contradictory experimental results.

7.53 The verb-complexity hypothesis

The **verb complexity hypothesis** is a special case of the exhaustive-computation hypothesis in that it says that the LCS does in fact compute all possible deep-structure configurations based on available information. Advanced by Fodor, Garrett, and Bever (1968), this hypothesis assumes that in addition to the meaning or meanings of the lexical items of an utterance being processed, the LCS also has access to information about what structures that lexical item can enter into. This kind of information is particularly relevant with respect to verbs. Consider, for instance, a verb such as 'expel'. It is a pure transitive verb in that it can only appear in a structure of the form $_S[NP \ V \ NP]_S$. It has a categorical restriction (section 3.63) that states that it must appear in such a structure, in which the second NP is its direct object.

(44)   The chemist expelled the air from the tube.
(45)   *The chemist expelled.

Thus sentence (44) is grammatical, but (45) is not because 'expel' can't be used intransitively. Sentences (46), (47), and (48) are ungrammatical because 'expel' will not take any kind of complement sentence.

(46)   *The chemist expelled that he hated his old professor.
(47)   *The chemist expelled the air to leave the tube.
(48)   *The chemist expelled the air's leaving the tube.

(In terms of the model of the LCS we have presented, the verb complexity hypothesis can be regarded as an hypothesis about the kind of lexical information that is retrieved during the lexical-search stage of processing as well as about how the information is used during the syntactic-processing stage.) Compare the pure transitive verb such as 'expel' to a more complex verb such as 'request', which will take not only a simple direct object but also complement sentences, as illustrated in sentences (49)–(52).

(49) Alice requested a raise.
(50) Alice requested that Bill leave immediately.
(51) Alice requested Bill to leave the room.
(52) Alice requested Bill's leaving the room.

Fodor et al. suggested that when the LCS receives a verb, it exhaustively computes all the possible underlying structures that would be compatible with well-formedness constraints in the language. These structures are then projected as guesses about the structure of the remainder of the clause being analyzed. Since all these hypotheses must be computed and retained by the LCS until sufficient information is obtained that enables a choice to be made among them, the greater the number of permitted structures associated with a verb, the more psycholinguistic complexity will be associated with the processing of that verb. Notice that the hypothesized effect of verb complexity is completely independent of what actually follows the verb. Since all predicted structures must be computed and all but one rejected, the presence of a complementizing verb should produce a more psycholinguistically complex sentence than a pure transitive verb even if both are followed by simple direct objects. Fodor et al. again used a paraphrase task to evaluate this hypothesis. They found that a sentence such as (53), with a complementizing verb (underlined), produced more paraphrasing inaccuracies than did a similar sentence (54) that differed only in that it contained a pure transitive verb (underlined).

(53) The box the man the child knew carried was empty.
(54) The box the man the child met carried was empty.

As a further test of the hypothesis they constructed a set of more natural sentences, such as (55) and (56).

(55) The man whom the child knew carried a box.
(56) The man whom the child met carried a box.

The subject's task in the second experiment was sentence construction. Each word of an experimental sentence was typed on a small piece of cardboard, the pieces were scrambled, and the subject was told to construct a sentence as quickly as possible using the words. This "anagram" task also confirmed the verb-complexity hypothesis in that more correct constructions were formed from word sets such as (56) than from sets such as (55).

A sentence-construction task such as this may seem of questionable validity in evaluating an hypothesis about sentence comprehension, but further confirmation of the hypothesis comes from Holmes and Forster (1972) with yet another measure of processing complexity. The rapid serial visual presentation technique (RSVP) was developed by Forster (1970) and also employed by Forster and Ryder (1971). In this paradigm the subject is visually presented with the words of a sentence in rapid succession and is then required to write down as many words as he can recall in the order in which they were presented. The number of words correctly recalled is taken as a measure of processing complexity. Holmes and Forster (1972) found that fewer words were recalled in sentences with complementizing verbs than in sentences with pure transitive verbs.

Since it is an hypothesis about immediate sentence processing, we would expect the phoneme-monitoring task also to confirm the verb-complexity hypothesis. However, in two experiments Hakes (1971) failed to obtain the predicted results. Monitor latencies were not longer for phonemes occurring after pure transitive verbs. In one of those experiments Hakes confirmed the hypothesis using a paraphrase task, so we have a situation where the paraphrase task yields a different result from the phoneme-monitoring task. Hakes suggests that the reason for this is that the phoneme-monitoring task measures decision processes in particular. That is, monitor latency is increased only when the LCS makes a decision of some sort. Immediately after the verb is received, however, the LCS does not make a decision. (This analysis would speak in favor of the immediate segmentation hypothesis to explain the phoneme monitor's sensitivity to extra processing in the case of the complement-deletion experiment.) In fact, Hakes suggests, the complex verb produces a local ambiguity that is not resolved by the LCS until the clause boundary, at which time structural decisions are made and the ambiguity is resolved. This suggestion brings us to another area of psycholinguistic research that has yielded insights into many of the operations of the LCS—this involves investigating how the LCS deals with ambiguous sentences.

7.54 Investigations dealing with ambiguous sentences

Earlier in this book (see section 2.21) we showed the importance of ambiguous sentences for competence theory. Now we want to explore the significance of the comprehension of ambiguous sentences for performance theory. The primary rationale for research into ambiguous sentence processing is simply that every ultimately unambiguous sentence is ambiguous for some period of time prior to its conclusion. Moreover, many of our completed utterances are ambiguous, but their ambiguity is never noticed.

It is believed, then, that if we can understand the psycholinguistic processes by which the LCS deals with ambiguity, we will understand some of the normal language-processing operations.

We have shown that it is possible to define levels of ambiguity that correspond to levels of linguistic description. In section 2.21 lexical ambiguities, surface-structure ambiguities, and underlying ambiguities were defined and illustrated. In an early investigation of the time required to perceive both meanings of ambiguous sentences, MacKay and Bever (1967) found that subjects perceived lexical ambiguities the fastest, then surface-structure ambiguities, then underlying ambiguities. This was considered early confirmation of the notion that at least three processing operations are involved in sentence comprehension—a lexical operation, which assigns a meaning to each lexical item; a parsing operation, which assigns constituent groupings to the string of lexical items; and an operation that assigns grammatical relations in the sentence.

Work with lexical ambiguities has dealt with two distinct areas of interest. Some research has contrasted the processing of lexically ambiguous sentences with that of other kinds of ambiguities. Another area of research has focused on the assignment of a meaning to the ambiguous lexical item itself. We shall discuss the former type of research first, although the findings of these two research areas are not independent of each other.

7.541 Research comparing the various types of ambiguities. The first and most reasonable question to ask about the processing of an ambiguous sentence is, In the absence of disambiguating context, does the LCS compute one meaning or does it exhaustively compute all meanings of the sentence? This has been investigated in an experimental paradigm where subjects hear an ambiguous sentence that is highly biased toward one of its meanings (that is, there is a high probability of one meaning's being perceived). Then they receive a stimulus—either a picture (Foss, Bever, and Silver, 1968) or a second sentence (Cairns, 1971 and 1973)—that is compatible with only the unexpected meaning of the sentence, after which they are asked to decide whether the stimulus is compatible with the sentence they have just heard. Decision latency is timed. The rationale for this paradigm is that a subject's LCS has produced only one meaning for the ambiguous sentence (the expected one), then in order for the stimulus and the sentence to be judged compatible, the subject would have to reprocess the sentence, which should take time.

Decision times associated with unexpected stimuli are compared to decision times associated with expected stimuli (in which case, presumably, the sentence would not be reprocessed). In all of the cited studies there was a large reprocessing effect associated with the lexical ambiguities. However, in the two studies (Foss et al. and Cairns, 1971) that compared lexical and underlying ambiguities there was no reprocessing effect associated with the underlying ambiguities. Foss et al. and Cairns suggest that there is strong evidence that only one meaning is computed by the LCS for lexical ambiguities. Cairns (1971) argues that two meanings are computed for the underlying ambiguities.

Another hypothesis that would account for these results is that underlying ambiguities are reprocessed more rapidly than are lexical ambiguities. There seems to be no supporting evidence for this latter hypothesis, which is completely ad hoc. There is, however, some additional evidence for the two-meaning hypothesis for underlying ambiguities. MacKay (1967) discovered that ambiguous sentence fragments take longer to complete than do unambiguous ones. Bever, Garrett, and Hurtig (1973), however, found that this is not true of all ambiguous sentences. They constructed ambiguous fragments that were either lexical or underlying ambiguities; some of the fragments ended within a clause, others at the end of a clause. The only ambiguous fragments that took subjects longer to complete were those that were underlying ambiguities ending within a clause. Bever et al. interpret the results as showing that during the processing of the ambiguous clause all possible structure assignments are being projected by the LCS. If the subject is required to complete such a fragment, his LCS must first choose which structure to complete. At the end of the clause perceptual closure takes place, the subject's LCS selects one structure (hence one meaning), and the fragment is no longer functionally ambiguous.

Notice that the Bever et al. hypothesis of perceptual closure at a clause boundary is exactly like Hakes' hypothesis of structural decision-making at a clause boundary. It is also compatible with the general hypothesis that the clause is the primary unit of comprehension. The Bever et al. data are compatible with the Cairns two-meaning hypothesis if one makes the additional assumption that perceptual closure can be delayed and both structures retained if the subjects' task demands it.

Recall that in the Foss et al. and Cairns experiments the subjects were performing a matching task and needed both structures to perform correctly. In the sentence-completion task the subject obviously needed only one structure to complete the fragment adequately. Notice that in the model of the LCS that we have been referring to, these are essentially hypotheses about the meaning(s) that are sent from the syntactic-processing stage to the memory-storage stage. The suggestion is that task demands may dictate exactly how many meanings are sent to the PWSGWTAU in the case of underlying ambiguities.

Let us now turn to the lexical ambiguities in the Bever et al. study. Completion time was not increased for lexically ambiguous fragments whether the break came within or at the end of a clause. Following the logic of Bever et al., then, we should conclude that the lexical ambiguity had been resolved very early in the clause. This is, of course, compatible with the one-meaning hypothesis for lexical ambiguities. It also implies that lexical decisions are made earlier in the comprehension process than are structural decisions. Notice that this is not just an hypothesis about lexical and structural decisions with regard to ambiguous elements, but rather an hypothesis about lexical and structural processing in general. Gough (1972) has made a similar claim about lexical decisions during the reading process.

7.542 Research investigating the assignment of meaning to lexical items. Foss (1970; 1973) has investigated the effect of an individual lexical item on the comprehension process using the phoneme-monitoring task. He found that monitoring latency is of longer duration following an ambiguous lexical item than following an unambiguous lexical item. If we assume that increased monitoring latencies reflect increased processing activity (perhaps a decision-making operation), then the Foss studies suggest two hypotheses. One is that lexical decisions are made immediately after the LCS receives each lexical item. In terms of our model this is an hypothesis about the lexical-search stage of the LCS—that words are assigned meanings in serial order as they enter the lexical-search stage from the speech-perception system, prior to syntactic processing. The second hypothesis that emerges from the Foss experiments is that ambiguous lexical items increase sentence complexity because both meanings must be stored in STM until the end of the clause, at which time lexical as well as structural decisions are made. The Bever et al. finding that lexical ambiguity does not increase sentence-completion time seems to speak against the hypothesis; more convincing are data from Cairns and Kamerman (1975) in which phonemes are monitored either immediately after an ambiguous lexical item or delayed until two words later (still within the same clause). Sentence (57) is an example of the immediate, while (58) illustrates the delayed, monitor condition. (The ambiguous word and the monitor phoneme are underlined.)

(57) Frank took the pipe down from the rack in the store.
(58) Frank took the pipe from the dollar rack in the store.

The effects of ambiguity on monitor latency were shown to disappear two words beyond the ambiguity. These data suggest strongly that the monitor effect is a decision effect.

To support this anaysis we need evidence that two meanings for the ambiguous lexical item are indeed present at some point in the comprehension process. (Clearly, two meanings must be present in order for a decision to take place.) An ingenious and fascinating experiment by Lackner and Garrett (1972) provides the evidence we require. Subjects in that experiment wore headphones and heard something different in each ear. In one ear they heard an ambiguous sentence (all three types of ambiguities were used); in the other ear they heard a sentence that would bias the ambiguous sentence toward one of its possible meanings. The second sentence was played at a lower volume than the ambiguous sentence, and subjects were told to pay attention only to the ear that was receiving the ambiguous sentence. Their task was simply to paraphrase the sentence. Even though subjects could never recall any part of the unattended sentence, their perception of the meaning of the ambiguous sentence was influenced by the biasing sentence.

(59) In the park we came upon a bat lying by an oak tree.

Thus, we would predict that an ambiguous sentence such as (59) would be perceived as being about flying rodents if a biasing sentence about caves and vampires were received simultaneously, but as being about a baseball bat if the biasing sentence were about home runs, players, and the like. This experiment is of far-reaching importance because it calls into question many of the theories of attention that psychologists have developed. A discussion of such matters is beyond the scope of this book. The point here is that both meanings of the ambiguous sentences must have been available to the subjects or it would not have been possible to swing the bias of the sentences either way by introducing different biasing sentences. So we have our evidence that there is a point in the processing of an ambiguous sentence when both meanings of an ambiguous lexical item are available to the LCS.

We can feel more confident of the hypothesis that increased phoneme-monitor latency following ambiguous lexical items is a result of a decision process in which the LCS chooses among possible readings for the ambiguous item. This hypothesis deserves a great deal more experimental testing. If further research continues to support it, an important next step will be to try to figure out why decisions are made so early. Many words are ambiguous before a sentence is completed but are disambiguated by the end of the sentence. It would seem likely, then, that an early-decision strategy would result in frequent errors—there would be many times when an incorrectly processed word would have to be reprocessed at the end of a sentence or clause. A good guess may be that limitations in STM force the LCS to make lexical decisions early, even though errors may result. For comprehension to proceed quickly and smoothly, then, there would have to be a rapid reprocessing routine available to the LCS (see section 8.642). Psycholinguistic research, then, must continue to test the early-decision hypothesis, attempt to explain the cognitive basis for early decisions, and account for the compensatory reprocessing routines that are operable.

7.543 The effects of prior context on the processing of ambiguous words. It is intuitively plausible that the context that precedes an ambiguous word will affect its comprehension. There are two possible mechanisms by which prior context could exert an effect. It could affect either the retrieval system or the decision procedure. Prior context could direct retrieval so that only one meaning is initially retrieved from the lexicon during the LSS—the meaning that is most compatible with the prior context. On the other hand, it could be that two meanings are retrieved in any context, but a biasing context may facilitate the decision of which meaning to retain in working memory. A study by Foss and Jenkins (1973) failed to decrease monitor latencies following ambiguous words by preceding them with a biasing context. Thus 'fly' produced increased monitor latencies whether it was preceded by a neutral context, as 'The youth caught the fly', or by a biasing context, as in 'The shortstop caught the fly'. These data would suggest that prior context does not affect retrieval and affects only the outcome, not the duration, of the decision process.

A subsequent experiment by Swinney (1974) presented contradictory results. He did in fact succeed in decreasing monitor latencies to ambiguous words by embedding them in biasing contexts. Other aspects of his experiment led him to conclude that the context is effective during decision rather than during retrieval.

Since context effects are only beginning to be investigated systematically, it would seem precipitous to state a theoretical position at this time. One point appears definite, however: whatever they turn out to be, context effects are not as simple or as automatic as our intuitions would have led us to believe.

7.55 Memory for sentences

In the early days of psycholinguistic research sentence memory was regarded primarily as another experimental task demonstrating the psychological reality of linguistic structures (recall section 7.4). A number of interesting claims were made about just exactly what was stored in memory. Blumenthal (1967) and Blumenthal and Boakes (1967) suggested that the deep structure was stored. Mehler (1963) suggested that the kernel and the transformational tags were stored, as did Savin and Perchonock (1965). Sachs (1967) called these hypotheses into question when she showed that semantic information, but little or no syntactic information, is recalled as soon as 27 seconds after hearing a sentence embedded in running discourse. Research by Bransford and Franks (1972) and Barclay (1973) has shown that not only is the meaning of a sentence stored in memory, but the meanings of several sentences may be integrated into one memory representation. Further, information that is inferable from a sentence, but not directly present in it, is also represented in memory. We will present evidence below that in memory for sentences, not only is the meaning of the sentence (in the sense of expressed grammatical relations) available to the hearer, but also integrative and inferred "extra" meaning.

In an experiment demonstrating the integration of atomic sentences in memory subjects were presented with four atomic (simple) sentences known as "ones," or with various combinations of two or three atomic sentences, called "twos" and "threes."

(60) The ants are in the kitchen.
(61) The ants ate the jelly.
(62) The jelly was sweet.

(63) The jelly was on the table.
(64) The ants in the kitchen ate the jelly.   (a "two")
(65) The ants in the kitchen ate the sweet jelly.   (a "three")

A "four" (66) was never presented to subjects, nor were all possible threes or twos presented for memory.

(66) The ants in the kitchen ate the sweet jelly which was on the table. (a "four")

Following the memory phase of the experiment there was a recognition phase, during which subjects were given sentences they had actually heard and "twos," "threes," and "fours" they had not heard. All the subjects had to do was identify the sentences they had heard and tell how confident they were about their identification. The results were that subjects claimed with a high degree of confidence to have heard sentences that they had in fact not heard, but that represented the integration of information from "smaller" sentences. Subjects were most confident about having heard "four" sentences, although they had not heard a single "four" in the initial presentation. It appears that information derived from the semantic interpretation of a number of sentences is integrated and stored in memory. One way of characterizing these data is to say that elements (sentences) that were distinct at one stage of processing (the immediate processing period when the original sentences were presented) lost their distinctiveness at the memory-storage stage. In this experimental paradigm we have an example of nondistinctiveness being produced by integration of information.

Further research by Bransford, Barclay, and Franks (reported in Bransford and Franks, 1972) shows a lack of distinctiveness in memory representations attributable to the addition in memory of inferred information. Consider sentences (67a) and (67b), which differ only in the underlined preposition.

(67a) Three turtles rested on the floating log and a fish swam beneath it.
(67b) Three turtles rested beside the floating log and a fish swam beneath it.

Subjects were presented with such sentences, then with sentences such as (68a) and 68b), for recognition three minutes later.

(68a) Three turtles rested on the floating log and a fish swam beneath them.
(68b) Three turtles rested beside the floating log and a fish swam beneath them.

Subjects who had heard (67a) believed that they had heard (68a), but subjects who had heard (67b) did not think that they had heard (68b). In other words (67a) and (68a), two distinct sentences, lose their distinctiveness in memory, while (67b) and (68b), which differ in exactly the same way, do not. How can we account for this difference? Notice that (68a) can be inferred from (67a), because if the turtles are *on* a log, then a fish swimming *under* the log is simultaneously swimming under the turtles. However, (68b) is not related to (67b) in this way. If the turtles are merely *beside* the log (and not on it), it does not follow that the fish is swimming under the turtles. In brief, (67a) and (68a) are confused in memory because if the former is true, the latter must be true.

What is stored in memory is not only a representation of the meaning of the sentence in terms of its grammatical relations but a representation that includes information that may be inferred from the stored meaning. It is important to note that the simultaneous truth of (67a) and (68a) is based on nonlinguistic considerations. The information creating the inferential relationship between those sentences is not information about noun phrases and clauses, but about spatial relationships and turtles and logs and fish. At the level of sentence memory the hearer brings all his knowledge of the world to bear in constructing a representation for the presented sentence.

Offir (1973) has shown, in a similar experimental paradigm, that presuppositional information (see Chapter 4) is also part of the memory representation of a sentence. She did this by showing that sentences that differ structurally will be distinct in memory if they differ in their presuppositions. Sentences that differ structurally but do not alter presuppositions will tend to be judged as nondistinct. For example, subjects in Offir's experiment would tend to confuse (69) and (70) in memory, but not (71) and (72).

(69) A Sioux Indian he befriended represented the Chief.
(70) He befriended a Sioux Indian who represented the Chief.
(71) That Sioux Indian he befriended represented the Chief.
(72) He befriended that Sioux Indian who represented the Chief.

Notice that neither (69) nor (70) contain any presuppositions. Hence they are perfect paraphrases of each other and lose their distinctiveness in memory. Sentences (71) and (72) make the same assertion in the sense that they describe the same event, but they differ in their presuppositions. In (71) the use of the determiner 'that' rather than 'a' presupposes that 'he' had befriended a Sioux Indian. The sentence tells the hearer something else about the Indian (that he represented the Chief). In (72) the determiner 'that' carries the presupposition that some Sioux Indian represented the Chief; the sentence tells the hearer something about that Sioux Indian— that 'he' befriended the Indian. These sentences do not lose their distinctiveness in memory and are not confused in recall. Offir argues that these data support the hypothesis that the presuppositional information associated with a sentence becomes part of its representation in memory.

It is crucial to determine whether the memory representation of the sentence, enriched as it is by inferences based on knowledge of the world, actually constitutes the output of the SPS. Alternatively, it could be that the output of the SPS is what we have called a basic meaning, based solely on the linguistic facts about the utterance (i.e., the meanings of individual words and the relationships among them), and that the basic meaning is enriched during storage with inferences and integration of information contained in other basic meanings. While it will take a great deal of careful research to demonstrate that one of these hypotheses is correct, a study by C. Jenkins (1971) supports the latter interpretation.

Jenkins attempted to demonstrate the immediate distinctiveness of sentences such as (67a) and (68a). He wanted to show that immediate comprehension processes did not involve the addition of inferred information. He did this by asking a question—(73)—after the presentation of (67a) or (68a).

(73) Did the fish swim beneath the turtles?

The correct answer in either case is yes, but the truth of (73) is based on the basic meaning of (68a), but on the inferred meaning of (67a). What interested Jenkins was the speed with which subjects answered yes. He hypothesized that if the representations of the two original sentences were distinct, then subjects should take longer to answer yes having heard (67a) than having heard (68a), because in the former case they would have to make the inference before answering. On the other hand, if the sentences were not distinct—if the inference had already been made during immediate comprehension—it should take the same amount of time to answer yes having heard either (67a) or (68a). Jenkins showed that immediately after presentation of the sentence it takes longer to answer yes to (73) if the subject had heard (67a) and not (68a), but a few seconds later there was no difference in the time required to answer yes. Jenkins argues (and we agree) that this provides strong evidence for the hypothesis that there are actually two representations of meaning available for each sentence, one a basic meaning derived by immediate-comprehension processes, the other an enriched meaning resulting from inference and/or integration as a sentence is stored in memory.

7.6
The Language-Comprehension System and Linguistic Competence

The LCS emerges as an immensely complex network of processing stages and memory systems. Its access to enormous amounts of stored information allows it to process incoming information with remarkable speed. Much of the information that is important for pairing sound with meaning is transient. Like the auditory information that is lost after it has been recoded as perceptual information, lexical and syntactic information is lost after it has been recoded semantically (perhaps twice).

In this chapter we have tried to introduce only those mechanisms for which there is some experimental evidence. We certainly anticipate that a complete model of the LCS will include many more sophisticated operations such as feedback systems among the levels and parallel processing capabilities, about which we could only speculate at this time. (For an idea of the complexity of such a system see Hunt, 1971.)

The largest gap in our understanding of the LCS seems to be our inability even to speculate about the interface between psychological processes and internalized linguistic knowledge. The grammar provides a formal mapping of deep structures with surface structures via T rules. The LCS that is confronted with an utterance must infer what surface structure and deep structure underly it. In order for the LCS to accomplish such a task not only must it have a rich array of cognitive strategies to facilitate the inferential process, it must also have some representation of the constraints on possible deep-structure–surface-structure pairs. The grammar of a language provides just this sort of information in that it provides rules that describe an infinite number of such pairs. But there is no existing evidence that grammatical rules are represented in the brain as they are represented in the linguist's notebook. We must therefore assume that this information is represented in the brain in a neural notation that we are not likely to decipher in the foreseeable future.

7.7
The Relationship between Linguistic Competence and Linguistic Performance

Throughout this book we have been concerned with the relationship between competence and performance. It seems clear that the language-production system as well as the language-comprehension system must have access to the information represented by the grammar. Put differently, these systems must make use of internalized linguistic knowledge if they are to produce understandable utterances, on the one hand, and assign meanings to utterances, on the other. Thus we have shown that while the grammar must not be taken as a theory about psychological states during sentence production or comprehension, the performance operations are dependent on competence.

It is interesting to ask if there is *mutual* dependence between the two systems: is there any sense in which the grammar can be said to depend upon performance operations? A number of linguists (Bever and Langendoen, 1972; Langendoen and Bever, 1973) have suggested that in fact the structure of some rules may be determined by comprehension strategies. Consider the fact that the relative-clause reduction transformation may be applied to (74) to produce (75) but may not be applied to (76) to produce (77) (see section 3.61).

(74)   The girl that John loved passed her comps.
(75)   The girl John loved passed her comps.
(76)   The girl that loved John passed her comps.
(77)   *The girl loved John passed her comps.

It has been suggested that this rule is blocked from application just because the immediate segmentation strategy of the LCS would lead to segmentation of the sentence after 'John', rendering the final portion of the sentence unanalyzable. All such sentences would be as difficult to process as 'The horse raced past the barn fell', which would clearly mean that English would be a difficult language to process.

Performance strategies can account for some restrictions on complementizer deletion in English, too. Note that 'that' can be deleted in (78) to produce (79) but not in (80) to produce (81).

(78)   It was evident that the giraffe was tired.
(79)   It was evident the giraffe was tired.
(80)   That the giraffe was tired was evident.
(81)   *The giraffe was tired was evident.

This prohibition may come from the requirement by the LCS that subordinate clauses be marked if they occur in sentence-initial position. Recall that Jarvella's data in section 7.61 indicated that subordinate clauses are processed differently from coordinate clauses. It may well be that the LCS needs to know in advance whether the clause it is processing is in fact subordinate or not. Clearly, the presence of 'that' in (80) blocks immediate segmentation, which seems to be the basic cause of difficulty in the processing of (81).

A great deal of research will be required to support the hypothesis that the form of grammars is to some extent dependent on comprehension strategies. Relevant research will be that which reveals properties of the performance system as well as that which reveals grammatical constraints that may be dependent on such properties. Clearly, production strategies as well as comprehension strategies will be relevant.

Another sense in which theories of competence may be dependent on theories of performance is that performance constraints may account for the unacceptability of sentences that cannot be ruled out by the grammar. Consider the relative acceptability of (82) and (83).

(82) Betty looked the address up.
(83) Betty looked the address of the man she had met in New York when she was attending a meeting of the Acoustical Society of America up.

It is obvious that (82) is a better sentence than (83) in some significant sense. It is also clear that the unacceptability of (83) is due to the "heaviness" of the noun phrase intervening between the verb 'looked' and the particle 'up.' Sentences (84) and (85) are equally acceptable.

(84) Betty looked up the address.
(85) Betty looked up the address of the man she had met in New York when she was attending a meeting of the Acoustical Society of America.

The only way to prevent the grammar of English from generating sentences such as (83) would be to write a constraint into the particle movement transformation that would allow it to apply only when the noun phrase around which the particle is moved is sufficiently "nonheavy." In the current formulation of transformational-generative grammar there is no way to formulate the notion of heaviness as a formal constraint on transformational operations. To modify the metatheory to allow such a formulation would result in a metatheory that generates a far larger class of grammars than does the current extended standard theory. As we explained in Chapter 4, the goal of linguistic theorists should be to further constrain the metatheory, not to increase its generative capacity. We are left with a paradox in that the grammar must be allowed to generate sentences such as (83), which are clearly not acceptable English sentences.

It seems obvious that the source of the difficulty in (83) is that it puts too great a load on short-term memory during the syntactic-processing stage of comprehension. An enormous amount of information must be held in working memory until the verb particle 'up' is received by the LCS. It is reasonable, then, to rule out such sentences on performance grounds—to disallow them by appeal to performance theory—and not to complicate the metatheory to such an extent that (83) would be ungenerable by the grammar of English. Such a theoretical move acknowledges the interdependence of competence theory and performance theory in the construction of a complete theory of linguistic activity.

As we move to the question of how the child learns his native language, we shall see that the boundary between competence and performance becomes similarly fuzzy. Language acquisition provides an excellent arena for the observation of the subtle interplay of competence and performance.

SUGGESTIONS FOR FURTHER READING

The following books deal primarily with adult psycholinguistics:

D'Arcais, G. B. F., and Levelt, W. J. M. (eds.). *Advances in Psycholinguistics.* New York: American Elsevier, 1970.

Fodor, J. A., Bever, T. G., and Garrett, M. *The Psychology of Language.* New York: McGraw-Hill, 1974.

Greene, J. *Psycholinguistics.* Baltimore, Md.: Penguin, 1972.

Slobin, D. I. *Psycholinguistics.* Glenview, Ill: Scott, Foresman, 1971.

The following journals publish reports of research in the areas of adult psycholinguistics:

Cognition
Cognitive Psychology
Journal of Experimental Psychology
Journal of Psycholinguistic Research
Journal of Verbal Learning and Verbal Behavior
Memory and Cognition
Perception and Psychophysics

The Child's Acquisition
of Language

Up to this point we have dealt exclusively with linguistic abilities and capacities of adult human beings; with the structure of the adult's linguistic competence; and with the psychological processes by which adults produce, perceive, and understand spoken messages. Behind the discussion of each point has been the question, implicit or explicit, How did adults ever develop such abilities? Babies are not born producing and understanding sentences, yet adults possess remarkably complex psychological systems for dealing with speech. Obviously something happens between infancy and adulthood. The question is, What? It is only fair at the outset to tell you that we do not know. There is as yet no satisfactory theory to account for this important developmental achievement. Of course, we do not know how children acquire the ability to think or how their personalities develop, either. The development of linguistic abilities occurs within the general context of the child's conceptual and intellectual development. Understanding the language-acquisition process will provide insight into the child's overall cognitive development; on the other hand, a complete understanding of the acquisition of language must await a more thorough understanding of general cognitive development.

Since the early 1960s an enormous amount of theoretical and empirical work has been done in the area of language acquisition. It would be far beyond the scope of this book to attempt a comprehensive review of all this research. Such an effort would require (at least) another book to be done properly. In fact, a number of excellent books exist that deal with the entire field of language acquisition. Our goal here is considerably more modest. We shall present some of the central questions on the subject of language acquisition and sketch the linguistic (production) stages through which most children pass as they acquire their native language. We shall also characterize the major theories that have been developed to account for language development and shall present some representative empirical studies as we go along.

There are two preliminary questions of crucial significance that must be considered in approaching the study of language acquisition: What is acquired? What cognitive (or linguistic) abilities is the child born with? We will consider these questions in turn.

8.1
What Is Acquired?

The child learns a language—what do we mean by that? It is conceptually useful to formulate the answer to this question in terms of the competence/ performance dichotomy we have developed during the course of this book. The child develops linguistic competence in that he develops an internal representation of the grammar of his language that eventually allows him to make the kinds of linguistic judgments an adult can make—judgments about grammaticality, ambiguity, paraphrase, and so on.

As the child develops linguistic competence, he also develops linguistic performance abilities, which allow him to encode his own thoughts into understandable utterances and to decode the speech of others so that he achieves some level of understanding. The issue of comprehension of language by the child is complicated, because one must attempt to unravel those factors that are linguistic in origin and those that are conceptual. Consider the following sentences:

(1) The girl was hit by the boy.
(2) Two is the square root of four.
(3) James is the name of the dog.

A child of about three years would not understand either (1) or (2), but for quite different reasons. As is discussed later in this chapter, research has revealed that children of this age cannot understand certain sentences in the passive voice. Since they can understand the active voice ('the boy hit the girl'), we explain their inability to understand passives as resulting from a purely linguistic factor—the inability to decode sentences that have undergone the passive transformation. The origin of the three-year-old's inability to understand (2) is of course completely different. His number concepts are limited to simple counting. Not only does he not know what a square root is, he is incapable of assimilating a definition. Syntax is not the problem with (2), since its structure is similar to the completely comprehensible (3). Sentence (2) is incomprehensible for conceptual reasons. This seems quite straightforward, but it is necessary to keep the distinction between linguistic processing and extralinguistic knowledge in mind when either doing or evaluating research in language comprehension and acquisition.

It is also important to remember that the child is developing perceptual and comprehension strategies that have very little relationship to formal linguistic structure. Pursuing the example of the passive a bit further, the child who cannot understand (1) because his linguistic competence does not yet include knowledge of the passive transformation in fine detail might be able to understand (4), which is also in the passive voice.

(4) The ice cream cone was eaten by the girl.

The child can correctly intepret such a sentence despite the lack of full competence with its syntax because children of age three know enough about the world to know that ice cream cones do not eat girls, so there is only one set of grammatical relations that is possible unless the sentence is semantically anomalous. It is not at all surprising to discover that children use their knowledge about the world (and, as we shall see later, about regularities in their language) to form strategies for figuring out what sentences mean before they have developed the competence to assign complete structural analyses to them. In fact a moment's reflection will convince us that it must be this way. How could children ever develop a formal system of knowledge relating sound to meaning if they did not have some way of identifying meaning independently of the formal system? Thus children develop performance skills as well as formal grammatical knowledge. The trick for the theorists and the experimentalists is to figure out ways to assess one independently of the other and to account for the way in which they relate to each other.

8.2
The Innateness Hypothesis

If an organism is born with an ability, it is meaningless to investigate its development unless we are embryologists. Human babies, for instance, are born with vision. This ability is part of being human (baby clams cannot see) and is not an acquired ability. Therefore, it is not an interesting question to ask how a child learns to see or how the child acquires vision.[1] It is, however, interesting to ask how a child learns to read (a visual activity), for no one naturally develops the ability to read. Everyone must be taught, although it is unquestionably true that only humans can learn.

There are abilities that are intermediary between seeing and reading. Walking, for instance, is an ability that is not present at birth but naturally develops as a child grows. All normal humans acquire the ability to walk without special instruction. While we use the term 'learn to walk' it is a different kind of 'learn' from the 'learn' in 'learn to read'. The inability to learn (in this case to develop the ability) spontaneously to walk, is a sign

---

[1] We refer here to vision as sensation, with which we assume the child is born. There are many fascinating questions about how the child learns to perceive objects in his environment, to recognize faces, to coordinate vision with motor skills, and so on.

of pathology in humans. This is not so for reading; if one is not taught to read, one is not expected to learn to read. Humans seem to be born with physical capacities that make it natural for them to walk but not necessarily to read and write. In this chapter we are not interested in walking or reading but in the production, perception, and comprehension of spoken language. Although babies are not born knowing a language (as they are born being able to see), they are born with a predisposition to develop a language in much the same way they are born with a predisposition to learn to walk. No language is present at birth, so it is possible to study linguistic development, just as it was possible to study the development of walking. Like the ability to walk, the ability to speak and understand spoken language seems to be a natural human activity.

The idea that human babies are somehow predisposed to acquire a language is called the **innateness hypothesis** ("innate" means inborn). This hypothesis states that there are aspects of linguistic organization that are basic to the human brain and that make it possible for human children to acquire linguistic competence in all its complexity with little or no instruction from family and friends. While children would certainly not learn a language if they did not hear speech, it is no more necessary to teach babies to talk than it is to teach them to walk.

It is necesary to clarify the innateness hypothesis because it has been greatly misunderstood and abused since it was revived by Chomsky in the late 1950s. The child is said to be born with a knowledge of Language. Put differently, his cognitive system is such that he is predisposed to develop a grammar that will incorporate all the linguistic universals. The common features of human Language are assumed to be determined by the unique properties of the human brain and cognitive system, so any creature who is born with a human brain is necessarily born with a cognitive system that is predisposed to develop those universals. The innateness hypothesis, then, is inseparable from a theory of Language that recognizes and attempts to discover universal features of human Language.

When the idea that the child is born with all the linguistic universals was first introduced, it was taken rather literally. David McNeill (1966), for example, suggested that infants are born with a hierarchy of linguistic categories—such as sentence, noun phrase, verb phrase, and the basic grammatical relations. One problem with this literal interpretation of the innateness hypothesis is that it tends to cut off research into the development of linguistic categories and grammatical relations. As we said above, it is not interesting to study the development of something the child is born with (i.e., something that does not develop but is just there). So there is a very real danger that in postulating innate linguistic structures theorists will reduce the probability that important research will be done to discover more basic structures and processes underlying the linguistic structures.

Another problem with a literal interpretation of the innateness hypothesis is that it makes linguistic knowledge seem qualitatively different from other kinds of cognition rather than intimately related to all forms of human intelligence. It could be true that linguistic knowledge is a unique type of human cognition, but such a suggestion should be put forth in the form of a hypothesis, not in the form of an assumption.

An alternative to the strong innateness position of McNeill was presented by Fodor (1966), who suggested that linguistic universals are intrinsic in the child rather than innate. By this he meant that there was something in the structure of the human brain that would lead it to develop a formal system of linguistic descriptions that would incorporate all universal properties of Language. This theoretical approach seems eminently reasonable to the cognitive psycholinguist, who believes that humans have unique language-learning capabilities but who does not want to stifle research into the basis of those capabilities.

There is abundant evidence that some sort of innate predisposition does exist. The mere fact that languages exhibit universal properties is one line of evidence. Another is the observation that children all go through similar sequences or stages of language acquisition (much like the stages of the development of walking), although these sequences are completely independent of the child's linguistic environment.

The child would never learn a language were he not reared in a language-using environment, but when he learns a language, he learns a great deal more than is available to him through his environment alone. Language learning, like the production, perception, and comprehension of language, is constructive, and the child (like the adult) uses both external and internal information to accomplish this task. Developmental psycholinguists are anxious to be able to characterize the nature of this internal information because only then will we know which cognitive and linguistic abilities are in fact innate.

We feel that Slobin's theory, sketched at the end of this chapter, offers great promise for development into a comprehensive theory of language development. At the very least this theory demonstrates the feasibility of an explanation that acknowledges the intrinsic linguistic capabilities of the human mind and goes on to account for them by hypotheses about general characteristics of human conceptual development and general principles by which the child organizes linguistic input.

Before we move on to a sketch of the linguistic and psycholinguistic development of the child, let us revisit the behaviorists, and see what kind of an account of language learning empiricist epistemology leads them to.

8.3
The Behaviorists' Hypothesis

Recall that in Chapter 5 we emphasized that the epistemology of empiricism has two components. First, there is the belief that mankind (in this case scientists) cannot know anything that is not observable, hence must construct theories whose elements are either observable events or direct reductions of observable events. Second, there is the epistemology as applied to the individual that says that an individual's personal knowledge can be no more than an integrated summation of all his experience—that is, the *individual* cannot know anything he has not observed. We have already shown that transformational-generative grammar contradicts empiricist epistemology on the first count because it is a theory that has as its elements abstract unobservable constructs. Now we come to the clash between empiricism and transformational-generative grammar (and cognitive psycholinguistics) on the issue of the development of the personal knowledge of the individual, of which linguistic knowledge is a central component.

The behaviorists' analog of the innateness hypothesis is the **tabula rasa, or blank slate, hypothesis.** In its strongest form this hypothesis says that at birth the infant's mind is a blank slate to be written on by experience. Early empiricists, such as John Locke (who first advanced this hypothesis), and behaviorists, such as John Watson, took this hypothesis quite literally with reference not only to Language but to all aspects of the psychological, social, and intellectual development of the individual. Today even quite radical behaviorists acknowledge that humans speak and that other creatures do not, so there is some kind of species-specific character to this ability. However, for them, this is like agreeing that birds have wings and feathers and bunnies have long ears and fur. The important point is that the behaviorist view of language learning is that all the internal linguistic knowledge of the individual is the direct result of integration of the linguistic events that the individual has observed.

Let us compare the innateness and the tabula rasa hypotheses. It is incorrect to say that the former denies the importance of the linguistic environment while the latter denies any role of inheritance within the species. Both hypotheses acknowledge the existence of both factors, although the tabula rasa hypothesis attributes virtually no theoretical importance to the fact that only humans possess Language. We do not want to create the image of two strong hypotheses being modified so they are more and more compatible with each other, however. These two hypotheses and the accounts of language learning compatible with each are fundamentally and qualitatively different. They cannot both be true.

The behaviorist assumption is that linguistic knowledge consists of chains of associations, so behavioristic accounts of language learning offer an explanation of how these chains are formed. In Chapter 5 we mentioned three principal means for building associations: classical conditioning, operant conditioning, and mediation. Of these three the latter two (slightly modified) have been developed as theories of language learning. (A Mowrer-like account of the development of meaning by classical conditioning (Chapter 5) could, of course, easily be extended to the child.)

The language-learning theory most closely related to operant conditioning states that the language behavior of the individual is shaped by sequences of differential rewards in his environment. This theoretical account claims that as babies babble, they produce all the sounds of all the languages of the world. A baby's parents, however, reward only sounds that are present in the native language of the household, and the baby becomes conditioned to produce only those speech sounds that have been rewarded. The sounds are combined into words—some accidentally by children, others by their imitation of adult utterances—and "correct" words gain rewards, while incorrect words do not. Thus a child's speech proceeds step by step . . . sounds, words, then short phrases (which are rewarded if grammatically correct) are combined to make whole sentences. Thus, the complex verbal behavior of the child (and ultimately of the adult) is seen as a huge set of response chains, constructed unwittingly by proud parents who know a language and are anxious for their children to learn the language of the community.

The mediation account of language acquisition, associated with Braine (1963), is essentially similar to the mediational account of linguistic structure developed by Jenkins (presented in some detail in Chapter 5). Braine's theory, known as **contextual generalization,** attempts to account for the development of simple, active, affirmative declarative sentences by the child. This is assumed to take place by Jenkins-type form class generalization and chaining. The difficulties with this theory have been pointed out by Bever, Fodor, and Weksel (1965) and answered by Braine (1965).

Contrasting operant and mediation theories, we see that Braine's theory has the distinct advantage of not relying on either imitation or reward to account for language learning. Its disadvantage, however, is that it only addresses simple, active, affirmative declarative sentences and does not postulate general processes powerful enough to account for the learning of complex sentences or transformations. The operant-type theory is by far the most well-known learning theory or stimulus-response theory of language learning. There are a number of variations on the central theme that we have sketched. Some accounts, for instance, try to adduce a kind of self-reinforcement to substitute for reward by the parent or by the linguistic community. While it is not the primary purpose of this chapter to develop an elaborate argument against stimulus-response theories of learning, we will note throughout the chapter facts about language acquisition that falsify such theories. (For the reader who is interested in polemics against stimulus-response theories of Language and language acquisition we recommend Fodor, Bever, and Weksel (1965), McNeill (1970), Slobin (1971a), and Chomsky (1959), to name but a few sources.) The most devastating argument against any stimulus-response theory of language learning is not to be found in facts about a child's acquisition of language, however; it is to be found in a description of Language itself. If Language is as the transformational-generative linguist says it is, then it cannot be described as associative chains; therefore it cannot be learned by principles of association. Thus the major arguments against a behaviorist account of language acquisition are in fact all the arguments in favor of a generative account of linguistic analysis.

We now turn to a brief description of the stages through which the child progresses in his development of language. These stages will serve as a broad outline that will be filled in throughout the remainder of the chapter by specific descriptions of phonological, syntactic, and semantic development. Finally, we will describe a most promising theory of cognitive and linguistic development.

8.4

Stages of Linguistic Development

All observers have noted that language development proceeds in a stage-like pattern. This means that a child's linguistic performance will remain essentially constant for a period of time (say a month or two), then will undergo a relatively sudden qualitative change. The alternative to this sort of development would be a gradual developmental pattern, which would result in the child's linguistic development progressing at a steady rate, improving a bit every day. (Behaviorist learning theory would predict incremental development.) It is much more accurate to describe language development as in stages, rather than incremental, but this does not mean that the stages do not overlap. They certainly do. Just as we can say that a baby is in a crawling stage, then a walking stage, we say that a baby is in a one-word stage followed by a two-word stage. Of course, babies continue to crawl even after they learn to take a few steps; walking gradually overtakes crawling, but the stages overlap. It is the same with the one-word and two-word stages of development. Children continue to use one-word-utterances after they have developed the skill to use two-word utterances, but the one-word utterances diminish in frequency.

The numbering of the stages of linguistic development is quite arbitrary and varies from author to author. When comparing written accounts of acquisition stages, the student should concentrate on the characterization of the various stages rather than on the numbering system of each author. We have decided not to number the two prelinguistic stages.

8.41 First (prelinguistic) babbling stage

In the first babbling stage, during the early months of life, babies cry, coo, gurgle, squeal, and laugh. They seem to produce every conceivable kind of noise. Many observers have characterized this as a stage when a baby produces all the speech sounds to be found in all the world's languages. It is interesting that a baby's productions should be characterized in this manner, but the characterization is probably not factually correct—especially in the case of very complicated consonants. In any case the important point is that the sounds of tiny babies are not linguistically organized utterances based on phonemic and phonetic organization. They are not speech sounds; they are acoustic signals generated by the babies as they move their articulators in every possible configuration. They "play" with their vocal tracts, just as they play with their arms and legs, but their babblings should not be characterized as linguistic performance. It is interesting to note that even profoundly deaf infants proceed rather normally through this initial stage.

8.42 Second (prelinguistic) babbling stage (the nonsense word stage)

The onset of the second babbling stage is usually early in the second half of the first year of life. Children do not produce any recognizable words, but they do seem to be organizing their utterances according to syllabic patterning. Many of the exotic chirps and vowel-like "coos" disappear from the infants' output, and they begin producing consonant(usually stop)-vowel sequences, with one syllable frequently repeated over and over again. While children cannot be said to be using language in any true sense, their production at this time seems much closer to speech than it did in the first babbling stage. An interesting characteristic of the babbling of this period is that it is frequently produced with sentence intonation, sometimes with falling pitch like a declarative English sentence, sometimes with the rising pitch associated with questions. One might ask whether the children associate any meaning to these speechlike babbles. Frequently in the presence of such children, one feels that they are trying to tell us something. It is meaningless to ask whether the sounds of this stage are paired with meaning, however, because it is impossible to think of any investigation we could carry out to answer that question. It does seem to be the case that auditory feedback is necessary to maintain vocalization during this period, because profoundly deaf children babble less and less and finally fall silent during this age period.

Sometime in the latter part of this period (around the end of the first year of life) the "first word" occurs. Usually it will not sound any more like an adult word than many of the babbles the baby has been producing during this stage, but it will count as the first word because it clearly has a meaning associated with it. Our baby, for instance, said [læ] and pointed to the chandelier, to the lamp, to a flashlight, to the car's headlights, even to the wall switch. We accepted [læ] as a word not because it sounded more like a word than his other utterances, but because it was obviously sound paired with meaning (in this case 'light'), and that is what speech —and language—is all about.

8.43 Stage I: (First linguistic stage)   The holophrastic stage

This is the one-word stage, which begins around the age of a year. It is at this point, however, that the stages of linguistic development cease to be related reliably to age. While all normal infants go through the two bab-bling stages during their first year and begin the holophrastic stage during the first half of the second year, there is a great deal of variability in the duration of Stage I for normal children. Some children are still holophrastic by the age of two; others progress much more rapidly. There is little re-lationship between speed of language development and degree of intelli-gence in normal children. Of course, retarded children are usually retarded in every form of development, and gifted children are usually precocious in both verbal and motor development. There are famous exceptions to this, however; it is said that Albert Einstein did not speak until he was three.

The one-word utterances of this period are called holophrases because the child expresses the meaning of an entire phrase, or sentence, in the one word which he utters. Thus the child who says 'milk' may mean that he wants some milk or he may be announcing that he has some milk or he may be reporting that he just spilled his milk. There is a great deal of ambiguity in a child's speech during this stage and the next. It is fre-quently necessary to observe what the child is doing in order to figure out what he means by what he is saying.

8.44 Stage II: Two-word utterances

The second linguistic stage usually begins near the second birthday, but as we said, there is a great deal of individual variation among normal children. The child enters this stage by first uttering two holophrases in rapid succession. For instance, the child who uses the holophrases 'baby' and 'car' may point to a toy car and say 'baby', followed by a slight pause, and then 'car'. The meaning will appear to be that of the possessive 'baby car', but the child has definitely used two holophrases to express that mean-ing. Very soon after this the child will begin to use two-word utterances such as 'baby dress', 'doll fall', 'no shoe', and so on.

It is interesting to note that during the two-word period children use no inflections. Their verbs have no tense or number markers; their nouns have no plural endings. While individual vocabularies differ greatly, children at this age very rarely use prepositions, articles, and conjunctions (called function words). Pronouns are not common (except the first person) and are frequently in the objective case. Thus many children say 'me' rather than 'I'. 'Her', 'him', and 'them', while rare, are more likely than 'she', 'he', and 'they'. Later in this chapter (in section 9.621) we shall examine both the structure and the meaning underlying these early utterances.

8.45 Stage III: Developing grammar

The age at which a child moves out of Stage II varies greatly. Some chil-dren are well into Stage III by the age of two, others will still be using two-word utterances almost exclusively until beyond their third birthday.

During Stage III children develop many grammatical devices. The length of their sentences increases, but this is of less importance as their utterances become more complex. Past tenses, plurals, and some function words emerge, but many are still omitted. This stage is primarily concerned with the development of grammatical devices that occur in single sentences. The negative and question forms are refined but not perfected during this stage. The child's speech at this period has been described as telegraphic because the omission of function words makes children's utterances sound like the telegrams adults write. They produce utterances like 'Put dolly table' and 'There Mommy shoe'. It is probably misleading to characterize children's language as telegraphic, however, because it seems to imply that a child's sentences are edited as are an adult's in a telegram. Instead, it is best to view children's speech as gradually increasing in number and types of words used as maturation progresses.

8.46 Stage IV: Near-adult grammar

In Stage IV children begin to use more complicated grammatical structures, many of which involve the combination of simple sentences by complementation, relativization, and conjunction. Limber (1973) reports the development of complex sentences in three children between the ages of two and three. The first complex constructions involved complements functioning as the object NP, such as 'I see you sit down', but there was not one single instance of a complement serving as the subject NP before the age of three. Second, but far less frequent, Limber observed relative clauses modifying object nouns, as 'I show you the ball that I got'. However, he never observed a relative clause following a subject NP. It is reasonable to speculate that neither complementation nor relativization follows the subject NP in the child's early complex sentences because to produce them would break the continuity of the main sentence, imposing a heavier load on short-term memory and making the planning of the utterance more complex.

Very difficult constructions like the subjunctive ('I wish we were going swimming today') and tag questions ('You are coming, aren't you?') have yet to emerge, and the child still makes many "mistakes" from the point of view of adult grammar. However, the emergence of complex sentences signals a qualitative improvement in the child's linguistic abilities. Limber quotes Leopold (1949) who did a classic study of his own child, as saying that "... with the mastery of complex sentences, the linguistic development has reached the last stage. In the future only refinements can be expected." (Leopold, 1949, vol. 4, p. 37).

The "refinements" required by the child at this period include learning many exceptions to syntactic and phonological regularities in the language. Carol Chomsky (1969) reports a series of studies showing that fine details of linguistic structure are still developing in children between the ages of five and ten.

8.47 Stage V: Full competence

By late childhood everyone who is not handicapped in some way has learned all the syntactic devices of his native language and sufficient performance skills to understand and produce ordinary language. Naturally one's vocabulary continues to grow throughout adulthood and one's lan-language changes in style and (hopefully) increases in eloquence beyond late childhood. There is, however, no evidence that syntactic competence or performance skills undergo any further alteration beyond puberty.

This concludes our brief overview of the developmental stages through which children pass. We have presented these as a broad outline to be filled in as we discuss the empirical and theoretical developments in the field of language acquisition. It happens that most of the work in this field has been concerned with early language development, up to and including Stage III (Developing Grammar). Little systematic research has been reported for the later stages. We now turn to a consideration of the phonological, phonetic, and perceptual aspects of the child's linguistic development. This section will be followed by a discussion of syntactic and semantic development and a consideration of the major theories that have been advanced in this area.

8.5
Perceptual, Phonetic, and Phonological Development

One aspect of the acquisition of linguistic competence is the child's learning of the sound pattern of his language. This task includes three components: (1) development of an inventory of the phonemic distinctions employed by the native language; (2) acquisition of the skill to articulate the speech sounds required by the native language; and (3) construction of internal representations of the phonological rules describing the sound pattern of the native language.

8.51 Perceptual development

In Chapter 6 we demonstrated that the perception of speech is determined both by the acoustic speech signal and by the hearer's knowledge of his language. Furthermore, we saw that the perception of speech is different from the perception of other acoustic stimuli precisely because it is based on internalized knowledge.

The question that comes immediately to mind is, How will a person who has not yet acquired knowledge of a particular language perceive a speech signal? On the tabula rasa view, the infant has no internalized linguistic information and therefore should perceive speech as the adult perceives nonspeech stimuli. His perceptions depend completely on the stimulus, or external information, whereas the adult's depend on both internal and external information. On this view we would not expect infants to perceive the first segments of [du] and [gu] as quite different, while perceiving the initial segments of [du] and [di] as the same. (See section 6.26 for a full discussion of the acoustic and perceptual properties of these syllables.) Another prediction from this hypothesis is that infants do not perceive speech categorically, as do adult speakers. The categorical perception of speech sounds is based on the phonemic categories defined by the phonology of the language. Recall the differential perception of Thai and English speakers (see section 6.261). Those perceptual differences are determined by phonemic differences in the two languages. A newborn baby, however, has learned no language. If phonemic categories must be learned, then the newborn should have none. A second hypothesis is related to the innateness hypothesis. We assume that babies' brains are not blank tablets but contain specialized language-learning systems with potential structural "knowledge" of the universal features of Language. The existence of phonemic distinctions is common to all languages, and it is believed that the categorical perception of speech sounds (especially stop consonants) is universal to the species. Therefore, the innateness hypothesis would predict that infants would be born with some specialized perceptual abilities to enable them immediately to begin perceiving speech in that special way in which speech is perceived by human beings.

Research in infant speech perception is sparse, primarily because of the immense difficulty of working with tiny babies as subjects. The evidence that does exist points clearly to support for the innateness hypothesis. A study by Eimas, Siqueland, Jusczyk, and Vigorito (1971) demonstrates that babies perceived speech categorically. Their perception of differences between pairs of stimuli differentiated by voice onset time (see section 6.261) was greater if the pair straddled a phoneme boundary than if it did not. In fact VOT differences within phoneme categories were not perceived as different by the one- and four-month-old babies of that study. Further research by Eimas and his colleagues has replicated these findings (Eimas, in press). This group has also obtained data that demonstrate the categorical perception of syllables with varying second formant transitions, simulating the labial and alveolar points of articulation. These experiments measure the discriminability of various stimuli for the infants by measuring the rate at which they suck pacifiers in response to a stimulus. It is possible to identify a stimulus which is novel to a baby because he will suck with greater frequency in response to a novel stimulus than to one to which he has become adapted. Clearly more research is required before we can make any definite statements about the exact nature of the infant's speech-perception system. Even the most conservative present assessment, however, leads to the conclusion that human infants are born with special perceptual capabilities that are related to the later development of linguistic knowledge and linguistic skills. Notice that we have been very careful to say that the infant "knows" that one speech signal is a [p] and another is a [b]. We would deny such an interpretation of Eimas et al.'s work. The infant's perception of speech stimuli provides a perfect example of intrinsic, as opposed to strictly innate, linguistic knowledge. The child learns phonological categories as he learns his language, but his specialized perceptual response to speech stimuli enables him to make the initial distinctions on which that knowledge must be based.

There is further evidence that even newborn infants respond uniquely to the organized pattern of adult speech. Condon and Sander (1971) report that studies of small rhythmic muscular movements (known as micro-kinesis) of infants have shown that the babies move in synchrony with the articulatory segments of adult speech in the immediate environment (either tape recorded or spoken by an adult near the baby). Further data of this type should demonstrate that the infant is attuned to human speech in a fascinating variety of unexpected ways.

8.52 Phonetic development

By phonetic development we mean the actual ability to articulate speech sounds in the child's language. A characteristic of "baby talk" is the mis-articulation of certain sounds and groups of sounds, but in the normal child this is not accompanied by inability to discriminate and perceive the correct articulation of those sounds. Thus children who say [gwɛs] for [drɛs] will not accept [gwɛs] from their mothers and fathers. A source of amusement for adults is the child who insists "Don't say [gwɛs], say [gwɛs]!" seemingly unaware that he has failed to produce the correct distinction. If children have the ability to discriminate and perceive but not produce speech sounds, we assume that their difficulty is simply a result of a lack of articulatory control. The difficulty does not reflect an immature linguistic competence: children have a systematic phonetic representation that allows them to distinguish between [drɛs] and [gwɛs]. Their articulatory mechanisms are simply not cooperative when they are given instructions. The same may be true of older children with speech impediments if they can discriminate, perceive, but not produce certain speech sounds.

Because articulation development reflects neither the development of competence in any clear manner nor the development of performance capabilities such as perception and discrimination, we shall not devote space to the discussion of articulation development. There is a very large literature in this area (see Irwin, 1947; Snow, 1963; Menyuk, 1971, for an excellent review; also Cairns and Williams, 1972), which should be of particular interest to the student of speech and language pathology.

In general the earliest speech of children (we are speaking now of Stage

I speech) consists of consonant–vowel alternations. While they produce all the vowels of the language (although not necessarily the right ones at the right times), they typically do not produce complex consonants, such as the affricates [č] and [j]. They frequently do not produce initial clusters of consonants until quite late. Thus 'spring' will be pronounced first as [pɪŋ], then later [prɪŋ] or perhaps [pwɪŋ]. Some cluster-reduction devices are similar for most children; in [s]+stop clusters, for instance, the [s] is almost always omitted, producing [kul] for [skul], [pun] for [spun], and so on. Others are idiosyncratic. We know a child who invariably substitutes [f] for the [sw] cluster, pronouncing [fɪm] for [swɪm] and [fiyt] for [swiyt]. Many children reduce this cluster by omitting the [w] instead. A fairly general expectation seems to be that an [s] will be omitted if it precedes a stop, as in 'school', but will be retained if it precedes a liquid or glide—many children produce [sɪp] for [slɪp] but [kɪl] for [skɪl].

Some speech sounds frequently give children trouble in the early years. The nonstrident dental fricatives [θ] and [ð] present problems and are substituted for by a number of other "easier" phones, such as [f], [t], [d], even [s]. There are two reasons why these speech sounds are difficult: first, they are produced with the tip of the tongue, and lingual sounds are typically more difficult than nonlingual ones; second, they require the maintenance of a very slight opening—not wide open like a vowel, nor completely closed like a stop. An additional difficulty is that these are mellow sounds ([-strident]), and it is more natural, given a slight constriction, to make a sound strident (such as [s], which is a much "easier" speech sound than [θ]).

Another apparently difficult speech sound is [r]. It is frequently either omitted or replaced by [w] even by children who are well into Stage IV with respect to grammatical development. The other liquid, [l], is not misarticulated nearly as frequently as is [r], and the differential difficulty is virtually impossible to account for (see Cairns, Cairns, and Williams, 1974, for a theoretical account of phoneme substitutions).

The speech of very young children frequently has subtle intonational differences from the speech of adults, so that it may have a singsong quality not heard in adult speech. Disfluencies are much more frequent, too. Many parents suffer groundless fears that their children will become stutterers because they produce stutterlike disfluencies in the early preschool years.

It is interesting to note that the development of articulatory proficiency produces difficulties for the learning, or tabula rasa, theory of language development. Such theories rely heavily on the child's imitation of adult forms as a prerequisite to his learning of those forms. It is obvious that children learn to perceive and discriminate speech sounds that they are unable to articulate (imitate) properly. This is but one instance of a general principle in language development—that in general receptive abilities precede productive ones. We shall see that this principle holds for grammatical development as well as for phonetic development.

8.53 Phonological development

We now turn to the development of phonological rules, a well-researched and fascinating aspect of linguistic development. We shall concentrate particularly on the development of rules for formation of the past tense and for expression of plurality in English. (The linguistic aspects of these rules were presented in Chapter 4.)

Let us look briefly at the development of the past-tense inflection in typical English-speaking children. (See Brown, 1973, for a detailed account of this period.) In Stage II the child's verbs are uninflected. Though it may be obvious to the adult listener that the child is talking about, say, past events, verbs will not be marked for past tense. An exception to this pattern is that early in Stage II the child may use the past tense of "strong" verbs (those whose past-tense formation is irregular) such as 'went' and 'ran'. The child entering Stage III develops a rather large set of strong verbs and also begins to inflect regular verbs for past tense, producing such words as 'walked', 'talked', 'believed', and so on.

It seems that as children are doing quite well with developing control of the past tense, something odd and interesting happens. "Correct" forms of strong verbs are replaced by the incorrect forms that would result if these verbs were subject to the regular rule of English past-tense formation. Thus the child who has said 'slept', 'ate', and 'went' now says 'sleeped', 'eated', and 'goed'. This is "apparent regression"—regression, because children at this stage produce incorrect forms where they previously produced correct forms and apparent because this development actually represents a progression in children's analysis of the sound pattern of their language. They have constructed (or learned) a rule of English. Whereas before they had internalized only a long list of correct forms, they have now figured out the generalization that predicts the past forms of the weak verbs. They "erase" their list of past-tense forms and now have only a list of verb stems and a rule for past tense formation.

A plausible explanation for this turn of events begins with the observation that the strong verbs which the child first correctly masters are among the most common English verbs, hence among the earliest acquired. Thus, assuming that children still have a small vocabulary early in Stage II, they do not have a large body of data on which to base a generalization concerning the formation of past tenses. They have no alternative but simply to list the present and past tense forms of verbs. As their vocabulary grows, the proportion of regular verbs increases until they finally have enough data to formulate the regular past tense rule. Once they have formulated the rule for regular past tense formation, they abandon their lists of present and past tense forms, and substitute instead the underlying forms of verbs and the rule. This means, of course, that the formerly "correct" past tense forms for the strong verbs are now temporarily lost, causing many parents to think that their children are learning "bad grammar" from the neighbors or the kids at nursery school, whereas in fact the children are showing linguistic progress. It frequently takes years to reinstate the strong verbs, since to do so involves learning lists of exceptions to regular processes; rule governed "errors" of this type frequently persist well into Stage IV, and some children are in school before they have all their verbs straight again.

An identical pattern can be found in the use of pluralization. There are irregular plurals, such as 'sheep', 'feet', 'teeth', etc. When the children learn the English pluralization rule, they begin to produce rule-governed errors such as 'sheeps', 'foots', 'tooths', and frequently a bit of overkill with such amusing forms as 'feets' and 'teeths'.

The pattern of acquisition of these two phonological rules is interesting when viewed in the context of a behaviorist account of language acquisition. We cannot claim that the rules for past-tense and plural formation are so abstract that they cannot *in principle* be learned by operant conditioning. In fact these low-level phonological rules make reference to observable aspects of the verb or noun that is to be inflected. The phonetic shapes of the past and plural inflections are primarily determined by the voicing value of the final segment of the stem. We can define the voicing feature acoustically; thus the rule that selects the appropriate suffix can be described as relating two observable physical events to each other in a systematic way. Therefore these two rules, unlike most abstract rules of language, are in principle amenable to being learned by operant conditioning. There are in fact instances in which past tenses and plurals have been taught to children with various types of language pathology using operant conditioning techniques.

However, in natural language acquisition, the observed developmental pattern proves that operant conditioning cannot be the process responsible for the acquisition of these rules by the child. A learning theory account is falsified by the phenomenon of apparent regression. If children have been producing the correct forms of the verbs, then, according to the learning theory account they are being rewarded for the production of those correct forms (presumably by the parents or other adult caretakers), which they have imitated from the adults around them. But then they stop using the correct forms that are in the language and for which they have presumably been rewarded and they begin using words that they have had no opportunity to imitate since they have never even heard such words. Most children never hear anyone say 'foots' or 'sleeped'. Remember that according to the learning theory account children are rewarded for correct (grammatical) responses and are not rewarded for incorrect ones. This concept of selective reward is central to stimulus-response theories of language acquisition. Therefore the behaviorist must postulate that the deviant forms (which we see can be described as rule-governed errors) are not rewarded. Yet these errors persist, sometimes for years. According to the predictions of learning theory (which is supported by extensive experimental work with animals) a response that is correct and that is being rewarded will not be extinguished. Thus the development of the past and plural forms of strong verbs and nouns demonstrates the inadequacy of a conditioning account of language learning.

This phenomenon also illustrates many of the most interesting aspects of language development. Children observe regularities in the language around them and construct their own rules. Many times when they apply their rules the result is speech adults would never say and children have never heard. Another important aspect of language acquisition illustrated here is the fact that all English-speaking children go through these stages of overregularization of past and plural markers. Children who speak other languages overregularize forms in their respective languages (Slobin, 1971c). This is an example of a **language-learning universal,** a feature of language acquisition that is common to all children learning language. We will have much more to say about language-learning universals later.

8.6
Syntactic and Semantic Development

With the rise of generative-transformational grammar in the late 1950s psychologists began to view language—of children and adults—in a new way. There was an emphasis in linguistic theory on rules and syntactic structure. Therefore the earliest research in child language (based on the transformational-generative linguistic model) was primarily concerned with an examination of the language (speech) produced by the child in an attempt to characterize the structure underlying the child's language.

8.61 The formal approach

The most popular approach of this period was to record the spontaneous speech of children at regular intervals. Researchers would then write a series of grammars to describe the linguistic output of one child at various stages of development. The most thorough investigation of this type (called a longitudinal study because the investigators studied the same child over an extended period of time) was carried out by Roger Brown and his associates at Harvard. They followed three children, with the pseudonyms Adam, Eve, and Sarah, for a number of years (Brown, 1973). Detailed analyses of the early linguistic stages have emerged from that study, although the later stages have yet to be reported.

Investigations of the speech of young children yielded astonishing insights into child language. We have always known that children talk differently from adults, but somehow we had always assumed that the difference was a result of an inability of the child to "talk right." Children's language was assumed to be a reduced version of adults'. They spoke in shorter sentences, sometimes in short phrases, frequently used incorrect forms, and misarticulated some sounds; in general "baby talk" was thought of as an imperfect mirroring of adult speech, which would improve with time.

The careful analyses of children's speech carried out during the 1960s dispelled the "adultomorphic" assumptions described above (Brown, 1970). Child language is not simply a reduced version of adult language. It has a structure, consistency, and elegance all its own. Furthermore its regularities can be captured by rules, just as the regularities in adult language can be. The rules, however, turn out to be different from the rules of adults. Then, too, the child's rules are unstable. A child will appear to use one rule for several months, then exchange it for another greatly modified one.

The new rules are always more complex than their predecessors and seem to be closer to the rules we postulate for the adult. In the case of syntactic development, then, we have a different situation from what we had with the previous examples of plural and past-tense formation, where children formulated the correct rule on the first try. While they overgeneralized that rule, the rule itself was exactly like the adult rule on first formulation by the child. In syntax, however, we see children developing a number of "trial grammars," each a bit more complicated than the one before. The rules that must be formulated to explain children's utterances are different from adult rules. Notice that even if one believed that an abstract rule of syntax could in any sense be imitated and rewarded—which is in itself an untenable position—we would have to ask ourselves where the child's rules come from, since they are not present in adult grammar.

Another point that should be made about the rules postulated for children is that they have a theoretical status different from that of the rules that linguists write to describe adult competence. A linguist tests hypotheses about adult grammars by eliciting judgments from speakers about whether a sentence is grammatical or ungrammatical, whether certain sentences are ambiguous, and whether sets of sentences are paraphrases of each other. This method of hypothesis testing allows linguists to claim that their theory (grammar) is a theory of a person's knowledge of his language. Notice that linguists do not simply record the speech of adults and then describe it using rules of syntax, semantics, and phonology. Unfortunately, however, little children cannot give the researcher information about which sentences are grammatical, ambiguous, and paraphrases of one another. Children are not capable of such metalinguistic judgments until late childhood, a fact that we will consider again in another context later in this chapter. The point here is that grammatical rules written for children are different from those written for adults because they are based on and tested by different kinds of data. The fact that child grammars merely describe regularities in the linguistic output of children does not mean that they are totally unrevealing of a child's competence. Speech performance is undoubtedly based on children's internalized grammar and can give us some information about that grammar. It is impossible, however, because of children's limitations in divulging their linguistic intuitions, to describe their competence with the subtlety and precision that is achieved in adult grammar.

We refer to this early approach to research in language acquisition as the **formal approach** because researchers were mainly interested in characterizing the form or structure of the child's utterances. It will be contrasted later with a **functional approach,** in which the emphasis is on what children mean by what they say and the manner in which children use language.

Some of the most interesting research has centered on the development of single-sentence structures. As an example of patterns of language development as well as examples of the kind of research that characterizes the formal approach to child language, we will present sketches of the development of three constructions in English: the negative, questions, and constructions involving the verb 'to be'.

8.611 Negation. The earliest form of negation for children is the head shake. This begins during the holophrastic period and declines steadily after linguistic forms of negation are used. So in this early period children may shake their heads and say 'home', meaning that they do not want to go home. One has to look at children to know what they mean, a situation that frequently leads to mildly traumatic misunderstandings between parent and child.

The first linguistic expression of negation arises in the two-word Stage II and frequently persists into Stage III. It is referred to as **extrasentential negation** because the negative element (usually 'no', sometimes 'not', in the early stages) is placed usually at the beginning and sometimes at the end of the child's sentence. Thus, Stage II children might say 'no fall', 'no medicine', or occasionally, perhaps, 'fall no'. In early Stage III these would become utterances like 'no me fall', 'me fall no', or 'no baby medicine'. The interposition of the negative element in the middle of a sentence is not observed during the period of extrasentential negation; thus children during this period would not say 'me no fall' or 'baby no medicine'.

The assumption is that the child has internalized a phrase-structure rule that introduces the negative element optionally at either the beginning or end of the sentence, but has no transformational rule that will move the negative element to embed it inside the sentence. It is believed (McNeill, 1970; Slobin, 1971c) that external sentential negation is a language-learning universal. So far no one has investigated the development of a language in which this was not the first form of negation. This fact is very significant because none of the languages in question uses such a simple form of negation. It seems that external negation represents the most primitive linguistic expression of negation, so all human children initially adopt a common primitive rule to express the universal concept of negation. Only later does the child's expression of negation seem to be a reflection of the structures of his native language.

During the next period of negation, which arises in Stage III, children develop a rule to embed the negative element in their sentences. Such utterances as 'me no fall' are the result. It is about this time that English-speaking children begin to use the negative contractions 'don't' and 'can't'. These forms are treated by children as unitary negative elements, exactly like 'no' or 'not', with sentences like 'baby don't fall' resulting.

Although 'don't' appears to be similar to the adult form of a contraction of 'do' and 'not', it should not be analyzed in this manner for the child because 'do' never appears in the speech of children at this period. Their grammar at this period shows no evidence of the existence of a rule of "do support". Children do not produce such forms as 'Did you fall?' Instead, yes/no questions at Stage II and early Stage III are marked only by rising intonation or rising pitch at the end of the utterance—'you fall?' Therefore 'don't' for children is a fixed form, not appropriately analyzed as a contraction of the two words 'do' and 'not'. Only when 'do' and 'can' (as an auxiliary element) enter the child's speech at the end of Stage III or the beginning of Stage IV should 'don't' and 'can't' be analyzed as contractions similar to the adult forms.

Another instance of apparent regression appears when the child realizes that there are some determiners, such as 'some', 'any', and 'none', that are related to the negative character of an entire sentence. Thus it is grammatical to say 'I want none' or 'I don't want any' (both negative utterances); 'some' is admissible only in such nonnegative utterances as 'I want some milk'. Typically, children use 'some' in all positions—'I don't want some milk'—which is ungrammatical according to rules of adult grammar. At some point, however, children realize that this is an oversimplification and that negative sentences require negative determiners. They then attempt to ascertain which determiners are appropriate, and the first hypothesis is frequently that the negative determiner 'no' is appropriate for negative sentences. Experimenting with this hypothesis leads to double-negative constructions such as 'I don't want no milk'. Thus children who previously have not produced double negatives begin using them, which is another instance of apparent regression that actually reflects the progressive attempt by the child to sort out the proper positive and negative determiners. When our little boy was three, he grasped the negative aspect of 'any' and used the word 'anything' with the meaning of 'nothing' for months. Thus if this child were asked "What are you doing?" he would answer "Oh, anything," as an adult would answer "Oh, nothing."

The development of the negative is replete with examples of children using forms they have never heard before and seemingly learning "incorrect" forms for which the behaviorist must predict they are not rewarded. It is much more accurate to view children as little linguists, developing their own theories about how their language works. When the speech they hear around them tells them that their theories (rules) are incorrect, they replace them with increasingly more complex and more nearly correct hypotheses.

8.612 The development of wh-questions. A yes/no question is one that is properly answered either 'yes' or 'no'. Another type of question is the wh-question, which begins with 'what', 'when', 'where', 'who', why', or 'how'. We are concerned here with the development of children's ability to formulate (rather than answer) such questions.

Stage II usually sees children asking such questions (usually with 'what' or 'where') in such constructions as 'Where dolly?' and 'What car?' (Slobin, 1971). The constructions become more interesting when they produce longer wh-questions in Stage III (Brown, 1968).

The analysis of the adult wh-question consists of essentially two transformational operations. The underlying structure for the question 'Where is the car?' is 'The car is where', and the surface structure is created by the application of two transformational rules. First, the 'wh' element is moved to the front of the sentence, producing an intermediate structure of the form 'where the car is'. Next, the inflected aux element (or the tense marker if there is no inflected aux) is moved to follow the 'wh' element, producing 'Where *is* the car' or 'Where *did* he go' (in the latter sentence the tense marker was moved and the "do-support" transformation applied). With an expanded aux element we get 'What *is* he making' or 'Where *had* he gone?'

The developmental pattern of the child's formulations of wh-questions seems to follow roughly the pattern we would expect if the two adult rules were formulated sequentially, rather than simultaneously, by the child. Thus children's early constructions are 'Where the car is?' and 'Where he goed?' It is as though children had first learned the rule that preposes the 'wh' element but have not yet learned the much more complicated rule for placement of the tensed element. After children develop command of the auxiliary in Stage IV, they go on to formulate the second rule of wh-question formation, which will produce the adult forms.

The development of wh-questions has proved to be an example of a developmental pattern that can be described and explained quite elegantly in terms of rule acquisition. The development of this construction also provides another excellent example of the development of a rule-governed intermediate form that children have never heard in adult speech. Since children have not heard the form, they could hardly have imitated it. Since it is incorrect from the adult point of view, it would not (presumably) be rewarded. A behaviorist account of language acquisition, then, could not account for either the initiation or the (temporary) maintenance of such an intermediary form.

8.613 Development of use of the verb 'to be.' In Chapter 4 three uses of the verb 'to be' were described—as copula, as progressive auxiliary, and as the aux element in passive sentences. Here we want to focus on the first two uses and show that they develop in completely different ways, though they employ what seem to be the same words. It is almost as though children do not realize that the linking verb and the aux form are phonetically identical. Neither form is used in Stage II. You never hear children say 'is new' or 'dolly is' during the two-word stage. In Stage III, however, 'to be' as linking verb enters a child's repertoire, although it is apparently optional. Thus we observe the same child producing utterances such as 'He is doggie' and 'He doggie' at the same stage. These constructions are apparently paraphrases of each other, so it is assumed that children have command of the semantic properties of the linking verb and that it is part of their grammar, but its appearance in this construction is optional.

At the same time 'to be' appears as a linking verb (copula) it does not appear in the progressive construction at all. Early progressive constructions employ the '-ing' suffix but not the aux element. Sentences of the form 'Doggie running' or 'Baby eating' are common. Many researchers (Bloom, 1970; Brown, 1970; Brown and Hanlon, 1970) have observed that only a limited amount of complexity can be tolerated by young children. An example of such a limitation can be found in section 8.612, development of the wh-question, where complexity is introduced bit by bit. To extend this analysis to the progressive, we can think of the progressive construction as consisting of two elements, the '-ing' suffix and the aux. Even though the child is quite capable of producing forms of the verb 'to be', a less complex form of the progressive is first used, with only the suffix being introduced. The fact that it is the suffix that first emerges is consistent with Slobin's finding that suffixes are universally among the early grammatical devices acquired by children (more about this in section 8.7).

8.62 Criticisms of a purely formal analysis of child language

As descriptions of the syntax of children's utterances became more and more detailed, many researchers began to consider two other areas of major importance that seemed to be neglected. One was the semantics of child language; the other, the child's comprehension (as opposed to his production) of speech. The late 1960s saw an upsurge in research in these two areas.

The analysis of semantics in child language has proceeded along three major avenues. The first, and most productive, approach has been functional, concerning itself with the meaning underlying the child's utterances and the functions of language for the child (Bloom, 1970; Slobin, 1971c; Dore, 1973). In Section 8.621 we will contrast a formal and functional analysis of one stage of language acquisition. It is clear that an inspection of the meaning of the utterances of children can reveal sound-meaning correspondences not found in a purely formal account. It is also true, however, that an exclusively functional account obscures the regularities in syntactic development, which give us such a revealing picture of the child's developing grammar. A severe problem with functional analyses of child language is that the meaning of children's utterances must be inferred by the observer from the context in which the utterances occur. This activity is fraught with difficulties as the linguistic and nonlinguistic contexts frequently are insufficient for judging meaning with a high degree of confidence.

The second major approach to semantics in child language is to investigate the semantic features that characterize individual items in the child's lexicon (McNeill, 1970; E. Clark, 1973; H. Clark, 1973; Donaldson and Wales, 1970). This line of research has led to some very interesting findings relating to children's understanding of various words. Children will tend to confuse two lexical items if they have not yet learned the semantic feature that separates the two. Section 8.622 will deal with this approach to the semantic structures of the child.

The third view of semantics in developmental psycholinguistics would be better characterized as conceptual. The utterances children produce are partially constrained by the kinds of things that they can think about. We would hardly expect children of three to talk about square roots; they do not know anything about them. Conceptual development then, may be seen as the foundation for all linguistic development. This conception has been elaborated by Slobin and is presented in Section 8.7 of this chapter.

The study of language comprehension in children is closely related to semantic questions. When children comprehend a sentence, they assign a meaning to it, so their comprehension ability is constrained by their semantic system as well as by their ability to decode syntactic structures. The issue of comprehension in children brings up a number of complicated theoretical questions. It is well known that comprehension precedes production in that children (as well as adults) can usually understand structures more complex than they can produce (Brown, Fraser, and Bellugi, 1963). On these grounds it was once argued that comprehension must be a better index of true competence than is production. Thus, since both comprehension and production skills are based on linguistic competence, it was believed that comprehension must reveal a more highly developed competence than does production. Therefore, so the argument went, comprehension must be a better mirror of competence.

The argument described above became less convincing with the hypothesis that children, like adults, have (as performance skills) strategies that allow them to understand some sentences even if they do not have full command of the underlying linguistic structures. In Section 8.63 we will address the general issue of a child's comprehension of language.

We now turn to an illustration of the functional as opposed to the purely formal approach to analysis of the language of children.

8.621. Formal and functional analyses of Stage II. The contrast between the earlier structural approach and the more recent functional approach is perhaps best exemplified by studies of the Stage II, two-word period of linguistic development. Early investigations revealed that some words always appeared in fixed position in children's two-word utterances. The majority of fixed-position words always appeared in first position; others, always in second position. Words that always appeared in the same position were rarely used alone or with each other. By contrast the vast majority of words children used could occur in either position in a two-word utterance or alone in a one-word utterance. The words appearing in fixed position are labeled **pivot words** (this term was first used by Braine, 1963). Examples of first-position pivots are 'that', 'there', 'allgone', 'my', 'dirty', 'more'. The class is called the pivot class because its members seem to form a sort of fulcrum, or point of departure, for the child's early constructions. Dozens of "open" class words, which are frequently nouns, may be appended to a pivot word to form a two-word utterance. Thus, if 'allgone', 'dirty', 'my', and 'more' are pivot words, and if 'cereal', 'dress', 'mommy', and 'ice cream' exemplify the open class, then utterances such as 'allgone cereal', 'dirty dress', 'my mommy', and 'more ice cream' might occur.

The words of the open class, unlike those of the pivot class, may appear alone. Thus a child might say either just 'mommy' or 'mommy dress'. A purely formal or syntactic analysis of utterances at this stage might consist of a rule such as illustrated here.

$$S \rightarrow \begin{Bmatrix} P + O \\ O + P \\ O + O \\ O \end{Bmatrix}$$

There are a number of rather interesting aspects of this analysis. In the first place it demonstrates that the very early utterances of children are not simply random groupings of words that they happen to know, but are groupings that have internal structural organization. It also shows that the children are not simply imitating word pairs they have heard in adult speech. A classical example from Brown's observations is the sentence 'Allgone outside', which was produced as a little fellow closed a door. It is clear that the very earliest utterances of children are characterized by structure and creativity, two of the most important aspects of human Language. It is also clear that the structure and creativity of these early utterances demonstrate the inadequacy of a behaviorist theory of language acquisition. The children are not imitating the utterances of the adults in their environment. They are producing creative constructions that are correct by their own rudimentary rules but that are certainly incorrect by adult standards. However, if you observe the interaction between parents and children who talk like this, you see that the parents reward everything the children say, whether grammatical or ungrammatical from the point of view of adult grammar. There is certainly nothing like selective reward taking place.

Another significant aspect of the pivot/open analysis of Stage II language is the fact that it seems to represent a language-learning universal. Just as all children, no matter what their native language, go through the babbling stages and begin their linguistic career with a holophrastic Stage I, so do they experience a Stage II during which their utterances can be analyzed in terms of pivot and open classes.

The pivot/open description of Stage II language, like the formal approach to the analysis of child language in general, provides interesting insights into the formal structure of early utterances, but a number of researchers have claimed that important questions were being ignored (Bloom, 1970; Slobin, 1971a). They have suggested that it is also necessary to explore the meaning of the child's early utterances. Since meaning can never be known with certainty, it is possible only to investigate the apparent function of the child's utterances—to ask what kinds of messages the child's sentences convey. This is an important consideration in child language because many of the superficial forms the child produces are structurally ambiguous. Consider, for instance, the utterance 'see doggie', a common pivot/open construction for many small children. While only having one superficial structural description (pivot + open), the utterance could have many different underlying meanings. It could be an imperative sentence, exhorting someone else to see a dog. It could be a request to see a dog. It could be an imperative sentence spoken to a dog, urging him to see something. In the first two cases 'doggie' would be the object of the utterance; in the latter case 'doggie' would be the subject. Similarly an open + open construction such as 'baby kitty' could indicate possession, a request to do something with the kitty, a report that the baby has done something to the kitty, or simply a report on the infancy of the cat. The pivot/open analysis is purely a surface-structure analysis. Looking for the function, or meaning, of the early utterances is a necessary step toward understanding the sound-meaning correspondence in the language of young children.

It appears that the earliest utterances from children from various different language groups have both structural and functional features in common. Cross-linguistic studies of language development are very recent and are being carried out primarily by Slobin and his associates at the University of California at Berkeley. They have now studied the acquisition of a number of languages other than English and report striking similarities among little language learners. These similarities are theoretically important because they cannot have their origin in the speech the children are exposed to. The origin must be related to a basic cognitive similarity among human children.

Slobin (1971a) reports the following list of functions characteristic of the two-word utterances of children from six different language communities (English, German, Russian, Finnish, Luo, and Samoan). Slobin's claim is that the universality of the functions of language is an important language-learning universal because it demonstrates that children of similar ages have the ability to encode similar kinds of meanings.

1. Utterances are used to locate or name objects and people: 'there book'
2. Utterances are used to request, demand, or indicate a desire for people, objects, or events: 'more milk'
3. Utterances are used to negate propositions or indicate refusal or rejection: 'no wash'
4. Utterances are used to describe situations or events: 'Bambi go'
5. Utterances are used to indicate possession of people or objects: 'mama dress'
6. Utterances are used descriptively: 'papa big'
7. Utterances are used as both wh-questions and yes-no questions: 'where ball?' and 'daddy go?'

The fourth function above, description of events, provides an interesting insight into the relationship between the child's linguistic and semantic knowledge at this stage of development. Consider the major grammatical relations—subject, verb, and object. We find that all of these relations are expressed in the child's earliest constructions. If the baby observes a dog chasing a cat, he may use any of the following constructions to describe the action: 'Puppy chase' (subject-verb); 'chase kitty' (verb-object); or 'puppy kitty' (subject-object). The fact that the child can express each pair of grammatical relations indicates that at some level he can conceptualize the complete subject-verb-object relationship. For some reason, not as yet understood, the child at this age cannot produce three-word utterances such as 'puppy chase kitty'. By investigating the function, rather than merely the form, of his utterances, however, it can be demonstrated that his inability to say 'puppy chase kitty' is not due to an inability to grasp two simultaneous grammatical relations, only to an inability to produce utterances of sufficient length or complexity to reveal his understanding in one utterance (Bloom, 1970). In this case, then, it is possible to distinguish between competence factors and performance factors. The child's underlying linguistic and conceptual knowledge includes a range of grammatical relations that he cannot express because of performance limitations.

8.622 The development of features in the child's semantic system. A number of semantic theorists (Bierwisch, 1970; Katz and Fodor, 1963) have suggested that the meaning of individual words may be characterized as a list of semantic features with a notation to indicate whether or not that feature inheres (see Chapter 4 for a discussion of semantic features in linguistic theory) in that lexical item. A nonexhaustive list of the features associated with the word 'man', for instance, would be [concrete], [human],

[male], and [adult]. It has been frequently suggested that the individual features are pan-linguistic and constitute linguistic universals in the sense that all languages of the world use a common set of semantic features. In this view the features represent dimensions of contrast available to all humans. The sufficiency of such a theory to characterize all readings of all lexical items in all the world's languages may be open to serious question, but it seems plausible that such an analysis is at least a central component of lexical meaning.

A number of psycholinguists have suggested that children's acquisition of the meaning of an individual lexical item is accomplished by adding features until they have the full adult feature list for that item (McNeill, 1970; E. Clark, 1973). The Clark version of this theory called the **semantic-feature hypothesis,** accounts for the fact that a very small child calls all four legged animals 'doggie' (or 'kitty' or whatever) with the explanation that for a small child the word 'doggie' has only the features [nonhuman], [animal], and [four-legged]. Thus this kind of overgeneralization is related to a sort of underspecification from the point of view of semantic features.

The semantic-feature hypothesis accounts for some experimental findings that demonstrate quite unexpected confusions among words. Donaldson and Wales (1970) showed that children confused the words 'more' and 'less', interpreting both as having the meaning of 'more' in a series of tasks and conversations (see also Donaldson and Balfour, 1968). E. Clark interprets these results as following from an incomplete feature specification for the word 'less'. Clark maintains that these children have developed the feature [amount] that is common to both 'more' and 'less'. The next feature to emerge is [polar], which has for the adult the '+' value for 'more' and '−' for 'less'. The child confuses the two words because he has added the feature [polar] to both words, assigning a positive value to each. A similar confusion is demonstrated between the words 'same' and 'different' (Donaldson and Wales, 1970), 'different' always being interpreted as meaning 'same', and between 'before' and 'after' in time (E. Clark, 1971). The latter confusion, where both are interpreted as meaning 'before', is accounted for by the hypothesis that the children have learned the features [+time] and [−simultaneous] for these words but have incorrectly learned [+prior] for both. Later, 'before' and 'after' become differentiated by the feature [prior] and are understood and used correctly.

The work cited above may be of great importance in accounting for the development of the child's lexicon, a component of linguistic competence. Important questions that remain to be investigated relate to the order in which semantic features develop, why some features differentiate later than others, and, most important, the universality of the development of the features. If it is in fact true that there exists a universal set of semantic features available to all members of the human race, then we would predict a language-learning universal such that similar features would develop in children from different linguistic communities in similar sequences. Such a finding would strengthen the semantic-feature hypothesis and would provide impressive confirmation of Slobin's theory of a universal sequencing of cognitive development.

8.63 The development of comprehension in the child

The general research strategy for investigating language comprehension in the child has involved testing the child's understanding of various types of sentence constructions. While research in adult language comprehension is concerned with hypotheses about *how* the adult understands sentences, research with children is concerned with *whether* children understand the structures in question. In cases where children misunderstand a particular structure the investigator will typically formulate hypotheses to account for why the sentence was misinterpreted in a particular way.

The child's comprehension of the passive construction has been investigated extensively. Passives such as 'the ice cream cone was eaten by the clown' are correctly understood even by very young children, while sentences such as 'the boy was hit by the girl' will be misunderstood as though it were 'the boy' who hit 'the girl'. While the syntactic characteristics of these two passive sentences are the same, the semantic characteristics are not. The former sentence is an irreversible passive; it is plausible to imagine a clown eating an ice cream cone, but it is implausible to imagine an ice cream cone eating a clown. The latter passive is reversible in that it is equally sensible for a boy to hit a girl as for a girl to hit a boy. Thus the child who correctly interprets the irreversible passive but not the reversible one must not be assumed to have a well-formed transformational rule for description of the passive construction as part of his linguistic competence. Instead, the young child uses a comprehension strategy, which is a performance skill, to understand such sentences (Bever, 1970). Such a strategy can be characterized as an instruction to sort out the subject, object, and verb into the most plausible semantic configuration without regard to the syntactic form of the utterance.

Another comprehension strategy can be inferred by examining the kinds of errors made by children when confronted with reversible passive sentences. Very young children choose the first noun phrase as the logical subject of the verb about half the time, as the object the other half. Older children, however, will make a fairly consistent error by interpreting the first noun phrase (e.g., 'the boy' in 'the boy was hit by the girl') as the subject of the sentence. Bever reports that this type of error reaches peak frequency just before the age of four. This consistent error indicates that the child has adopted a comprehension strategy that tells him to interpret the first noun as the subject of the sentence (if no semantic cues are available). The existence of such a comprehension strategy is further supported by the child's misinterpretation of sentences (called cleft sentences) such as 'It was the cow the horse kissed'. It is frequently found that children who err on reversible passives also misunderstand cleft sentences such that they would report that 'the cow' is the subject of the above sentence.

The existence of comprehension strategies further complicates the assessment of the actual syntactic competence of the child. Considering only the production of the child leads us to underestimate his underlying linguistic competence. But it would appear that the consideration of comprehension per se could lead to an overestimation of competence. We would make a mistake if we leaped to the conclusion that the child who correctly interprets an irreversible passive sentence has full command of the passive construction at a level of competence.

Cromer (1970) studied slightly older children, all of whom were able to understand even reversible passive constructions. Using a puppet game format, he tested the children's interpretations of ambiguous sentences such as (5), in which 'the wolf' can be interpreted either as the subject of the verb 'bite', as in (6), or as the object, as in (7).

(5) The wolf is nice to bite.
(6) The wolf is eager to bite.
(7) The wolf is easy to bite.

The children indicated their understanding of each sentence by acting it out with the puppets. The less linguistically sophisticated children interpreted 'the wolf' as subject in sentences such as (5) and even misinterpreted sentences such as (7) so that the wolf was doing the biting. These results point to a continuing bias toward the interpretation of first nouns as subjects, even in embedded sentences.

An alternative explanation for Cromer's findings could be that since 'the wolf' is the surface subject of 'is', it is more natural for the child to interpret it as the subject of the embedded sentence. This interpretation is suggested by the results of an experiment by Sheldon (1974), investigating the comprehension of sentences with relative clauses by children between the ages of three and five. She distinguishes between two types of sentences with relative clauses—parallel-function and nonparallel-function sentences. A parallel-function sentence is one where the relativized NP in the relative clause has the same syntactic function in the embedded sentences as does the head NP in the matrix sentence. Sentences (8) and (9) illustrate these types.

(8) The dog that jumped over the pig bumped into the lion.
(9) The dog stood on the horse that the giraffe jumped over.

'That' in (8) is the revitalized NP, representing a deep-structure NP, 'the dog' (see section 3.61). It functions as the subject of the embedded sentence. Similarly, the NP 'the dog' that appears in (8) is the subject of the matrix sentence. In (9) the relative pronoun 'that' functions as the object of the relative clause, and the head noun 'the horse' is an object of the matrix sentence.

An example of a nonparallel sentence is given in (10), where the relative pronoun 'that' is the subject of the embedded sentence. The head NP 'the horse', however, is the object of the matrix sentence.

(10) The dog stood on the horse that bumped into the lion.

All children performed better on parallel-function sentences than on nonparallel-function sentences. Sheldon suggests that children (and perhaps adults as well) operate with a parallel-function strategy in which the grammatical relations within relative clauses (and across coordinate sentences) are interpreted as parallel to those of coreferential phrases.

Although it may be the case that adults and children alike use various strategies to understand sentences, there is a crucial difference between the ways they apply them. Children tend to actually misunderstand sentences that violate their strategies, while adults usually understand the sentences correctly at the cost of a little extra processing complexity. Children, then, tend to be more dependent on their strategies than are adults. This may be the case because children have nothing but comprehension strategies to rely on until they have developed full competence in their language. As Bever (1970) has said, it seems only reasonable to expect that a child would have to develop some ad hoc way of achieving at least partial understanding of the speech in his environment before he could begin to develop a systematic grammar to account for the observed pairings of sounds and meanings.

8.7
A Theory of Language Acquisition

The inadequacy of traditional behaviorist learning theories to account for the acquisition of language by the child has been a continuing theme throughout this chapter. In contrast, a cognitive theory of linguistic development has emerged. The essence of this theory is that human infants are born with a predisposition to develop a language with certain universal characteristics (linguistic universals) according to a universal developmental pattern (language-learning universals). The child then develops systems of rules (grammars) to describe the structure of the language he hears. Early grammars are simple but are gradually restructured and become increasingly more complex, and by adulthood (or early adolescence) the child's grammar is complete and essentially identical to those internalized by other speakers of his native language. It is traditional in developmental psycholinguistics to depict this theory in the following diagram:

Primary linguistic data → Language → Grammar
                                Acquisition
                                Device

The primary linguistic data is, of course, the speech the child hears around him during his years of language development. An important fact about language acquisition that must be accounted for is the fact that while all children even in the same language community, hear vastly differing primary linguistic data, they construct essentially identical grammars. This phenomenon can be understood only as we realize that the primary linguistic data for each child, while acoustically different, is based on essentially similar grammars. This commonality in grammar underlying the sentences of the primary linguistic data is, while unobservable, the sole basis for the similarity of grammars developed by thousands of individual children. The child himself is whimsically referred to as a **Language-acquisition device** (LAD) or perhaps a **Language-acquisition system** (LAS). The LAD or LAS is said to incorporate the universals of Language and Language development.

Recent theoretical contributions by Slobin (1971c) provide a more detailed account of the language-acquisition process within the broad outlines of a cognitive theory of language development. Slobin suggests that the conceptual development of all human children is the same with regard to the order of attainment of conceptual categories. When the child acquires a new conceptual category, he first attempts to express it by means of the linguistic structures that he has at his disposal. When those structures prove to be inadequate to communicate his new concept, he attempts to restructure his linguistic system to accommodate the new concept. Slobin characterizes this development in the following way: "New functions are first expressed in old forms."

An example will make this formulation clear. At some point in the child's life he develops the concept of past action, which underlies the grammatical form of past tense. He learns that one can think and talk about events that have already taken place and are no longer observable. During the holophrastic period and perhaps early in Stage II, however, he has no command of tense formations of any type. He must express his concept of past action, then, by using the same uninflected verbs that he uses for expression of present action. Thus he will use the utterance 'kitty run' to express his conceptualization that the kitty ran yesterday as well as that the kitty runs at the present time. Gradually children become aware of the inadequacy of their linguistic system (old forms) to communicate the concepts (new functions) they have acquired. They are also aware that the adults they know are not so handicapped by their linguistic system. Children then begin to examine the speech around them to discover the grammatical device appropriate to their new concept, and they begin to develop (in our example) the past tense in their speech, which is ultimately incorporated into their linguistic knowledge as a general rule for past-tense formation.

It is easy to see the role that comprehension strategies can play in such a theory. Between the time children develop a new concept and the time they develop a method of expressing that concept in their own language system, they must analyze the speech they hear around them without the benefit of an internalized linguistic description. For this reason children must develop ad hoc performance skills to figure out how their new concept is expressed in adult language.

The similarities in patterns of linguistic development—which we have called language-learning universals—have been constantly emphasized throughout this chapter. We hasten to point out, however, that there are great differences in patterns of development from one language to another. It might be reasonable to ask, If Slobin's theory is correct, why isn't there even more similarity in patterns of language development? Slobin's theory claims that linguistic development lags behind, though it mirrors, conceptual development. It seems that such a theory would predict a universal pattern of linguistic development. This is not the case, however, because Slobin's theory also states that some grammatical devices are more easily learned than others.

Based on his research in the learning of many languages other than English, Slobin has developed a set of operating principles (1971c) by which children formulate hypotheses about the grammar of their particular language. Linguistic devices that are discoverable by children's initial hypotheses will be more easily learned than those that require falsification of early hypotheses and the development of new ones. Slobin is in fact the first theorist to develop substantive claims about the conception that children behave like little linguists, making and testing hypotheses about the language in which they find themselves immersed. The operating principles are phrased as imperative sentences; in Slobin's words they are "... 'self-instructions' for language acquisition."

8.71 Operating Principle A: Pay attention to the ends of words

Evidence from a number of languages suggests that grammatical markers that are suffixes are easier to learn than those that are prepositional. For example, in English young children omit the articles ('a', 'an', 'the') before words, but children speaking Bulgarian do not. Slobin suggests that this is because the article in Bulgarian appears as a noun suffix. He adduces a number of other examples demonstrating that similar semantic devices in different languages will be learned earlier if encoded as a suffix. The implication of Operating Principle A is that when children are confronted with masses of primary linguistic data, they first scan the ends of words for grammatical devices. If such devices are there, they will be learned quickly. If they are not, the children must reject the initial end-of-the-word hypothesis and try something else (such as looking for prepositional de-vices).

8.72 Operating Principle B: The phonological forms of words can be systematically modified

This principle combines with Operating Principle A to allow children to learn inflectional morphology. It would hardly do children any good to pay attention to the ends of words if they were not set to observe systematic variation in suffixes. Slobin cites a number of reports of children "playing" with words, systematically varying their pronounciation before inflections are learned. This demonstrates that a child's language-acquisition device knows that linguistic units are smaller than the word and expects to see such units as the suffix vary in systematic ways.

8.73 Operating Principle C: Pay attention to the order of words and morphemes

Children usually use the standard word order of their language in their own sentences. In fixed-word-order languages, structures that violate standard order (such as the passive in English) are more difficult for children to understand than those that do not. It seems that children are predisposed to look to word order for the encoding of grammatical relations. Even in languages such as Russian, in which grammatical relations are marked by inflections and word order is freer than in English, children go through an early period (before they develop the inflections) in which they adopt a fixed word order to encode grammatical relations in their own speech.

8.74 Operating Principle D: Avoid interruption or rearrangement of linguistic units

There are many examples of early grammatical development in which chil-dren seem to formulate rules in order not to violate the internal integrity of their own sentences. Extrasentential negation is such a phenomenon, as is the early form of such wh-questions as 'Where that doggie is?' Early relative clauses are extensions of the object NP, rather than following and modifying the subject NP, which would require embedding. In terms of sentence processing (as opposed to formulation of grammatical rules) sen-tences will be more difficult the greater the separation between related parts of the sentence. It may be that the child's limited short-term memory contributes to this principle.

8.75 Operating Principle E: Underlying grammatical relations should be marked overtly and clearly

This principle suggests that well-marked grammatical relations will be learned earlier and also that in the child's own speech there will be a pressure to mark grammatical relations. It would seem also to predict that marked relations will be more easily understood in individual sentences. This seems quite consistent with the child's development of fixed word order (which is a way of marking grammatical relations). Slobin gives a number of examples from languages other than English in which children will mark a form that is not properly marked in the language. In Russian, for instance, masculine, nonhuman, and neuter nouns are not inflected in the accusative case (or, put differently, they are inflected with a zero morpheme). There is an accusative marking for feminine nouns, however, an /-u/ suffix. Russian children tend to add the /-u/ suffix to masculine and neuter nouns, in this case presumably because there is some pressure from this operating principle to formulate rules that mark all grammatical relations.

Slobin extends this operating principle to explain why sentences with deleted grammatical relations are more difficult to understand than are those with the material present. Thus "Tell Laura what to feed the doll" is more difficult than "Tell Laura what she should feed the doll." (Chomsky, 1969).

8.76 Operating Principle F: Avoid exceptions

One of the most striking aspects of child language is the tendency of children to overgeneralize rules once they are learned. Not only do children populate their early grammars with very general rules, it is also true that it is easier for them to develop rules that describe very general phenomena. The more widespread a syntactic or morphological process, the earlier it will be learned by a child in that linguistic community.

8.77 Operating Principle G: The use of grammatical markers should make semantic sense

Although the grammar of a language constitutes the rules by which meanings are encoded into sounds in that language, there are many linguistic devices that are semantic-free. Such forms are very difficult for children to learn. Slobin points out that in languages where grammatical relations are marked with case endings the cases themselves are mastered early but the inflections are more difficult, especially those inflections that mark gender. Gender markings usually have no semantic significance, since most common nouns have no sex, and even when they do, gender marks do not always reflect facts about the world. For instance, in German the noun meaning 'girl' is neuter! Such formal distinctions are learned late by children. This is hardly surprising if we have an image of children as valiantly trying to discover how their language relates sound with meaning.

8.78 An example

Slobin's theory predicts that even though two children learning different native languages develop a concept at the same time, the linguistic device for expressing that concept might be more easily learned in one language than the other. Therefore one child would be able to develop a new form to express the new function more quickly, while the other child would have to use old forms to express the new function for a longer period. There would be a gap in the linguistic development of the two children, as one child would be able to express the new concept linguistically, while the other would not.

The principle of "universal conceptual development, but uneven linguistic development" is best illustrated by an example, reported by Slobin, of one child learning two languages. Obviously, the one child had only one pattern of conceptual development. Therefore any linguistic differences can be ascribed to the differential acquisition of linguistic devices in the two languages. The child in question is a little girl who is bilingual in Hungarian and Serbo-Croatian. The example deals with the concept of location, expressed in English by such locative prepositions as 'in', 'on', 'above'. Serbo-Croatian uses a similar grammatical device—the preposition —to express the locative concept, while Hungarian expresses location with a suffix appended to the noun in the locative phrase. Thus a Serbo-Croatian-type expression would appear like the English 'ball in box,' while the analogous Hungarian expression would be something akin to 'ball box-in'.

The little girl Slobin tells about began using grammatical locatives when she was speaking Hungarian but not when she was speaking Serbo-Croatian. This is because, according to Operating Principle A, the suffix is one of the most easily learned grammatical devices, while prepositions are more difficult. Slobin and his associates have established this fact independently, of course, of the evidence from this one bilingual child, who offers only one example.

Suppose that instead of one child we had two children to observe—one learning Hungarian and the other learning Serbo-Croatian. We would observe that the Hungarian child had linguistic command of the locative but the Serbo-Croatian child did not. It would be incorrect to conclude, however, that the Serbo-Croatian child did not have the locative concept. We could ascertain this by observing whether she seemed to be attempting to communicate the locative concept with her old linguistic forms—such as carefully putting a ball in a box and announcing 'ball box'. We could also give her a series of commands that, if she were able to carry them out, would be very good evidence that she had command of locative concepts. (We have oversimplified this account by writing as though the locative is a unitary concept. In point of fact some locatives, such as 'in' and 'on', are learned earlier than others, such as 'above' and 'below'.)

This theory, then, predicts that with regard to any particular concept, a child will go through three periods:

During the first period he does not have the concept within his cognitive repertoire. At this point he will not understand the concept and will not attempt to use it in any way in his own communication system.

The child develops the concept within his cognitive repertoire during the second period. He begins to construe events in the world in terms of that concept. At this stage he does not express the concept in his linguistic production by means of grammatical devices. Therefore his linguistic output is the same as it was during the first period. However, he may be using his old linguistic forms in new functional patterns in an attempt to communicate the new concept. At this point he is attempting to discover a linguistic device with which to encode the new concept. When he discovers the linguistic device, he will almost certainly understand others' use of it, even though he cannot produce it yet himself.

During the third period he develops the ability to communicate his new concept via linguistic devices in his own speech. At this point his linguistic production will change and show development of the new form.

With respect to linguistic competence we would definitely say that the child in the first period has no internalized knowledge of the new form, while the child in period three definitely does. But what can we say about the child in the second period? Perhaps we can say that he lacks linguistic competence with regard to the form in question, although he does have some sort of communicative or performative ability with regard to the concept that consists of a receptive capacity for the linguistic form.

8.8
Language Development and Cognitive Development

If we put together everything that we know about language acquisition, it seems that children proceed in the following manner, with at least four interlocking activities:

The development of concepts
↓

The development of strategies for understanding and producing sentences before he knows the full grammar of his language
↓   ↓

The development of strategies for figuring out the grammar of his language (bit by bit)
↓   ↓

The development of internalized linguistic rules.

Children at the very beginning of language learning would follow the broken arrows rather directly. (This would probably be during the holophrastic period of development, or perhaps even earlier). Once children have learned one linguistic device, however, that device will serve to help them do three things—to understand the speech around them, to produce understandable utterances, and to learn other grammatical devices in the language. In the meantime the rule is being revised from the children's original hypothesis, new rules are being added, new strategies are being devised, and the entire process becomes a mutually dependent developing system until the children have acquired full adult competence. Of course the comprehension strategies do not go away—in fact, as we argued in Chapter 7, a large component of adult language comprehension is probably mediated by comprehension strategies.

8.81 Cognitive aspects of language learning

One must be very careful about the use of the word 'cognitive' in psycholinguistics. In the mid- to late sixties there was no question what a psycholinguist meant who used the word 'cognitive'. It meant 'mental' or, more specifically, 'nonbehaviorist'. (This was discussed in some detail in Chapter 5.) In the mid-seventies, however, 'cognitive' frequently means nonlinguistic. Theorists would like to account for the development of linguistic knowledge by a more general theory of cognitive development. Used in this way, 'cognitive' still means 'mental' and 'nonbehaviorist', but it also refers to mental activity that is more general than that associated with linguistic functioning. If we had a complete general theory that accounted for the information-processing capabilities and styles of the human brain, we would be able to predict the organization of linguistic information, visual information, auditory information, motor information—any kind of information that is organized in the human brain. Such a theory would be a 'cognitive' theory in the nonlinguistic sense intended. It would also be nonvisual, nonauditory, and so on. Such a theory would predict the linguistic universals because they are exactly universals of the organization of linguistic information. Thus a complete cognitive theory would explain linguistic universals. Unfortunately there is not even the glimmer of such a theory on the psycholinguistic horizon; in the meantime a lot of people are wasting a lot of time trying to decide, without the benefit of a cognitive theory, what is 'cognitive' and what is 'linguistic'. To demonstrate the futility of this activity, consider the little diagram above that described the four types of language learning activity. Which of those would you say are 'cognitive' as opposed to 'linguistic'? Which are 'linguistic' as opposed to 'cognitive'? Everyone would probably agree that the first activity is 'cognitive' and the fourth 'linguistic' (if we are forced into such a dichotomy). However, we would be at a loss to argue for either the uniquely linguistic status of the two intermediate-level activities. Until a general theory of neural information processing is developed, it seems premature to attempt to distinguish very sharply between 'cognitive' and 'linguistic'.

8.82 Piaget's theory as an explanatory cognitive theory

By far the best available theory of cognitive development is that of Jean Piaget, the Swiss psychologist and philosopher. His career and theory spread over many years and many volumes, and it would be beyond the scope of this chapter to review his work in sufficient detail to do it justice. (The best summary of Piaget's thought is in Flavell, 1963.) Piaget has theorized that children experience four major periods of cognitive functioning.

8.821 The sensory-motor period. The years (roughly two) immediately after birth comprise the sensory-motor period of development. At birth the infant's entire world is an extension of himself. The sensory-motor period consists of a gradual disengagement of the infant from the rest of the world as he gradually develops the ability to distinguish himself from other things and finally other objects from each other. During this period children literally construct their own reality in the motor patterns they develop. They are unable to represent activities or cognitions symbolically, but the beginning of symbolization is the internalization of the action schemata (motor patterns) with which they have learned to deal with the world.

8.822 The preoperational period. The preoperational period extends from the end of the sensory-motor period (around the age of two) until the beginning of the period of concrete operations (six to seven years). The latter years of the preoperational span have been studied much more extensively than the first two. This is unfortunate from the point of view of developmental psycholinguistics because the rate of language acquisition is at its peak during the early years of this period. During this period representational thought develops, which is characterized by the development of internal symbols. Piaget is careful to point out that the earliest symbols are not verbal. It is the symbolic development of this period that enables children to learn language, not the learning of language that brings children to this symbolizing period.

The preoperational period has a number of related cognitive characteristics. Children are said to "center" on one single, striking aspect of an object or array and by so doing distort their analysis of the object. It is this characteristic that prevents children from "conserving." Thus, if preoperational children see liquid being poured from a short, wide glass into a tall, skinny one, they will say that the tall glass contains more water. While this belief is quite remarkable to an adult, it is the result of the children centering their attention on one feature of the situation, the level of liquid.

Another related and very important aspect of this development period is the fact that children's thought processes are not reversible. This means that they can't conceive of something changing in shape or arrangement, then changing back again to the original. If such children are shown a spherical piece of clay that is then rolled out in a long, thin, snake, they will say that there is now a greater quantity of clay than there was in the sphere. They would not suffer from this confusion if they could imagine the rolling-out operation as being reversed, leading back to the original sphere. Because their cognitions are not reversible, they cannot conceive simultaneously of the clay being the sphere and the snake—cannot think of them as being two states of the same object.

Thus preoperational children differ radically from sensory-motor children in that the former function at a "... wholly new plane of reality, the plane of representation as opposed to direct action" (Flavell, 1963, p. 164). Clearly they are operating on a fairly primitive cognitive level compared to full adult cognitive competence.

8.823 The period of concrete operations. Late childhood, ages approximately seven to eleven is the period of concrete operations. The important difference between this period and the preoperational is that now children have a well-organized cognitive system that underlies all their cognitions and perceptions. Their thinking is reversible, so that when things change, they do not become totally different things. Children are able to "decenter" and attend to all relevant aspects of an object or an array simultaneously, thus they can "conserve" volume and other physical dimensions. While a child's cognition is well-organized and stable during this period, it operates very much in the here-and-now and tends to have as its object concrete things and events in the world.

8.824 The period of formal operations. Around adolescence children enter the period of formal operations, which frees them from the world of the actual and allows them to enter the world of the possible. They can conceive now not only of what is, but of what might be. Their temporal world view expands enormously, and they develop a sense of historical time. This period ushers in a lifetime of cognitive maturity.

8.83 Relevance of Piagetian theory to language learning

There are two aspects of Piaget's study that may be relevant to our thinking about language development. First, there is the suggestion of Sinclair (1971) that the ability to conceptualize grammatical relations of actor-action-object arises during the sensory-motor period of development as the children learn to distinguish themselves from other things in the world and learn that they can be effective in their operations on other physical objects. Following this, children observe that other objects in the world can affect each other. Thus infants emerge from the sensory-motor period with the conceptions of effector (i.e., actor—either the child or someone or something else), action (from the motor patterns with which the child has organized the world during the period) and of object (as the child has recognized the effectiveness of his own and others' actions). These representations are nonverbal, but they form the conceptual, cognitive foundation for underlying grammatical relations. Says Sinclair "The child at this stage can ... classify in action, that is to say, he can use a whole category of objects for the same action, or apply a whole category of action schemes to one object. ... The linguistic equivalents of these structures are ... the major categories and functional grammatical relations" (p. 126). Thus Sinclair is using Piagetian theory as a general explanation of cognitive development from which the linguistic universals can be derived.

The possibility of using Piagetian theory from which to derive linguistic universals is a suggestion that has some appeal. However, it seems too early to do much more than talk about linguistic constructs using vocabulary from Piagetian theory. That is, it seems to be possible to talk about grammatical relations in terms of action patterns, but there is nothing about the Piagetian conception of the sensory-motor period from which one could deduce the cognitive categories of actor-action-object or by which one would predict that the child would be led ineluctably to those linguistic formulations. In fact one could make a good case for the opposite—that the conceptual categories do not exist in any sense that is real to the child until the language provides a method of verbally encoding the cognitive categories. This hypothesis is probably wrong, but it is no more or less plausible or testable than Sinclair's position. There seem to be two basic problems with a Piagetian approach to linguistic development. First, Piaget's theory is not yet sufficiently explicit to predict precisely occurring aspects of language and language developments while ruling out nonoccurring aspects. A second problem is that when one moves from grammatical relations to other linguistic universals, such as transformational rules, the existence of nouns and verbs, recursive properties of grammar, deep and surface structure, and others that are formulated with great precision, it becomes impossible to use Piagetian theory even metaphorically. On balance, then, it seems reasonable to conclude that while it would be possible in principle to predict linguistic universals from a cognitive theory, such a theory is not yet available.

Another more promising application of Piagetian theory to language acquisition regards the emergence of metalinguistic judgments in the child, particularly the ability of the child to perceive ambiguous sentences as ambiguous and to recognize when two sentences are paraphrases of each other. As we mentioned earlier, these abilities do not seem to emerge until late childhood, around the ages of six to eight. It has been suggested by some (Hakes, 1974; Beilin and Spontak, 1969) that the abilities emerge as a direct result of the child's emergence from the preoperational period to that of concrete operations.

In order to judge that a sentence is ambiguous, more is required than that children be able to understand both meanings of the sentence. The further requirement must be satisfied that they *simultaneously* understand both meanings of the sentence. That is, they must be able to hold in awareness the sentence itself and both meanings derivable from it. Preoperational children tend to focus on one meaning, making it impossible for them to perceive the ambiguity, even though they are capable of understanding the other meaning of the sentence during some other comprehension event. While their cognitive system lacks the characteristic of reversibility, children are unable to conceive of one (surface structure) sentence as simultaneously representing two underlying structures.

The process required to perceive that two sentences are paraphrases of each other is essentially a mirror image of that required for ambiguity perception. Thus the two abilities emerge together and are dependent on the same cognitive ability. In order to perceive that two sentences mean the same thing, children must process and retain both meanings simultaneously. Only then can they compare them and determine that the two meanings are the same. They must then be able to conceive of the reversible process of converting the (one) meaning back into both (or either) sentence in order to judge that the two original sentences mean the same thing.

The hypothesis that the emergence of linguistic intuitions is related to cognitive development does not postulate a cognitive basis for grammatical development per se. Instead it relates an ability to perform linguistic judgments to general aspects of cognitive structure. This seems to be a promising way to relate psycholinguistic functioning to cognitive development, a connection that is required of a complete theory of psycholinguistic development.

The point is that we are no longer discussing linguistic competence versus linguistic performance as though that were all there is to say about language acquisition. Just as behaviorist psychology found that its conception of language was not sufficiently rich to deal with natural language and natural language users, perhaps cognitive psycholinguistics has also discovered that it is insufficient to speak merely of linguistic competence and linguistic performance. We cannot discuss linguistic development without beginning to talk about conceptual development and the growth in the child of the fundamental ability to communicate. We cannot talk about syntax in the child and ignore the semantic aspects of his developing linguistic system. Most important, we can no longer speak of linguistic performance as consisting of skills based on an abstract competence because we have seen that performance skills are in a very real sense precursors of linguistic competence.

As we conclude this book, we are reminded of the words of Miller, in concluding his almost revolutionary "Some Preliminaries to Psycholinguistics":

In a word, what I am trying to say, what all my ... admonitions boil down to, is simply this: Language is exceedingly complicated. Forgive me for taking so long to say such a simple and obvious thing.

SUGGESTIONS FOR FURTHER READING

The following are but a few of the many books which deal with language acquisition in the child. Some of the books also address the relationship between language acquisition and general cognitive development:

Brown, R. *A First Language: The Early Stages.* Cambridge, Mass.: Harvard University Press, 1973.

Dale, P. S. *Language Development: Structure and Function.* Hinsdale, Ill.: The Dryden Press, 1972.

Ferguson, C. A., and Slobin, D. I. (ed.). *Studies of Child Language Development.* New York: Holt, Rinehart and Winston, 1973.

Hayes, J. R. (ed.). *Cognition and the Development of Language.* New York: John Wiley & Sons, 1970.

Huxley, R., and Ingram, E. (eds.). *Language Acquisition: Models and Methods.* New York: Academic Press, 1971.

Menyuk, P. *The Acquisition and Development of Language.* Englewood Cliffs, N.J.: Prentice-Hall, 1971.

Moore, T. E. (ed.). *Cognitive Development and the Acquisition of Language.* New York: Academic Press, 1973.

McNeill, D. *The Acquisition of Language: The Study of Developmental Psycholinguistics.* New York: Harper & Row, 1970.

Slobin, D. I. (ed.). *The Ontogenesis of Grammar.* New York: Academic Press, 1971.

The following journals contain reports of research in language acquisition:

Child Development
Journal of Child Language
Journal of Psycholinguistic Research

Bibliography

Abramson, A. S., and Lisker, L. 1965. Voice onset time in stop consonants: Acoustic analysis and synthesis. *Status Report on Speech Research,* Haskins Laboratories, August.

Anderson, S. R. 1974. *The Organization of Phonology.* New York: Academic Press.

Anisfeld, M. 1969. Psychological evidence for an intermediate stage in a morphological derivation. *Journal of Verbal Learning and Verbal Behavior,* 8, 185–190.

Bach, E. *Syntactic Theory.* 1974. New York: Holt, Rinehart and Winston.

Barclay, J. R. 1973. Comprehension and sentence memory. *Cognitive Psychology,* 4, 229–254.

Beilin, H., and Spontak, G. 1969. Active-passive transformations and operational reversibility. Paper presented at the Biennial Meetings of the Society for Research in Child Development, Santa Monica, California, March.

Berko, J. 1958. The child's learning of English morphology. *Word,* 14, 150–177.

Bever, T. G. 1970. The cognitive basis for linguistic structures. In J. R. Hayes (ed.), *Cognition and the Development of Language.* New York: Wiley.

Bever, T. G. 1973. Serial position and response bias do not account for the effect of syntactic structure on the location of brief noises during sentences. *Journal of Psycholinguistic Research,* 2, 287–288.

Bever, T. G., Fodor, J. A., and Garrett, M. F. 1968. A formal limitation of associationism. In T. R. Dixon and D. L. Horton (eds.), *Verbal Behavior and General Behavior Theory.* Englewood Cliffs, N.J.: Prentice-Hall.

Bever, T. G., Fodor, J. A., and Weksel, W. 1965. On the acquisition of syntax: A critique of "contextual generalization." *Psychological Review,* 72, 467–482.

Bever, T. G., Garrett, M. F., and Hurtig, R. 1973. The interaction of perceptual processes and ambiguous sentences. *Memory and Cognition,* 1, 277–286.

Bever, T. G., Lackner, J., and Kirk, R. 1969. The underlying structure sentence is the primary unit of speech perception. *Perception and Psychophysics,* 5, 225–235.

Bever, T. G., and Langendoen, D. T. 1972. The interaction of speech perception and grammatical structure in the evolution of language. In R. Stockwell and R. Macaulay (eds.), *Linguistic Change and Generative Theory.* Bloomington, Indiana: University Press.

Bierwisch, M. 1970. Semantics. In J. Lyons (ed.), *New Horizons in Linguistics.* Baltimore: Penguin.

Bloom, L. 1970. *Language Development: Form and Function in Emerging Grammars.* Cambridge, Mass.: M.I.T. Press.

Bloomfield, L. 1933. *Language.* New York: Holt, Rinehart and Winston.

Blumenthal, A. L. 1967. Prompted recall of sentences. *Journal of Verbal Learning and Verbal Behavior,* 6, 203–206.

Blumenthal, A. L. 1970. *Language and Psychology.* New York: Wiley.

Blumenthal, A. L., and Boakes, R. 1967. Prompted recall of sentences. *Journal of Verbal Learning and Verbal Behavior,* 6, 674–676.

Braine, M. D. S. 1963. On learning the grammatical order of words. *Psychological Review,* 70, 323–348.

Braine, M. D. S. 1965. On the basis of phrase structure: A reply to Bever, Fodor, and Weksel. *Psychological Review,* 72, 483–492. Reprinted in L. A. Jakobovits and M. S. Miron (eds.), 1967. *Readings in the Psychology of Language.* Englewood Cliffs, N.J.: Prentice-Hall.

Bransford, J. D., Barclay, J. R., and Franks, J. J. 1970. Linguistic inputs and knowledge-enriched ideas. Prepublication ms, University of Minnesota.

Bransford, J. D., Barclay, J .R., and Franks, J. J. 1972. Sentence memory: A constructive versus interpretive approach. *Cognitive Psychology,* 3, 193–209.

Bransford, J. D., and Franks, J. J. 1972. The abstraction of linguistic ideas: A review. *Cognition,* 1, 211–249.

Brown, R. *Words and Things,* 1958. Glencoe, Ill.: Free Press.

Brown, R. 1968. The development of Wh questions in child speech. *Journal of Verbal Learning and Verbal Behavior,* 7, 279–90.

Brown, R. 1970. *Psycholinguistics.* New York: Free Press.

Brown, R. 1973. *A First Language: The Early Stages.* Cambridge, Mass.: Harvard University Press.

Brown, R., Cazden, C., and Bellugi, U. 1970. The child's grammar from I to III. In R. Brown (ed.), *Psycholinguistics.* New York: Free Press.

Brown, R., Fraser, C., and Bellugi, U. 1963. Control of grammar in imitation, comprehension, and production. *Journal of Verbal Learning and Verbal Behavior,* 2, 121–135. Reprinted in R. Brown (ed.), *Psycholinguistics.* New York: Free Press, 1970.

Brown, R., and Hanlon, C. 1970. Derivational complexity and order of acquisition in child speech. In J. R. Hayes (ed.), *Cognition and the Development of Language*. New York: Wiley.

Cairns, C. E., and Williams, F. 1973. Language. In F. D. Minifie, T. J. Hixon, and F. Williams (eds.), *Normal Aspects of Speech, Hearing, and Language*. Englewood Cliffs, N.J.: Prentice-Hall.

Cairns, H. S. 1971. Ambiguous sentence processing. Paper presented at Mid-Western Psychological Association.

Cairns, H. S. 1973. Effects of bias on processing and reprocessing of lexically ambiguous sentences. *Journal of Experimental Psychology*, 97, 337–343.

Cairns, H. S., and Blank, M. 1974. Word recognition latency and the duration of clausal processing. Unpublished manuscript.

Cairns, H. S., Cairns, C. E., and Williams, F. 1974. Some theoretical considerations of articulation substitution phenomena. *Language and Speech*, 1974, 17, 160–173.

Cairns, H. S., and Foss, D. J. 1971. Falsification of the hypothesis that word frequency is a unified variable in sentence processing. *Journal of Verbal Learning and Verbal Behavior*, 10, 41–43.

Cairns, H. S., and Kamerman, J. 1975. Lexical information processing during sentence comprehension. *Journal of Verbal Learning and Verbal Behavior*, 14, 170–179.

Cairns, H. S., and Williams, F. 1972. An analysis of the substitution errors of a group of standard English-speaking children. *Journal of Speech and Hearing Research*, 15, 811–820.

Caplan, D. 1971. Probe tests and sentence perception. Unpublished doctoral dissertation, Massachusetts Institute of Technology.

Caplan, D. 1972. Clause boundaries and recognition latencies for words in sentences. *Perception and Psychophysics*, 12, 73–76.

Carroll, J. B. (ed.). 1956. *Language, Thought and Reality: Selected Writings of Benjamin Lee Whorf*. Cambridge, Mass.: M.I.T. Press.

Chapin, P. G., Smith, T. S., and Abrahamson, A. A. 1972. Two factors in perceptual segmentation of speech. *Journal of Verbal Learning and Verbal Behavior*, 11, 164–173.

Chistovich, L. A., Fant, G. C., De Serpa-Leitao, A., and Tjerlund, P. 1966. Mimicking and perception of synthetic vowels: Part II. Speech Transmission Laboratory, Royal Institute of Technology, Stockholm, Sweden. QPSR 3.

Chomsky, C. 1969. *The Acquisition of Syntax in Children from 5 to 10*. Cambridge, Mass.: M.I.T. Press.

Chomsky, N. 1957. *Syntactic Structures*. Janua Linguarum 4. The Hague: Mouton.

Chomsky, N. 1959. Review of Skinner's *Verbal Behavior. Language*, 35, 26–58. Reprinted in Jakobovits and Miron (eds.), 1967. *Readings in the Psychology of Language*. Englewood Cliffs, N.J.: Prentice-Hall.

Chomsky, N. 1965. *Aspects of the Theory of Syntax*. Cambridge, Mass.: M.I.T. Press.

Chomsky, N. 1966. *Cartesian Linguistics*. New York: Harper & Row.

Chomsky, N. 1972. *Language and Mind*. New York: Harcourt, Brace.

Chomsky, N. 1972b. Some empirical issues in the theory of transformational grammar. In S. Peters (ed.), *Goals of Linguistic Theory*. Englewood Cliffs, N.J.: Prentice-Hall.

Chomsky, N., and Halle, M. 1968. *The Sound Pattern of English*. New York: Harper and Row.

Clark, E. 1971. On the acquisition of the meaning of 'before' and 'after.' *Journal of Verbal Learning and Verbal Behavior,* 10, 266–275.

Clark, E. 1973. What's in a word: On the child's acquisition of semantics in his first language. In T. E. Moore (ed.), *Cognitive Development and the Acquisition of Language*. New York: Academic Press.

Clark, H. H. 1971. The importance of linguistics for the study of speech hesitations. In Horton and Jenkins (eds.), *The Perception of Language*. Columbus, Ohio: Chas. Merrill.

Clark, H. H. 1973. Space, time, semantics, and the child. In T. E. Moore (ed.), *Cognitive Development and the Acquisition of Language*. New York: Academic Press.

Clifton, C., and Odom, P. 1966. Similarity relations among certain English sentence constructions. *Psychological Monographs,* 80 (Whole No. 613).

Condon, W. S., and Sander, L. W. 1974. Neonate movement is synchronized with adult speech: Interactional participation and language acquisition. *Science,* 183, 99–101.

Cooper, F. S., Delattre, P. C., Liberman, A. M., Borst, J. M., and Gerstman, L. J. 1952. Some Experiments on the Perception of Synthetic Speech Sounds. *Journal of the Acoustical Society of America,* 24, 297–606. Reprinted in I. Lehiste (ed.), 1967. *Readings in Acoustic Phonetics*. Cambridge, Mass.: M.I.T. Press.

Cromer, R. F. 1970. 'Children are nice to understand.' Surface structure clues for the recovery of a deep structure. *British Journal of Psychology,* 61, 3, 397–408.

Dale, P. S. 1972. *Language Development: Structure and Function*. Hinsdale, Ill.: The Dryden Press.

D'Arcais, G. B. F., and Levelt, W. J. M. (eds.), 1970. *Advances in Psycholinguistics*. New York: American Elsevier.

Delattre, P. C., Liberman, A. M., and Cooper, F. S. 1955. Acoustic loci and transitional cues for consonants. *Journal of the Acoustical Society of America,* 27, 769–773. Reprinted in I. Lehiste (ed.), 1967. *Readings in Acoustic Phonetics*. Cambridge, Mass.: M.I.T. Press.

DeVito, J. 1970. *The Psychology of Speech and Language*. New York: Random House.

Dingwall, W. O. (ed.), 1971. *A Survey of Linguistic Science*. Linguistics program, University of Maryland.

Dixon, T. R., and Horton, D. L. (eds.) 1968. *Verbal Behavior and General Behavior Theory*. Englewood Cliffs, N.J.: Prentice-Hall.

Donaldson, M., and Balfour, G. 1968. Less is more: A study of language comprehension in children. *British Journal of Psychology*, 59, 461–471.

Donaldson, M., and Wales, R. 1970. On the acquisition of some relational terms. In J. R. Hayes (ed.), *Cognition and the Development of Language*. New York: Wiley.

Dore, J. 1973. A developmental theory of speech act production. *Transactions of the N. Y. Academy of Sciences*, 35, 623–630.

Eimas, P. D. (in press) Speech perception in early infancy. In L. B. Cohen and P. Salapatek (eds.), *Infant Perception: From Sensation to Cognition*. New York: Academic Press.

Eimas, P. D., and Corbit, J. D. 1973. Selective adaptation of linguistic feature detectors. *Cognitive Psychology*, 4, 99–109.

Eimas, P. D., Siqueland, E. R., Jusczyk, P., and Vigorito, J. 1971. Speech perception in infants. *Science*, 171, 303–306.

Epstein, W. 1969. Recall of word lists following learning of sentences and of anomalous and random strings. *Journal of Verbal Learning and Verbal Behavior*, 8, 20–25.

Ervin-Tripp, S. 1970. Discourse agreement: How children answer questions. In J. R. Hayes (ed.), *Cognition and the Development of Language*. New York: Wiley.

Ferguson, C. A., and Slobin, D. I. (eds.) 1973. *Studies of Child Language Development*. New York: Holt, Rinehart and Winston.

Fillmore, C. 1968. The case for case. In E. Bach and R. T. Harms, (eds.), *Universals in Linguistic Theory*. New York: Holt, Rinehart and Winston.

Fillmore, C. J., and Langendoen, D. T. 1971. *Studies in Linguistic Semantics*. New York: Holt, Rinehart and Winston.

Flavell, J. H. 1963. *The Developmental Psychology of Jean Piaget*. Princeton, N.J.: Van Nostrand.

Fleming, J. D. 1974. Field report: The state of the apes. *Psychology Today*, January, 31–46.

Fodor, J. A. 1966. How to learn to talk: Some simple ways. In F. Smith and G. A. Miller (eds.), *The Genesis of Language*. Cambridge, Mass.: M.I.T. Press.

Fodor, J. A. 1968. *Psychological Explanation: An Introduction to the Philosophy of Psychology*. New York: Random House.

Fodor, J. A., and Bever, T. G. 1965. The psychological reality of linguistic segments. *Journal of Verbal Learning and Verbal Behavior*, 4, 414–420.

Fodor, J. A., Bever, T. G., and Garrett, M. F. 1974. *The Psychology of Language*. New York: McGraw-Hill.

Fodor, J. A., Fodor, J. D., Garrett, M. F., and Lackner, J. R. 1974. Effects of surface and underlying clausal structure on click location. *Quarterly Progress Report*, 113, Research Laboratory of Electronics, M.I.T.

Fodor, J. A., Garrett, M. F., and Bever, T. G. 1968. Some syntactic determinants of sentential complexity. II: Verb structure. *Perception and Psychophysics*, 3, 453–461.

Fodor, J. A., and Garrett, M. F. 1967. Some syntactic determinants of sentential complexity. *Perception and Psychophysics*, 2, 289–296.

Fodor, J. A., and Katz, J. J. (eds.). 1964. *The Structure of Language: Readings in the Philosophy of Language*. Englewood Cliffs, N.J.: Prentice-Hall.

Forster, K. I. 1970. Visual perception of rapidly presented word sequences of varying complexity. *Perception and Psychophysics*, 8, 215–221.

Forster, K. I., and Ryder, L. A. 1971. Perceiving the structure and meaning of sentences. *Journal of Verbal Learning and Verbal Behavior*, 10, 285–296.

Foss, D. J. 1969. Decision processes during sentence comprehension: Effects of lexical item difficulty and position upon decision times. *Journal of Verbal Learning and Verbal Behavior*, 8, 457–462.

Foss, D. J. 1970. Some effects of ambiguity upon sentence comprehension. *Journal of Verbal Learning and Verbal Behavior*, 9, 699–706.

Foss, D. J., Bever, T. G., and Silver, M. 1968. The comprehension and verification of ambiguous sentences. *Perception and Psychophysics*, 4, 304–306.

Foss, D. J., and Cairns, H. S. 1970. Some effects of memory limitation upon sentence comprehension and recall. *Journal of Verbal Learning and Verbal Behavior*, 9, 541–547.

Foss, D. J., and Jenkins, C. M. 1973. Some effects of context on the comprehension of ambiguous sentences. *Journal of Verbal Learning and Verbal Behavior*, 5, 577–589.

Foss, D. J., and Lynch, R. H. 1969. Decision processes during sentence comprehension: Effects of surface structure on decision times. *Perception and Psychophysics*, 5, 145–148.

Frisch, K. von. 1950. *Bees: Their Vision, Chemical Senses, and Language*. Ithaca, New York: Cornell University Press.

Frisch, K. von. 1953. *The Dancing Bees: An Account of the Life and Senses of the Honey Bee*. (trans. Dora Ilse.) New York: Harcourt, Brace.

Frisch, K. von. 1962. "Dialects in the language of the bees." *Scientific American*, 207, 78–87.

Fromkin, V. A. 1973. Slips of the tongue. *Scientific American*, 229, 6, 110–117.

Fromkin, V. A., and Rodman, R. 1974. *An Introduction to Language*. New York: Holt, Rinehart and Winston.

Gardner, R. A., and Gardner, B. T. 1969. Teaching sign language to a chimpanzee. *Science*, 165, 664–672.

Garrett, M. F., Bever, T. G., and Fodor, J. A. 1966. The active use of grammar in speech perception. *Perception and Psychophysics*, 1, 30–32.

Garrett, M. F., and Fodor, J. A. 1968. Psychological theories and linguistic constructs. In T. R. Dixon and D. L. Horton (eds.), *Verbal Behavior and General Behavior Theory*. Englewood Cliffs, N.J.: Prentice-Hall.

Glucksberg, S., and Danks, J. H. 1969. Grammatical structure and recall: A function of the space in immediate memory or of recall delay? *Perception and Psychophysics*, 6, 113–117.

Gough, P. B. 1965. Grammatical transformations and speed of understanding. *Journal of Verbal Learning and Verbal Behavior*, 4, 107–111.

Gough, P. B. 1966. The verification of sentences: The effects of delay of evidence and sentence length. *Journal of Verbal Learning and Verbal Behavior*, 5, 492–496.

Gough, P. B. 1972. One second of reading. In J. F. Kavanagh and I. G. Mattingly (eds.), *Language by Ear and Eye*. Cambridge, Mass.: M.I.T. press.

Greenberg, J. H., and Jenkins, J. J. 1967. Studies in the psychological correlates of the sound system of American English. L. A. Jakobovits and M. S. Miron (eds.), *Reading in the Psychology of Language*. Englewood Cliffs, N.J.: Prentice-Hall.

Greene, J. 1972. *Psycholinguistics*. Baltimore, Md.: Penguin.

Hakes, D. T. 1971. Does verb structure affect sentence comprehension? *Perception and Psychophysics*, 10, 229–232.

Hakes, D. T. 1972. Effects of reducing complement constructions on sentence comprehension. *Journal of Verbal Learning and Verbal Behavior*, 11, 278–286.

Hakes, D. T. 1974. The emergence of linguistic intuitions in children. Annual report submitted to Grant Foundation of the University of Texas at Austin.

Hakes, D. T., and Cairns, H. S. 1970. Sentence comprehension and relative pronouns. *Perception and Psychophysics*, 8, 5–8.

Hakes, D. T., and Foss, D. J. 1970. Decision processes during sentence comprehension: Effects of surface structure reconsidered. *Perception and Psychophysics*, 8, 5–8.

Halle, M., and Stevens, K. N. 1964. Speech recognition: A model and a program for research. In J. A. Fodor and J. J. Katz (eds.), *The Structure of Language: Readings in the Philosophy of Language*. Englewood Cliffs, N.J.: Prentice-Hall.

Harris, K. S. 1974. Physiological aspects of articulatory behavior. In T. A. Sebeok (ed.), *Current Trends in Linguistics*. The Hague: Mouton.

Hayes, J. R. 1970. *Cognition and the Development of Language*. New York: Wiley.

Hilgard, E. R., and Marquis, D. G. 1961. *Conditioning and Learning*. New York: Appleton-Century-Crofts.

Holmes, V. M., and Forster, K. T. 1972. Perceptual complexity and underlying sentence structure. *Journal of Verbal Learning and Verbal Behavior*, 11, 148–156.

Horton, D. L., and Jenkins, J. J. 1971. *The Perception of Language.* Columbus, Ohio: Charles E. Merrill.

Hunt, E. 1971. What kind of a computer is man? *Cognitive Psychology,* 2, 57.

Huxley, R., and Ingram, E. (eds.), 1971. *Language Acquisition: Models and Methods.* New York: Academic Press.

Hyman, L. M. 1975. *Phonology: Theory and Analysis.* New York: Holt, Rinehart and Winston.

Irwin, O. C. 1947. Infant speech: consonant sounds according to the manner of articulation. *Journal of Speech Disorders,* 12, 397–401.

Jackendoff, R. S. 1972. *Semantic Interpretation in Generative Grammar.* Cambridge, Mass.: M.I.T. Press.

Jacobs, R. A., and Rosenbaum, P. S. 1968. *English Transformational Grammar.* Waltham, Mass.: Blaisdell.

Jakobovits, L. A., and Miron, M. S. 1967. *Readings in the Psychology of Language.* Englewood Cliffs, N.J.: Prentice-Hall.

Jarvella, R. J. 1971. Syntactic processing of connected speech. *Journal of Verbal Learning and Verbal Behavior,* 10, 409–416.

Jenkins, C. M. 1971. Memory and linguistic information: A study of sentence memory, linguistic form, and inferred information. Unpublished Ph.D. dissertation, The University of Texas at Austin.

Jenkins, J. J. 1964. A mediational account of grammatical phenomena. *Journal of Communication,* 14, 86–97.

Jensen, A. R. 1969. How much can we boost IQ and scholastic achievement? *Harvard Educational Review,* 39, 1–123.

Just, M. A., and Clark, H. G. 1973. Drawing inferences from the presuppositions and implications of affirmative and negative sentences. *Journal of Verbal Learning and Verbal Behavior,* 12, 21–31.

Katz, J. J. 1964. Mentalism in linguistics, *Language,* 40, 124–137. Reprinted in Jakobovits and Miron (eds.), 1967. *Readings in the Psychology of Language.* Englewood Cliffs, N.J.: Prentice-Hall.

Katz, J. J. 1966. *The Philosophy of Language.* New York: Harper & Row.

Katz, J. J. 1972. *Semantic Theory.* New York: Harper & Row.

Katz, J. J., and Fodor, J. A. 1963. The structure of a semantic theory. *Language,* 39, 170–210. Reprinted in J. A. Fodor and J. J. Katz (eds.), 1964. *Readings in the Philosophy of Language.* Englewood Cliffs, N.J.: Prentice-Hall.

Katz, J. J., and Postal, P. M. 1964. *An Integrated Theory of Linguistic Descriptions.* Cambridge, Mass.: M.I.T. Press.

Kavanagh, J. F., and Mattingly, I. G. (eds.), 1972. *Language by Ear and by Eye.* Cambridge, Mass.: M.I.T. Press.

Kimball, J. 1973. Seven principles of surface structure parsing in natural language. *Cognition,* 2, 15–48.

Klima, E. S., and Bellugi, U. 1966. Syntactic regularities in the speech of children. In J. Lyons and R. Wales (eds.), *Psycholinguistic Papers.* Edinburgh: Edinburgh University Press.

Kornfeld, J. R. 1973. Clause structure and the perceptual analysis of sentences. Massachusetts Institute of Technology, Research Laboratory of Electronics, *Quarterly Progress Report,* 108, January 15.

Kuhn, T. S. 1962. *The Structure of Scientific Revolutions.* Chicago: University of Chicago Press.

Lackner, J. R., and Garrett, M. F. 1972. Resolving ambiguity: Effects of biasing context in the unattended ear. *Cognition,* 1, 359–372.

Ladefoged, P. 1962. *Elements of Acoustic Phonetics.* Chicago: University of Chicago Press.

Ladefoged, P. 1967. *Three Areas of Experimental Phonetics.* London: Oxford University Press.

Ladefoged, P., and Broadbent, D. E. 1957. Information conveyed by vowels. *Journal of the Acoustical Society of America,* 19, 98–104. Reprinted in I. Lehiste (ed.), 1967. *Readings in Acoustic Phonetics.* Cambridge, Mass.: M.I.T. Press.

Langendoen, D. T., and Bever, T. G. 1973. Can a not unhappy person be called a not sad one? In S. R. Anderson and P. Kiparsky (eds.), *A Festschrift for Morris Halle.* New York: Holt, Rinehart and Winston.

Lehiste, I. (ed.), 1967. *Readings in Acoustic Phonetics.* Cambridge, Mass.: M.I.T. Press.

Lenneberg, E. H. 1964. The capacity for language acquisition. In J. A. Fodor and J. J. Katz (eds.), *The Structure of Language.* Englewood Cliffs, N.J.: Prentice-Hall.

Lenneberg, E. H. 1967. *Biological Foundations of Language.* New York: Wiley. (With an appendix by Chomsky: The formal nature of language.)

Leopold, W. F. 1949. *Speech Development of a Bilingual Child: A Linguist's Record.* Vol. 4, Diary from age two. Evanston, Ill.: Northwestern University Press.

Lettvin, J. Y., Maturana, H. R., McCulloch, W. S., and Pitts, W. H. 1959. What the frog's eye tells the frog's brain. *Proc. Inst. Radio Engr.,* 47, 1940–1951.

Liberman, A. M., Cooper, F. S., Harris, K. S., MacNeilage, P. F., and Studdert-Kennedy, M. Some observations on a model for speech perception. In W. Wathen-Dunn (ed.), *Models for the Perception of Speech and Visual Form.* Cambridge, Mass.: M.I.T. Press.

Lieberman, P. 1973. On the evolution of language: A unified view. *Cognition,* 2, 59–94.

Lieberman, P., Crelin, E. S., and Klatt, D. H. 1972. Phonetic ability and related anatomy of the newborn and adult human, Neanderthal, and the chimpanzee. *American Anthropologist,* 74, 187–307.

Limber, John. 1973. The genesis of complex sentences. In T. E. Moore (ed.),

Cognitive Development and the Acquisition of Language. New York: Academic Press.

Lindauer, M. 1967. *Communication Among Social Bees.* New York: Atheneum.

Lindblom, B. E. F., and Studdert-Kennedy, M. 1967. On the role of formant transitions in vowel recognition. *Journal of the Acoustical Society of America,* 42, 830–843.

Lisker, L., and Abramson, A. S. 1964. A cross-language study of voicing in initial stops: Acoustic measurements. *Word,* 20, 384–422.

Lyons, J. 1970. *Noam Chomsky.* New York: Viking Press.

Lyons, J., and Wales, R. J. 1966. *Psycholinguistics Papers.* Chicago: Aldine.

MacKay, D. 1966. To end ambiguous sentences. *Perception and Psychophysics,* 1, 426–436.

MacKay, D., and Bever, T. G. 1967. In search of ambiguity. *Perception and Psychophysics,* 2, 193–200.

MacNeilage, P. F. 1970. Motor control of serial ordering of speech. *Psychological Review,* 77, 182–196.

MacNeilage, P. F. 1972. Speech physiology. Paper presented to conference on "Speech production and perception: Their relation to cortical function," Vancouver, B. C., Canada, April.

McNeill, D. 1966. Developmental psycholinguistics. In F. Smith and G. A. Miller (eds.), *The Genesis of Language.* Cambridge, Mass.: M.I.T. Press.

McNeill, D. 1970. *The Acquisition of Language: The Study of Developmental Psycholinguistics.* New York: Harper & Row.

Martin, J. G. 1971. Some acoustic and grammatical features of spontaneous speech. In Horton and Jenkins (eds.), *The Perception of Language.* Columbus, Ohio: Merrill.

Matthews, W. A. 1968. Transformational complexity and short-term recall. *Language and Speech,* 11, 120–128.

Mehler, J. 1963. Some effects of grammatical transformations of the recall of English sentences. *Journal of Verbal Learning and Verbal Behavior,* 2, 340–351.

Menyuk, P. 1971. *The Acquisition and Development of Language.* Englewood Cliffs, N.J.: Prentice-Hall.

Miller, G. A. 1956. The magical number seven, plus or minus two: Some limits on our capacity for processing information. *Psychological Review,* 63, 81–97.

Miller, G. A. 1962. Some psychological studies of grammar. *American Psychologist,* 17, 748–762.

Miller, G. A. 1965. Some preliminaries to psycholinguistics. *American Psychologist,* January, 20, 15–20.

Miller, G. A. 1967. *The Psychology of Communication.* Baltimore, Md.: Penguin.

Miller, G. A. (ed.), 1973. *Communication, Language, and Meaning*. New York: Basic Books.

Miller, G. A., and McKean, K. O. 1964. A chronometric study of some relations between sentences. *Quarterly Journal of Experimental Psychology,* 16, 297–308.

Minifie, F. D., Hixon, T. J., and Williams, F. (eds.), 1973. *Normal Aspects of Speech, Hearing, and Language*. Englewood Cliffs, N.J.: Prentice-Hall.

Moore, T. E. (ed.), 1973. *Cognitive Development and the Acquisition of Language*. New York: Academic Press.

Mowrer, O. H. 1954. The psychologist looks at language. *The American Psychologist,* 9, 660–694. Reprinted in L. A. Jakobovits and M. S. Miron (eds.), 1967. *Readings in the Psychology of Language*. Englewood Cliffs, N.J.: Prentice-Hall.

Norman, D. A. 1972. The role of memory in the understanding of language. In J. F. Kavanagh and I. G. Mattingly (eds.), *Language by Ear and by Eye*. Cambridge, Mass.: M.I.T. Press.

Obusek, C. J., and Warren, R. M. 1973. Relation of the verbal transformation and the phonemic restoration effects. *Cognitive Psychology,* 5, 97–107.

Offir, C. 1973. Recognition memory for presuppositions of relative clause sentences. *Journal of Verbal Learning and Verbal Behavior,* 12, 636–643.

Öhman, S. E. G. 1966. Coarticulation in VCV utterances: Spectographic measurements. *Journal of the Acoustical Society of America,* 39, 151–168.

Osgood, C. E. 1963. On understanding and creating sentences. *American Psychologist,* 18, 735–751. Reprinted in L. A. Jakobovits and M. S. Miron (eds.), *Readings in the Psychology of Language*. Englewood Cliffs, N.J.: Prentice-Hall, 1967.

Pavlov, I. P. 1902. *The Work of the Digestive Glands*. Trans. W. H. Thompson. London: Charles Griffin.

Penfield, W., and Roberts, L. 1966. *Speech and Brain Mechanisms*. New York: Atheneum.

Perfetti, C. A. 1973. Retrieval of sentence relations: Semantic vs. syntactic deep structure. *Cognition,* 2, 95–106.

Perkell, J. S. 1969. *Physiology of Speech Production*. Cambridge, Mass.: M.I.T. Press.

Pisoni, D. B. 1971. On the nature of categorical perception of speech sounds. Supplement to Status Report on Speech Research, New Haven: Haskins Laboratories, November.

Polanyi, M. 1958. *Personal Knowledge: Towards a Post-Critical Philosophy*. Chicago: University of Chicago Press.

Postal, P. M. 1968. *Aspects of Phonological Theory*. New York: Harper & Row.

Postal, P. M. 1970. On coreferential complement subject deletion. *Linguistic Inquiry,* 1, 439–500.

Putnam, H. 1973. Reductionism and the nature of psychology. *Cognition*, 2, 131–146.

Pylyshyn, Z. W. 1973. The role of competence theories in cognitive psychology. *Journal of Psycholinguistic Research*, 2, 21–50.

Reber, A. S. 1973. Locating clicks in sentences: Left, center, and right. *Perception and Psychophysics*, 1, 133–138.

Reber, A. S., and Anderson, J. R. 1970. The perception of clicks in linguistic and nonlinguistic messages. *Perception and Psychophysics*, 8, 81–89.

Reibel, D. A., and Schane, S. A. 1969. *Modern Studies in English: Readings in Transformational Grammar*. Englewood Cliffs, N.J.: Prentice-Hall.

Rosenbaum, P. S. 1967. Phrase structure principles of english complex sentence formation. *Journal of Linguistics*, 3, 103–118. Reprinted in D. A. Reibel and S. A. Schane (eds.), 1969. *Modern Studies in English*. Englewood Cliffs, N.J.: Prentice-Hall.

Ross, J. R. 1969. A proposed rule of tree-pruning. In D. A. Reibel and S. A. Schane (eds.), *Modern Studies in English: Readings in Transformational Grammar*. Englewood Cliffs, N.J.: Prentice-Hall.

Ross, J. R. 1972. Doubl-ing. *Linguistic Inquiry*, 3, 61–86.

Sachs, J. 1967. Recognition memory for syntactic and semantic aspects of connected discourse. *Perception and Psychophysics*, 2, 437–442.

Sapir, E. 1921. *Language*. New York: Harcourt, Brace.

Savin, H. B., and Perchonock, E. 1965. Grammatical structure and the immediate recall of English sentences. *Journal of Verbal Learning and Verbal Behavior*, 4, 348–353.

Schane, S. A. 1973. *Generative Phonology*. Englewood Cliffs, N.J.: Prentice-Hall.

Schlesinger, I. M. 1971. Production of utterances and language acquisition. In D. I. Slobin (ed.), *The Ontogenesis of Grammar*. New York: Academic Press.

Sheldon, A. 1974. The role of parallel function in the acquisition of relative clauses in English. *Journal of Verbal Learning and Verbal Behavior*, 13, 272–281.

Sinclair, H. 1971. Sensorimotor action patterns as a condition for the acquisition of syntax. In R. Huxley and E. Ingram (eds.), *Language Acquisition: Methods and Models*. New York: Academic Press.

Sinclair-deZwart, H. 1973. Language acquisition and cognitive development. In T. E. Moore (ed.), *Cognitive Development and the Acquisition of Language*. New York: Academic Press.

Skinner, B. F. 1957. *Verbal Behavior*. New York: Appleton-Century-Crofts.

Skinner, B. F. 1973. *Beyond Freedom and Dignity*. New York: Knopf.

Slobin, D. I. 1966. Grammatical transformations and sentence comprehension in childhood and adulthood. *Journal of Verbal Learning and Verbal Behavior*, 5, 219–227.

Slobin, D. I. 1971a. *Psycholinguistics.* Glenview, Ill.: Scott, Foresman.

Slobin, D. I. (ed.), 1971b. *The Ontogenesis of Grammar.* New York: Academic Press.

Slobin, D. I. 1971c. Developmental psycholinguistics. In W. O. Dingwall (ed.), *A Survey of Linguistic Science,* Linguistics Program, University of Maryland. Reprinted in C. A. Ferguson and D. I. Slobin (eds.), 1973. *Studies of Child Language Development.* New York: Holt, Rinehart and Winston.

Smith, C. S. 1969. Determiners and relative clauses in a generative grammar of English. In D. A. Reibel and S. A. Schane (eds.), *Modern Studies in English: Readings in Transformational Grammar.* Englewood Cliffs, N.J.: Prentice-Hall.

Snow, K. 1963. A detailed analysis of the articulation responses of normal first grade children. *Journal of Speech and Hearing Research,* 6, 277–290.

Steinberg, D. D., and Jakobovits, L. A. 1971. *Semantics.* Cambridge, Mass.: Cambridge University Press.

Stevens, K. N. 1972. Segments, features, and analysis by synthesis. In J. F. Kavanagh and I. G. Mattingly (eds.), *Language by Ear and Eye: The Relationships Between Speech and Reading.* Cambridge, Mass.: M.I.T. Press.

Studdert-Kennedy, M. 1974. The perception of speech. In T. A. Sebeok (ed.), *Current Trends in Linguistics.* The Hague: Mouton.

Swinney, D. A. 1974. Effects of context upon the processing of Lexical Ambiguities during Sentence Comprehension. Unpublished Ph.D. Dissertation, University of Texas at Austin.

Tash, J., and Pisoni, D. B. 1973. Auditory and phonetic levels of processing as revealed by reaction time. Paper presented at the Acoustical Society of America convention, April.

Warren, M., and Warren, P. 1970. Auditory illusions and confusions. *Scientific American,* 223, 30–43.

Wathen-Dunn, W. (ed.), 1967. *Models for the Perception of Speech and Visual Form.* Cambridge, Mass.: M.I.T. Press.

Whitaker, H. A. 1971. Neurolinguistics. In W. O. Dingwall (ed.), *A Survey of Linguistic Science,* Linguistics Program, University of Maryland.

Williams, F. 1972. *Language and Speech.* Englewood Cliffs, N.J.: Prentice-Hall.

Williams, F., and Cairns, H. S. 1973. Linguistic performance. In F. D. Minifie, T. J. Hixon, and F. Williams (eds.), *Normal Aspects of Speech, Hearing, and Language.* Englewood Cliffs, N.J.: Prentice-Hall.

Index

Name Index